**RENEWALS 458-4574**

| DATE DUE | | | |
|---|---|---|---|
| ILL: | 6775818 | | ANM |
| | JUL 1 | | |
| | JUL 11 2009 | | |
| | NO RENEWALS | | |

GAYLORD　　　　　　　　　　　　　PRINTED IN U.S.A.

**WITHDRAWN**
UTSA Libraries

# BONHOEFFER ON FREEDOM

Dietrich Bonhoeffer lived most of his adult life in Hitler's Germany, under one of the last century's most restrictive regimes. He spent his final years in a Nazi prison, deprived of the basic freedoms which most of us take for granted. Against this backdrop, his theological reflections on the true nature of freedom make compelling reading.

This new study takes the theme of freedom as a lens through which to offer a fresh and insightful reappraisal of this major theologian in the light of the new critical edition of his writings.

ASHGATE NEW CRITICAL THINKING IN RELIGION, THEOLOGY
& BIBLICAL STUDIES

The *Ashgate New Critical Thinking in Religion, Theology & Biblical Studies* series brings high quality research monograph publishing back into focus for authors, international libraries, and student, academic and research readers. Headed by an international editorial advisory board of acclaimed scholars spanning the breadth of religious studies, theology and biblical studies, this open-ended monograph series presents cutting-edge research from both established and new authors in the field. With specialist focus yet clear contextual presentation of contemporary research, books in the series take research into important new directions and open the field to new critical debate within the discipline, in areas of related study, and in key areas for contemporary society.

*Series Editorial Board:*

David Jasper, University of Glasgow, UK
James Beckford, University of Warwick, UK
Raymond Williams, Wabash College, USA
Geoffrey Samuel, University of Newcastle, Australia
Richard Hutch, University of Queensland, Australia
Paul Fiddes, University of Oxford, UK
Anthony Thiselton, The University of Nottingham, UK
Tim Gorringe, University of Exeter, UK
Adrian Thatcher, College of St Mark and St John, Plymouth, UK
Alan Torrance, University of St Andrews, UK
Judith Lieu, King's College, London, UK
Terrance Tilley, University of Dayton, USA
Miroslav Volf, Yale Divinity School, USA
Stanley Grenz, Carey Theological College, Canada
Vincent Brummer, University of Utrecht, The Netherlands
Gerhard Sauter, University of Bonn, Germany

*Other Titles in the Series:*

Feminist Biblical Interpretation in Theological Context
*J'annine Jobling*
John Hick's Pluralist Philosophy of World Religions
*Paul Rhodes Eddy*

# Bonhoeffer on Freedom
Courageously grasping reality

ANN L. NICKSON

**ASHGATE**

© Ann L. Nickson 2002

All rights reserved. No part of this publication may be reproduced, stored in a retrieval system or transmitted in any form or by any means, electronic, mechanical, photocopying, recording or otherwise without the prior permission of the publisher.

The author has asserted her moral right under the Copyright, Designs and Patents Act, 1988, to be identified as the author of this work.

Published by
Ashgate Publishing Limited
Gower House
Croft Road
Aldershot
Hampshire GU11 3HR
England

Ashgate Publishing Company
131 Main Street
Burlington, VT 05401-5600 USA

Ashgate website: http://www.ashgate.com

**British Library Cataloguing in Publication Data**
Nickson, Ann L.
 Bonhoeffer on freedom : courageously grasping reality. -
 (Ashgate new critical thinking in religion, theology & biblical studies)
 1. Bonhoeffer, Dietrich, 1906-1945 2. Theology - Germany
 3. Liberty - Religious aspects - Christianity
 I. Title
 230'.044'092

**Library of Congress Cataloging-in-Publication Data**
Nickson, Ann L. 1958-
 Bonhoeffer on freedom : courageously rasping reality / Ann L. Nickson.
     p.cm. – (Ashgate new critical thinking in religion, theology & biblical studies)
 Includes bibliographical references and index.
 ISBN 0-7546-0452-7
   1. Bonhoeffer, Dietrich, 1906-1945. 2. Liberty. I. Title. II. Series.

BX4827.B57.N53 2002
230'.044'092–dc21
                                                                                      2002024888

ISBN 0 7546 0452 7

Printed and bound in Great Britain by MPG Books Ltd, Bodmin, Cornwall

# Contents

| | | |
|---|---|---:|
| *Acknowledgements* | | *vi* |
| *List of Abbreviations* | | *vii* |
| 1 | Setting the Scene | 1 |
| 2 | Freedom and Knowledge | 14 |
| 3 | Freedom in the Image of God | 48 |
| 4 | Freedom in Community | 84 |
| 5 | Freedom and Responsibility | 116 |
| 6 | Freedom in a World Come of Age | 147 |
| *Bibliography* | | *180* |
| *Index* | | *191* |

# Acknowledgements

My study of Bonhoeffer has impressed upon me the corporate nature of the theological task and whilst any errors remain my responsibility alone, this volume would not have emerged in its current form without the challenge and stimulation of theological engagement with others. This book began life as doctoral thesis within the Faculty of Divinity at Cambridge University and I remain deeply grateful to my doctoral supervisor Professor David Ford, for inspiration, lively theological exchange and patient encouragement. My thanks are also due to the Revd. Dr. Jeremy Begbie, who first nurtured my love of theology and persuaded me to embark on research and to Dr. Graham Davies for his support and encouragement, particularly during the initial stages of the project. I am also indebted to many within the worldwide family of Bonhoeffer scholarship, not least to the late Professor Eberhard Bethge and his wife Renate who, despite declining health and advancing age, offered hospitality and graciously made time for yet another Bonhoeffer scholar. Professors John de Gruchy, Clifford Green, Christopher Morse, Walter Lowe, Dorothee Sölle, Christian Gremmels, Peter Selby, F. Burton Nelson and Drs. Ralf Wüstenberg, Andreas Pangritz and Wayne Whitson Floyd Jr. also gave generously of their time or answered specific queries. My thanks are also due to the staff and students of Ridley Hall Theological College, especially to the 'Grads Group' and to the staff of the University Library in Cambridge and the Burke Memorial Library at Union Theological Seminary, New York whose assistance and efficiency were invaluable. Finally I must express my warm appreciation to the staff of Ashgate Publishing Ltd for their guidance throughout the pre-publication process.

# List of Abbreviations

**Dietrich Bonhoeffer Werke in 16 Bande (München Chr Kaiser Verlag 1986-present)**

DBW 1 *Sanctorum Communio* ed. von Soosten J. (1986)
DBW 2 *Act und Sein* ed. Reuter H-R. (1988)
DBW 3 *Schöpfung und Fall* ed. Rüter M. and Tödt I. (1989)
DBW 4 *Nachfolge* ed. Kuske M. and Tödt I. (1994)
DBW 5 *Gemeinsames Leben; Das Gebetbuch der Bibel* ed. Müller G. L. and Schönherr A. (1987)
DBW 6 *Ethik* ed. Tödt I., Tödt H.E. and Green C. (1992)
DBW 6 (Ergänzungsband) *Zettelnotizen für eine 'Ethik.'* ed. Tödt I. (1993)
DBW 7 *Fragmente aus Tegel* ed. Bethge R. and Tödt I. (1994)
DBW 9 *Jugend und Studium 1918-1927* ed. Pfeifer H. (1986)
DBW 10 *Barcelona, Berlin, Amerika 1928-31* ed. Staats R. and von Hase H.C. (1991)
DBW 11 *Okumene, Universität, Pfarramt 1931-1932* ed. Amerlung E. and Strohm C. (1994)
DBW 13 *London 1933-1935* ed. Goedeking H., Heimbucher M. and Schleicher H-W. (1994)
DBW 14 *Illegal Theologen-ausbildung Finkenwalde 1935-1937* ed. Dudzus O. and Henkys J. (1996)
DBW 15 *Illegale Theologen-ausbildung Sammelvikariate 1937-1940* ed. Schulz D. (1998)
DBW 16 *Konspiration und Haft 1940-1945* ed. Glenthøj J., Kabitz U. and Krötke W. (1996)

**Other Primary Texts in German**

WE *Widerstand und Ergebung* (Chr. Kaiser/Gütersloher Verlaghaus, Gütersloh 1951; 15., durchgesehene Auflage, 1994 )

GS I-VI *Gesammelte Schriften Bds I-VI* (München: Chr. Kaiser Verlag 1965-1974)

**English Primary and Secondary Texts**

DBWE 2 *Act and Being* ed. Floyd W.W. trans. Rumscheidt H. M. (Minneapolis: Fortress 1996)
DBWE 3 *Creation and Fall* ed. de Gruchy J. W. trans. Bax S. D. (Minneapolis: Fortress 1997)
DBWE 5 *Life Together* ed. Kelly G. B., trans. Bloesch D. (Minneapolis: Fortress 1996)

C *Christology* trans. Robertson E. H. (London: Collins 1978)
CD *The Cost of Discipleship* trans. Fuller R. H. (London: SCM 1959)
E *Ethics* trans. Horton Smith N. (London: SCM 1955)
LPP *Letters and Papers from Prison* trans. Fuller R. Clarke F. and Bowden J. (London: SCM 1971)
NRS *No Rusty Swords* ed. Robertson E. H. (London: Collins 1965)
WTF *The Way to Freedom* ed. Robertson E. H. (London: Collins 1966)
TP *True Patriotism* ed. Robertson E. H. (London: Collins 1973)
DB *Dietrich Bonhoeffer: Theologian, Christian, Contemporary* Bethge E. (London: Collins 1970)
WCOA *World Come of Age: A Symposium on Dietrich Bonhoeffer* Gregor Smith R. (ed.) (London: Collins 1967)
IKDB *I Knew Dietrich Bonhoeffer* Zimmermann W-D. and Gregor Smith R. eds. (London Collins 1966)

I have worked from the revised German edition of the DBW and where this is cited in footnotes, the translation is my own. Where an English translation of the new edition is available (DBWE), this has been used, except where otherwise indicated in the footnotes. Because of the major re-ordering of the new edition of *Ethik* (DBW 6), I have included parallel references to the 1955 English translation. Biblical quotations are from the New Revised Standard Version.

## Chapter One
# Setting the Scene

**Introduction**

On 9th July 1998 ten statues celebrating the lives and deaths of twentieth-century martyrs were unveiled at Westminster Abbey. Among them was a statue of Dietrich Bonhoeffer, the Lutheran theologian and pastor executed on 9th April 1945 for his involvement in von Stauffenberg's unsuccessful plot to overthrow Hitler.[1] Bonhoeffer's ambiguous status as a martyr has made assessment of his theological legacy problematic. In some circles he has become the victim of a misguided hagiography, in others he has been dismissed as a theological lightweight who owes his fame to the tragic circumstances of his death rather than to the depth or originality of his theological insight. In his prison letters, Bonhoeffer made it clear that he harboured no ambitions of sainthood[2] and this study has no intention of lapsing into an uncritical martyrology. However, there are major reasons why a critical reassessment of Bonhoeffer's theological achievement is both necessary and possible.

Such a fresh appraisal is necessary because Bonhoeffer reception, particularly in the UK, has tended to trap the theologian and his writings in a 1960s time warp. It is possible because of the availability, for the first time, of a definitive critical edition of the entire Bonhoeffer corpus *Dietrich Bonhoeffer Werke,*[3] complete with sophisticated critical apparatus.

**Problems in Bonhoeffer Reception**

Bonhoeffer first came to the notice of the English speaking world in the 1950s after the publication of the letters written from Tegel prison to Eberhard Bethge, his closest friend, under the title *Letters and Papers from*

---

[1] The so-called 20th July Plot.
[2] LPP 369.
[3] Chr. Kaiser Verlag 1986-1999.

*Prison.*[4] This prison correspondence, popularised in John Robinson's *Honest to God*[5] was for many, their first and decisive contact with Bonhoeffer. There has been relatively little recent academic interest in Bonhoeffer in the UK and interpretation remains heavily influenced by his reception in the 1960s, which tended to seize upon a number of eminently quotable but esoteric sentences from the *Letters*, without much regard for context.[6] Amid the apparently rampant secularisation of that decade, terms such as 'religionless Christianity', culled from the prison letters, seemed to epitomise the spirit of the times, and Bonhoeffer was embraced by a number of diverse and at times mutually contradictory causes and movements. *Honest to God* bracketed Bonhoeffer with Bultmann and Tillich in a re-interpretation of God as the non-personal 'ground of our being', an interpretation which is hard to sustain, even on a superficial reading of the prison letters.[7]

However, even in the United States, where interest in Bonhoeffer has been more evenly sustained, and Robinson's influence has been less pervasive, there has been a tendency to privilege the prison theology over earlier writings. This tendency is closely linked to what has long been assumed to be a key issue confronting any interpreter of Bonhoeffer's fragmentary output, that of continuity or discontinuity within his writings. Perhaps inevitably, in attempting to answer this question, the prison correspondence has been used as a plumbline against which to measure Bonhoeffer's earlier output. Is there a significant shift between *Ethics* and *Letters and Papers*, or can a linear development be traced between the earliest writings and the theology which emerged from the Tegel prison cell? Even where the interpreter's expressed aim is a survey of Bonhoeffer's work as a whole, the earlier writings are often read almost exclusively in the light of the *Letters*, as if the 'Tegel correspondence' were the summit of Bonhoeffer's theological achievement.

One of the earliest examples of this linear approach can be seen in the interpretation of the American theologian John Phillips who reads Bonhoeffer in terms of the gradual freeing of christology from

---

[4] First published by SCM in 1953, second edition 1956.
[5] Robinson J. A. T. *Honest to God* (SCM 1963).
[6] The work of Keith Clements is a notable exception. cf. Clements K. *What Freedom: The Persistent Challenge of Dietrich Bonhoeffer* (Bristol Baptist College 1990).
[7] Chapter 3 is headed 'The ground of our Being: A depth at the centre of life'. Robinson readily admits that he had not read much beyond *Letters and Papers*, commenting in a footnote, 'I have made no attempt to give a balanced picture of Bonhoeffer's theology as a whole, which cannot be done by concentrating, as I have been compelled to do, on this final flowering of it.' *Honest to God* (SCM 1963), 36, footnote 1.

ecclesiology.[8] Phillips' work, published in 1967, was only the third full-length study of Bonhoeffer to appear.[9] He begins uncontroversially, suggesting christology as the unifying theme of Bonhoeffer's writings. However, like many interpreters writing in the 1960s, the study proceeds, at least implicitly, from the standpoint of the prison correspondence. Phillips claims to identify two conflicting christologies, a christo-ecclesiology in *Sanctorum Communio* and *Act and Being*, and a 'transcendent person' christology which, he argues, first emerges in the 1933 *Christology* lectures as a preliminary and unsuccessful attempt to free christology from ecclesiology.[10] *The Cost of Discipleship*, is viewed as a regrettable relapse into a world-denying ecclesiology[11] from which Bonhoeffer's involvement in the secular plot against Hitler eventually provided an escape. However, according to Phillips, it is only in the prison letters that christology is finally released from its bondage to ecclesiology. In his forward, Phillips discloses his underlying agenda with the revealing comment 'We have reached the point now where it is impossible to explore the fascinating region of the prison letters ... without a serviceable map of Bonhoeffer's earlier theological journeys. It is hoped that the present work will provide such a map.'[12] His preoccupation with the Tegel correspondence is amply evidenced by the fact that discussion of its various themes comprises more than half the book.[13] Perhaps inevitably therefore, discussion of the earlier works is cursory, the necessary if unexciting appetiser to the more exotic menu served up in the final correspondence.

Undoubtedly one of the outstanding contributions to the field of Bonhoeffer interpretation is Ernst Feil's *The Theology of Dietrich Bonhoeffer,* first published in German in 1971 and extensively revised by the author in preparation for the English translation which appeared in 1985. Feil is particularly concerned to elucidate Bonhoeffer's theology of the world and succeeds in placing *Letters and Papers from Prison* firmly

---

[8] Phillips J. A. *The Form of Christ in the World* (Collins 1967).
[9] Earlier studies being John Godsey's *The Theology of Dietrich Bonhoeffer* (SCM 1960), which traced a development of christology and ecclesiology through Bonhoeffer's writings and Hanfried Müller's *Von der Kirche zur Welt* (Leipzig 1961), written from an avowedly Marxist perspective.
[10] Phillips op. cit. 75.
[11] Phillips at times appears to confuse the bourgeois compromise with the world which Bonhoeffer attacks in *Cost of Discipleship* as the result of the peddling of cheap grace, with the 'worldliness' which is positively endorsed in LPP, op. cit. 104.
[12] Phillips op. cit. xii.
[13] Pages 48-127 discuss the writings from *Sanctorum Communio* to *Cost of Discipleship*. Discussion of *Letters* (with a few references to *Ethics*) runs from pages 128-245.

within the context of Bonhoeffer's earlier works, exposing the shallowness of many interpretations which see the prison correspondence as a major shift in Bonhoeffer's theology. Nevertheless, Feil's agenda becomes clear in the Introduction, where he writes: 'all texts lead again and again to those last letters from prison which stimulated all the interest in Bonhoeffer and without which little notice would be paid today to the earlier writings.'[14] In his preface to the English translation, Feil states his own concern 'to avoid making an interpretation of Bonhoeffer that is based on a prior point of departure.'[15] Nevertheless, he approaches his task, confident of finding that 'Christ and the world come of age ... is the theme of Bonhoeffer's life and theology.'[16] Such a bold and at this stage unsubstantiated assertion that a concern expressed in *Letters and Papers from Prison* holds the key to Bonhoeffer's life and theology is surely scarcely compatible with a claim not to impose a pre-understanding on the material. Whilst Feil's concern to place *Letters and Papers from Prison* within the context of Bonhoeffer's work as a whole enables him to trace a unity of development which Phillips and Müller reject, it means nevertheless that his interpretation is inevitably dominated by the final writings.

Heinrich Ott, writing in the 1960s took the concept of 'reality', which he saw as a crucial issue in contemporary theology, as an interpretative key to Bonhoeffer.[17] In methodological terms, his approach is a dialogical one, in which he argues from a 'phenomenology of discussion' that 'as a rule what he [i.e. a discussion partner] says last is authoritative', so that *Letters and Papers from Prison* becomes definitive for Ott's interpretation.[18] Hence although by his choice of the concept of reality as a starting point, the reader might expect a discussion which focused on the *Ethics*, where Christ and reality are identified, Ott in fact takes *Letters and Papers from Prison* as his starting point. Strangely, without any attempt to substantiate the claim, he repeatedly asserts the contemporaneity of *Letters and Papers from Prison* and *Ethics*.[19] This contention forms the basis of his assertion that '*Letters and Papers from Prison* and *Ethics* are one single drive towards reality, a reality which is nobody and nothing other than Jesus

---

[14] Feil E. op. cit. 3.
[15] Ibid. xvi.
[16] Ibid. xv.
[17] Ott H. *Reality and Faith: The Theological Legacy of Dietrich Bonhoeffer* trans. A. A. Morrison (London Lutterworth 1971).
[18] Ibid., 89.
[19] Ibid. 107 note 3; 171; 192; 204 Presumably Ott has in mind a perceived identity of content rather than strict chronology, although this is never made clear.

Christ himself.'[20] Ott identifies Bonhoeffer's understanding of Christ as reality in *Ethics*, with the 'non-religious interpretation' of *Letters and Papers from Prison* and purports to find a similar approach as early as the *Christology* lectures, which he interprets as an attempt 'to structure the ontology of all that is real as christology, or in other words, to develop christology as the ontology of all that is real'.[21] However, despite his protestations that 'we are not mistakenly importing into the early context of the christology lectures his late thought about non-religious interpretation', it is in fact difficult to avoid such a conclusion.

Dumas whose *Dietrich Bonhoeffer, Theologian of Reality* is undoubtedly one of the best of the early group of interpretations, stresses continuities within Bonhoeffer's output. For Dumas, Bonhoeffer is a theologian of paradox who seeks to hold together a theology of the word and a theology of ontological presence. Dumas was the first commentator to give serious consideration to the influence of Hegel on Bonhoeffer, suggesting that in Bonhoeffer, we see the fulfilment of the 'great promise' which the later Barth saw in Hegel.[22] As with Ott, for Dumas, the key word is 'reality'. However where Ott viewed Bonhoeffer as an existential theologian, Dumas suggests that Bonhoeffer's theology is 'best described as structural',[23] arguing that the German word *Gestalt*, used repeatedly by Bonhoeffer and variously translated into English as form, figure or shape should be translated as 'structure'. He asserts that Bonhoeffer's writing is generally characterised by the use of 'non-religious language', citing his use of the words 'structure' and 'deputy' (*Stellvertretung*).[24] However this is one of the less convincing aspects of his thesis, given that *Stellvertretung* is the word consistently used in German theology to describe the representative or substitutionary work of Christ, whilst the decision to translate *Gestalt* as 'structure' rather than the more usual 'form', seems to owe more to Dumas' interpretation of Bonhoeffer as a 'structuralist' than to any textual evidence.[25] Again one can perhaps detect an undue concern to bring the earlier works into continuity with *Letters and Papers*, where the question of non-religious language is a major issue.

Allied to the problems which arise from reading Bonhoeffer 'backwards' through the lens of *Letters and Papers*, is the reality that even

---

[20] Ibid., 204.
[21] Ibid., 169.
[22] Ibid. 83, citing Barth's *From Rousseau to Ritschl* (SCM 1959), 305.
[23] Dumas A. *Dietrich Bonhoeffer Theologian of Reality* trans. McAfee Brown R. (SCM 1971), 31, 34.
[24] Ibid. 32, 36, 286; cf. Chapter 5 for a detailed discussion of Bonhoeffer's use of this term.
[25] Ibid., 34.

where the prison letters are not used explicitly as an interpretative key, when a linear interpretation is operative, the position of the letters at the 'end of the line' often renders their influence disproportionate. As a result, Bonhoeffer is often marooned in a time warp, viewed in terms of the sort of liberal theology which today seems somewhat outdated and stale. As Rowan Williams has aptly remarked 'We did a very terrible thing ... in the 1960s. We made [Bonhoeffer] an Anglican and a liberal Anglican at that.'[26]

The German theologian Andreas Pangritz suggests that Bonhoeffer's theological development be viewed in terms of a 'spiral' or 'helix',[27] that is, a return to a familiar theme on a different level. The language of intensification or improvisation on a theme might also be helpful. However, the real problem with the continuity/discontinuity debate is that it remains trapped within a linear view of development, whereas, as we will argue, Bonhoeffer's thought is too complex and rich for such un-nuanced categorisation.

**The New Critical Edition**

Despite the inadequacies of an approach to Bonhoeffer interpretation which whether implicitly or explicitly takes the Tegel correspondence as its starting point, the place of *Letters and Papers from Prison* among religious classics is undoubtedly deserved. In its wake Bonhoeffer's lesser known early writings, *Sanctorum Communio* and *Act and Being* were translated, bringing these works to the attention of an English speaking audience. However the lack of a consistent editorial policy meant that they were flawed by inconsistencies of translation, which masked the recurrence of language and phraseology throughout the corpus.[28] Second, given that any translation is inevitably an interpretation,[29] the emergence of most translations in the 1960s, when the concern to trace the roots of the theology of the prison letters was at its height, has inevitably, even if subliminally, influenced the translations, giving them a somewhat anachronistic feel, which is not the case with the original German text. In

---

[26] Paper entitled *Bonhoeffer, the Sixties and After* at the Consultation on Bonhoeffer, Britain and British Theology 1991 (Union Theological Seminary International Bonhoeffer Society Archive).

[27] Pangritz op cit. 7.

[28] e.g. The translation of *Stellvertretung* as 'vicarious action' in *Sanctorum Communio* but 'deputyship' in *Ethics*, led some commentators to trace a move towards 'non religious' language in *Ethics* which has no foundation at all in the German text.

[29] cf. Steiner G. *Real Presences* (University of Chicago Press 1991), 15.

Germany, the six volume *Gesammelte Schriften* edited by Eberhard Bethge gradually emerged, and in due course, English translations of selections from these volumes were published under the editorship of Edwin Robertson.[30] However, the bulk of Bonhoeffer's sermons and occasional writings have never been translated into English, and this has seriously hindered critical appraisal. Even where English speaking scholars worked from the German texts, there remained significant amounts of unpublished material.

In 1981 the West German section of the International Bonhoeffer Society, in conjunction with the parallel organisation in the German Democratic Republic, decided that a new critical edition of Bonhoeffer's work had become necessary.[31] The two committees were motivated both by the fact that new unpublished material had come to light, and by the need for a fresh critical edition which would place the better known works within the context of less familiar material. The fact that the number of friends and contemporaries of Bonhoeffer was steadily decreasing added urgency to the task. A sixteen volume work, amounting to around 8000 pages of text was proposed. The first eight volumes were to be revised editions of Bonhoeffer's published works, including the three which had been posthumously edited by Eberhard Bethge. The remaining eight volumes would comprise letters, lectures, sermons and other occasional writings, assembled in chronological order. 1986 saw the publication of the first volume of the new edition, Bonhoeffer's doctoral dissertation *Sanctorum Communio*. All sixteen volumes and an expanded index are now available,[32] and an English translation is in preparation. Of particular significance amongst the previously published works, is the revised and re-ordered edition of *Ethics*, which will be discussed in detail in Chapter 5.[33]

The new and definitive critical edition of the *Dietrich Bonhoeffer Werke* gives the contemporary interpreter the inestimable advantage of access to all the available material, enabling Bonhoeffer's more familiar work to be read in the context of lesser known or previously unpublished material. Furthermore, the quality of the editorial team, headed by the late Eberhard Bethge and including Bonhoeffer's niece Renate, a number of Bonhoeffer's former colleagues and students as well as an international

---

[30] *No Rusty Swords* (hereafter NRS) (Collins 1965); *The Way to Freedom* (hereafter WTF) (Collins 1966); *True Patriotism* (hereafter TP) (Collins 1973).
[31] In what follows, I draw upon Heinz Eduard Tödt's 'Introduction' to the new edition in DBW 1.
[32] Dietrich Bonhoeffer Werke in 16 Bande (München Chr Kaiser Verlag 1986-present).
[33] DBW 6 (München Chr Kaiser Verlag 1992).

collection of Bonhoeffer scholars, ensures a high standard of critical apparatus. An English translation is under way and a number of volumes have already been published. The editorial process is moderated by a team of Bonhoeffer scholars to ensure a consistency of translation which was previously lacking. [34]

**This Study**

I have already criticised interpretations of Bonhoeffer's work which give disproportionate emphasis to the prison correspondence and particularly its 'creative misappropriation'[35] in the 1960s. Certainly, any single interpretation is unlikely to do justice to this 'open and rich and at the same time deep and disturbing man'[36] and his writings. In a symbiosis between his life and theology which is entirely fitting, the Bonhoeffer who in his *Christology* lectures, opposed all attempts to categorise Christ, himself refuses facile categorisation.

Hence, in focusing on the motif of freedom, my concern is not to offer some alternative interpretative key by which Bonhoeffer can be clinically systematised and packaged, or to create another procrustean bed upon which to constrict him, but rather to highlight a motif which runs like a unifying thread through his writings, giving shape and coherence to the variety of texts and genres within the Bonhoeffer corpus. It is my case that no previous scholarship has done justice to this motif which is central to Bonhoeffer's theology,[37] and that this approach offers a more adequate reading of Bonhoeffer's life and theology than many other interpretations.

Freedom is only one of many rich and varied themes within Bonhoeffer's theology. And yet, its central place within Bonhoeffer's understanding of creation and redemption, and indeed the doctrine of God itself, means that other motifs continually engage with and are enlivened by their reference to it. In this study, I will show that the theme of freedom

---

[34] Inconsistencies of translation are numerous. To cite just one, the famous phrase translated as 'costly grace' in *Cost of Discipleship* is rendered as 'dear mercy' in *Ethics*.
[35] John de Gruchy speaks of a 'creative misuse' of Bonhoeffer in *Dietrich Bonhoeffer, Witness to Jesus Christ* (Collins 1988), 36.
[36] Karl Barth 'Letter to Landsessuperintendent Herrenbrück 21/12/52' quoted in WCOA, 131.
[37] Donald Bachtell's *Freedom in the Theology of Dietrich Bonhoeffer* Unpublished Ph.D. dissertation Drew University 1973 (Microfilm British Library) is a rare exception. There are shorter articles, for example Eberhard Bethge's 'Freiheit und Gehorsam bei Bonhoeffer' in *Am gegebenen Ort: Aufsätze und Reden* (Chr. Kaiser Verlag 1979).

illuminates the relationship between doctrine and ethics, faith and discipleship, Christ and reality, which is absolutely fundamental to Bonhoeffer's life and theology. It offers a perspective from which to survey his life and theology as a whole, avoiding the tendency to abstract theology from its personal or historical context. In the course of the discussion, I will offer a new reading of a number of the familiar texts. Further, whilst the prison correspondence can never be disregarded, and will be the focus of the final chapter, it is my hope that the theme of freedom will both help to relativise the *Letters* within the Bonhoeffer corpus, and cast them in a fresh and compelling light.

**The Rhetoric of Freedom**

Questions of freedom were high on the theological and political agenda in the 1920s and 1930s. In the aftermath of the First World War, the Western world underwent seismic cultural and political shifts, the latter evidenced in the rise of communism and the European dictators. Friedrich Gogarten famously spoke of a era 'Zwischen den Zeiten',[38] where the old certainties of state, culture, rationalism and scholarship were in the process of dissolution and what might replace them was as yet unseen.

In post-world war Germany, the humiliation of the Treaty of Versailles, and in particular the notorious Article 231, which required an admission that 'as the originators of the war, Germany and her allies are responsible for all losses and damage which the allied ... governments and members of their states suffered as a result of the war forced upon them by Germany's attack'[39] had fuelled a longing for a restoration of national freedom and dignity. Although the signal failure of the Weimar Republic meant that many saw the democratic option as a spent force, in the years leading up to Hitler's assumption of power, the rhetoric of 'freedom' retained its resonance, becoming the watchword of Social Democrats and National Socialists alike.

However, in the Germany of the 1920s and 1930s, under the influence of the Cartesian 'turn to the subject' and its Nietzschean and existentialist

---

[38] Gogarten F. *Anfänge* 2, 95, cited in Scholder K. *A Requiem for Hitler and other Perspectives on the German Church Struggle* (London: SCM 1989) The phrase became the title of a journal published by young dialectical theologians in the 1920s in Germany.

[39] Berber G. *Das Diktat von Versailles, Enstehung-Inhalt-Zerfall. Eine Darstellung in Dokumenten*, Essen 1939, article 231, p.1224 cited by Scholder K. *A Requiem for Hitler and other Perspectives on the German Church Struggle* (London SCM 1989), 24.

interpretations, the governing model of freedom was the autonomy of the individual human subject, a freedom from God, from others and for self. With hindsight, the inauspicious conjunction between this philosophical and cultural climate, severe economic hardship and the emergence of Hitler under the banner of freedom and national regeneration, could only end in dictatorship. As Michael Polanyi has convincingly argued, the logical outcome of total individual freedom is tyranny. Polanyi's argument is compellingly simple: If there is no God (or if God is reduced to the image of national self-expression), and human beings are free, then they are free to change society. But in order to make the necessary changes, one must seize power and that power must be absolute, brooking no resistance.[40] Hence despite the lip service paid to freedom, the Nazi assumption of power was characterised by a gradual and persistent erosion of freedom. W. Allen, in his groundbreaking study of the German town of Northeim during Hitler's rise to power, has cogently exposed the gap between the rhetoric and the reality. Allen writes of the totalising influence of National Socialism, subsuming everything into itself, which led at the same time to the atomising of German society. His research reveals a systematic attempt to destroy freedom of association and with it, the freedom of true community, as youth organisations were subsumed into the Hitler youth, sports and social clubs and finally the church were incorporated under the banner of the Reich. He comments: 'By the process of *Gleichschaltung* individuals had a choice: solitude or mass relationship via some Nazi organisation.'[41] As German society was forced into subordination to the image of a malign Messiah, any ethical grounding of freedom was quickly abandoned. There could be no price too high to pay for the freedom of German self expression.

## Bonhoeffer and Freedom

Bonhoeffer does not set out to produce a treatise on freedom, and his thoughts on the issue are incomplete. However, as he sought to engage

---

[40] Polanyi M. *Knowing and Being* (London Routledge and Kegan 1969), 13; cf. also the analysis of Dostoevsky's Grand Inquisitor, to whom Bonhoeffer refers in DBW 10, 311 cf. also DBW 6, 145; DBW 14, 321f.

[41] Allen W. S. *The Nazi Seizure of Power: The Experience of a Single German Town 1922-1945* Revised Edition (New York: Franklin Watts 1984), 232. 'Gleichschaltung' or 'co-ordination' meant the imposition of a National Socialist majority on every committee or governing body in order to bring them into line with the Nazi majority in the Reichstag and so achieve 'national unity'.

theologically with life, especially against the backdrop of National Socialism, the theme resonates as a leitmotif throughout his writings.

Although conditions under National Socialism were exceptional, we would suggest that the very extremity of the situation causes the difference between authentic and inauthentic freedom to be thrown into sharp relief. It is precisely this understanding of freedom as individualistic, atomising and at best ethically neutral, an abstract concept floating free of the practicalities of historical, political and social reality, which Bonhoeffer addresses, challenges and subverts in his christologically framed understanding of freedom in relational, social and ethical terms. Although the long trumpeted demise of modernity will continue to be disputed and the exponents of post-modernity are often much clearer in their denunciation of the past than in their vision for the future, there is a sense in which contemporary culture, in the early years of a new millennium, once again finds itself 'between the times'. Whilst we must be careful not to draw too facile a comparison between Bonhoeffer's situation in those early decades of the twentieth century and our own position at the beginning of the third millennium, a number of parallels suggest themselves. The rhetoric of freedom, at least, retains a powerful resonance and the questions, though differently phrased, are no less urgent. In the political arena, the dismantling of the Berlin Wall and the peaceful overthrow of the Eastern European dictatorships have heralded the decline of communism as a significant world force. But these peaceful revolutions in the name of freedom pose as many questions as they purport to answer. If freedom is from the monolithic rule of the Soviet Union and the rigidity of the command economy, what is freedom for? The resurgence of nationalism and tribalism suggest that the old notion inherited from the Enlightenment, which saw freedom as freedom from God, from others and for self has, as in the 1920s and 1930s, proved palpably inadequate. The struggle for national self-determination, whether in the former Yugoslavia, the Baltic states or in the former African colonies of Rwanda and Burundi, offer chilling parallels with National Socialist Germany. Where freedom means only 'freedom from' the other, who must be demonised in the process, the price of freedom of national expression and identity in the post-Holocaust world can be that late twentieth century euphemism for genocide, 'ethnic cleansing'.

At the level of economics, freedom from the repression of the communist command economy has led to an eager embracing of western style materialism with its attendant problems of rampant individualism and the vagaries of the market. The ideology of the so-called 'free market economy' enshrines an understanding of freedom in terms of the free choice of autonomous individuals which, as Peter Selby and others have ably demonstrated, brings an apparent freedom for the few but imprisons much of the southern hemisphere in a debt economy.[42] The ethical implications of the western consumer's individual freedom of choice on the two thirds world go largely unheeded, although, even within the prosperous Western nations, the illusion of a benign free market is cruelly exposed when the 'freedom' of home ownership is turned into the crippling bondage of negative equity.

Although Bonhoeffer's engagement with issues of politics was largely confined to the very particular circumstances of the Third Reich, his theology has already proved influential in the political arena, in the former GDR, where his legacy was interpreted by his former friend and pupil Albrecht Schönherr,[43] in the struggle against apartheid in South Africa[44] and amongst exponents of liberation theology in South America.[45] Again, despite the absence of much by way of direct comment in the area of economics, Bonhoeffer's work, and in particular his famous question 'who Christ really is for us today', provides the starting point for Peter Selby's recent analysis of the Western financial hegemony, in terms of an economy of debt or mortgage rather than grace.[46]

**The Structure of this Study**

In the chapters which follow, the theme of freedom in Bonhoeffer's work is addressed from five distinct yet complementary perspectives. Chapter 2, 'Freedom and Knowledge' lays some epistemological foundations for the study as a whole. Then in 'Freedom in the Image of God', I trace the pervasive influence of the theme of freedom in Bonhoeffer's exposition of the central Christian doctrines of creation, sin and redemption. Chapter 4,

---

[42] Selby P. *Grace and Mortgage* (Darton Longman and Todd 1997).
[43] Schönherr A. and Krötke W. *Bonhoeffer-Studien: Beiträge zur Theologie und Wirkungsgeschichte Dietrich Bonhoeffers* (Berlin: Evangelische Verlagsanstalt 1985).
[44] cf. De Gruchy, J. W. *Bonhoeffer and South Africa: theology in dialogue* (Grand Rapids: Eerdmans 1984).
[45] cf. Gutierrez's constructive but critical engagement with Bonhoeffer in *The Power of the Poor in History* (Maryknoll: Orbis Books 1983) cited by Clifford Green in 'Bonhoeffer, Modernity and Liberation Theology' in Floyd W. W. and Marsh C. eds. *Theology and the Practice of Responsibility: Essays on Dietrich Bonhoeffer* (Trinity Press International 1994).
[46] Selby op. cit., 4, 11 and passim.

'Freedom in Community', sets Bonhoeffer's understanding of freedom within the context of sociality, offering a critique of individualist approaches, whilst Chapter 5 takes up the ethical implications of freedom in its exploration of the relationship between freedom and responsibility. In the final chapter, I offer a reassessment of the prison correspondence in the light of the motif of freedom, suggesting that questions of authentic and inauthentic freedom stand at the heart of Bonhoeffer's approach to the 'world come of age', which for Bonhoeffer, as we will argue, is primarily the world of the latter days of the Third Reich.

The subtitle of this study 'Courageously Grasping Reality' arises out of Bonhoeffer's poem on the subject of freedom, written in the final year of his imprisonment in Tegel. Freedom, says Bonhoeffer 'exists not in hovering between possibilities but in courageously grasping reality.'[47] It draws upon the importance of the concept of reality throughout Bonhoeffer's writing, not least in his *Ethics*, where Bonhoeffer sees the ethical task in terms of 'the realisation of the real'[48] and asserts that free and responsible action is action 'in accordance with reality'.

---

[47] My translation. The German reads 'nicht im Möglichen schweben, das Wirkliche tapfer ergreifen ... ist die Freiheit'.*Widerstand und Ergebung* (1998 Chr. Kaiser Verlag, München) 571.

[48] *Ethik* (1992 Chr. Kaiser Verlag, München), 34.

# Chapter Two
# Freedom and Knowledge

**Introduction**

In the last months of his life, Bonhoeffer wrote to Eberhard Bethge from Tegel prison about the draft book on which he was working, and commented: 'It's as you say "Knowing" is the most exciting thing in the world.'[49] The manuscript, to which he refers, has never been found. It seems that Bonhoeffer continued to work on it, keeping it with him until the end, leaving his readers with this tantalising comment, but no possibility of comparing his thoughts from Tegel with his early writings on the subject. Nevertheless, it is striking that at the end of his life, Bonhoeffer should return to the subject which had been the focus of his youthful dissertation *Act and Being*.

This chapter, which focuses on the relationship between knowledge and freedom, is foundational to the argument of this book, not merely because it focuses on one of Bonhoeffer's earliest works *Act and Being*, but also because, although Bonhoeffer will never again address epistemological issues in such detail, many of the concepts which he develops and the conclusions which he reaches within this context, will become fundamental to our discussion of freedom in the chapters which follow. Bonhoeffer's understanding of divine freedom in christological terms as 'freedom-for', and of redemption as freedom from the *cor curvum in se*, will underlie much of what we will discuss in our next chapter on 'Freedom in the Image of God'. The stress on the personal and yet communal nature of 'ecclesial' knowing, questions the individualist assumptions which are implicit in many interpretations of freedom, and as such is foundational to our discussion in Chapter 4 on 'Freedom in Community', while the ethical implications of knowing and the place of responsibility undergird much of what will emerge when we consider 'Freedom and Responsibility' in Chapter 5. Bonhoeffer's search for an epistemology which subverts

---

[49] LPP 384.

competitive understandings of freedom and breaks the tacit connection between freedom, knowledge and control of others, lays the foundations for our final chapter on the Tegel theology.

*Act and Being*[50] which began life as Bonhoeffer's *Habilitationschrift*, the post-doctoral dissertation required to qualify him as a lecturer within the German university system, will be the main focus of this chapter, but reference will also be made to his doctoral thesis *Sanctorum Communio*, to the *Christology* lectures delivered in Berlin in 1933 and to various occasional lectures. We aim to show that questions of divine and human freedom underlie Bonhoeffer's discussions of revelation and epistemology. On this basis, we will examine Bonhoeffer's critique of the dominance of the subject-object paradigm in epistemology, looking at its implications for the relationship between human knowledge and freedom, and its inadequacy for a theology of revelation which takes seriously both God's freedom as revealer and the reality of what is revealed. The distinction which Bonhoeffer draws between formal and substantial understandings of freedom will prove crucial here. Another foundational concept, which we will discuss at some length, is Bonhoeffer's use of the social category of 'person', which undergirds his attempt to develop an ecclesial epistemology in which both sociality and ethics are taken with due seriousness. We will also give critical attention to his advocacy of the church or Christian community as 'the place where human existence is understood.'[51]

We would suggest that a number of salient issues arise from the standpoint of our theme: Can an epistemology of revelation be constructed which both affirms the freedom of God as revealer and yet takes seriously the human, cognitional end of the equation? Does the very concept of revelation constitute a threat to, or infringement upon human freedom? Must theology bypass epistemology and conceptualise revelation purely in terms of feeling or direct experience as in Romanticism, or reduce the Christian faith to ethics, or can it engage fruitfully with epistemological structures so that they give space for revelation? What might an epistemological reticence, with the intrinsic capacity to be self-critical and self-subverting, rather than systematising, look like?

---

[50] *Act and Being* trans. Rumscheidt H. M. ed. Floyd W. W. (Harper Collins 1996) (hereafter referred to as DBWE 2).

[51] DBWE 2, 109. The new English translation leaves the word 'Dasein', which I have rendered 'human existence', untranslated.

## The Key Issues

Until recently, *Act and Being*, was one of the most neglected works in the Bonhoeffer corpus.[52] This is understandable, given that it is perhaps Bonhoeffer's least accessible work. However, two recent studies, which see an understanding of *Act and Being* as crucial to our interpretation of Bonhoeffer's work as a whole, must be mentioned at the outset of our discussion. The first is Charles Marsh's *Reclaiming Dietrich Bonhoeffer*,[53] which focuses on Bonhoeffer's engagement with post-Enlightenment philosophy as well as offering some cogent analysis of his critique of the early Barth. The second is Wayne Whitson Floyd's, *Theology and the Dialectics of Otherness*, which uses the writings of Bonhoeffer and Theodor Adorno, the philosopher of the Frankfurt school, as lenses through which to reassess the response of twentieth-century theology and philosophy to the subject-object paradigm.[54] Both of these works will be referred to throughout this chapter.

In his seminar paper delivered at Union Theological Seminary in 1931, *The Theology of Crisis and its attitude towards Philosophy and Science*, Bonhoeffer had written that philosophy must recognise its limits. 'By so doing', he writes, 'it gives room so far as it can, for God's revelation, which indeed makes room for itself by itself.'[55] Floyd grounds his study of Bonhoeffer on this assertion, viewing Bonhoeffer's writing as an 'attempt to push the transcendental tradition to "give room", so far as it can, for God's revelation'.[56] Bonhoeffer, of course is always clear that it is God who 'makes room' for himself. Here is no 'God of the gaps,' rather Bonhoeffer is concerned that theology should not retreat from the sphere of epistemology but must engage creatively with its questions.

One of the greatest difficulties which *Act and Being* poses for the would-be interpreter, is the lack of clarity or consensus about the theme or

---

[52] Clifford Green's discussion of the text in *Bonhoeffer: A Theology of Sociality* (Revised Edition Eerdmans, Grand Rapids, Michigan, 1999, first published as *The Sociality of Christ and Humanity: Dietrich Bonhoeffer's Early Theology* Scholars Press American Academy of Religion, Missoula. 1972), being an honourable exception to the general picture. cf. also Franklin Sherman's short essay in *The Place of Bonhoeffer* ed. Marty M. E. (SCM 1963).
[53] Marsh C. *Reclaiming Dietrich Bonhoeffer: The Promise of his Theology* (Oxford 1994).
[54] Floyd W. W. *Theology and the Dialectics of Otherness* (University Press of America 1988).
[55] *The Theology of Crisis and its attitude towards Philosophy and Science*, DBW 10, 448.
[56] Op. cit., 10.

purpose of the work. Here is not the place to enter into that debate in any depth.[57] However, whilst the search for an interpretative key to Bonhoeffer's *Habilitationschrift* may prove as unprofitable as attempts to construct a hermeneutic to Bonhoeffer's work as a whole, one clear theme which emerges from this early thesis is the whole question of the relationship between divine and human freedom. At the heart of Bonhoeffer's exploration of the concept of revelation and his attempt to construct a Christian, or, as he describes it in his introduction, an 'ecclesial' epistemology of revelation, lies the deeper question of freedom. Indeed, at the outset of the thesis, in his overview of recent theological developments, Bonhoeffer couches the question in terms of this issue. 'Barth', he asserts, 'by means of his "critical reservation", seeks to hold onto the freedom of God's grace, and thereby to provide a foundation for human freedom', whereas Gogarten and Bultmann, on the other hand, 'wish to free the human being in its "concrete situation" or "historicity" from the delusion of being at its own disposal.'[58] As we will see, Bonhoeffer offers a solution which goes beyond this apparent polarisation between divine and human freedom.

*The Epistemological Problem*

However, first Bonhoeffer analyses the problem as he perceives it. He argues that post-Enlightenment theology can be viewed as an attempt to deal with the questions raised for theology by Kant and Idealism with regard to the 'objectivity' of the concept of God and the question of human cognition. These appear to offer a choice between objectifying God and drawing him into the power of the human knower, or withdrawing from the realm of cognition and maintaining a place for God within the realm of ethics or feeling:

> At the heart of the problem is the formulation of the question that Kant and idealism have posed for theology... It is a question of the 'objectivity' of the concept of God and an adequate concept of cognition, the issue of determining the relationship between 'the being of God' and the mental act which grasps

---

[57] For a comprehensive discussion of the different views see Clifford Green's *Bonhoeffer: A Theology of Sociality* (op. cit.) and the Introduction to DBWE 2, by the editor Wayne Whitson Floyd Jr.
[58] DBWE 2, 25.

that being. In other words, the meaning of 'the being of God in revelation' must be interpreted theologically.[59]

Later in *Concerning the Christian Idea of God*,[60] Bonhoeffer again identifies, what he sees as the critical epistemological problem. '[H]ow can theology state the reality of God without thinking it? And if it thinks it, how can it be avoided that God should again be pulled into the circle of thought?'[61] He concludes that theology must recognise its limits and 'leave room for the reality of God, which can never be conceived by theological thinking.'[62] If, as the Christian faith maintains, God has revealed himself in Christ, then if revelation is in any real sense knowledge, theology must develop an epistemology of revelation. In his lecture *The History of Systematic Theology in the Twentieth Century*,[63] Bonhoeffer refers to 'Feuerbach's two questions to religion', which 'in essence, theology has left unanswered' namely '(1) about the truth of its statements (illusion) (2) about correspondence with real life.' In *Act and Being*, Bonhoeffer is concerned to address the first of these questions.[64] The key issue is whether God can be known, or whether human knowledge of God is always a reflection on an ungraspable *actus directus*. If revelation is defined purely in terms of act then God remains free from the power of the human knower, but is rendered unknowable. However, if revelation is defined as being, as in the Roman Catholic identification of revelation and church, or the conservative Protestant equation of revelation and the Bible, it becomes knowable, but at the cost of becoming an object to be possessed, something within the control of the human knower. Bonhoeffer asks whether there might be a third way, which can affirm both the act and being of revelation without opting for the dialectical approach of the early Barth in which all our knowing must be qualified as not knowing. As I understand the text, Bonhoeffer is not dealing here with questions of the use of *language* about God and hence with issues of univocal, equivocal and analogical usage, but rather with the question of whether an adequate epistemology of revelation can be constructed, given the danger that if 'knowing' is qualified too heavily, the believer lives in doubt and the church cannot proclaim the

---

[59] Ibid., 27, 28.
[60] DBW 10, 424.
[61] Ibid., 425.
[62] Ibid., 426.
[63] DBW 11, 148.
[64] cf. Chapter 5 for a discussion of the Feuerbach's second question.

Gospel.⁶⁵ Hence Bonhoeffer defines his aim in *Act and Being*, as 'to unify the concern of true transcendentalism and true ontology in a ecclesial form of thinking'.⁶⁶ As will become clear, this concern to find an 'ecclesial form of thinking' goes to the very heart of his thesis.

## The Argument of *Act and Being* in Outline

However, before putting forward a solution to the problem as he perceives it, Bonhoeffer offers an analysis of post-Enlightenment philosophy and in particular the question of the autonomy of the thinking subject over against God and the other, in other words, the question of the relationship of knowledge and human freedom. It is important to note that at the outset, Bonhoeffer himself recognises that his approach, both to Kant and to Idealism, is stylised rather than nuanced and that his concern is with systematic rather than historical questions.⁶⁷ At the heart of his argument in the first half of the thesis, is the assertion that since human knowledge operates by classifying its object, placing the unknown into a category of the known, philosophy, of whatever hue, tends inevitably towards the totalising system and as such displays an inherent antipathy to the possibility of revelation.⁶⁸ In making this assessment, Bonhoeffer is not working to some anti-philosophical agenda, or engaging in theological imperialism, but defines his remit with care. Given the way in which human knowledge operates, how can revelation be conceptualised in epistemological terms, without being reduced to an entity or forced into a pre-existing category? Hence his concern is not to polarise faith and reason but, working from the standpoint that revelation has in fact been given, he proposes to stretch the categories of cognition to give room for a cognitive conceptuality of revelation, a way of articulating something which the philosophical tradition, turned in upon itself, is impotent to grasp.

---

⁶⁵ For a detailed discussion and analysis by Bonhoeffer of Barth's early theology, cf. *Jungste Theologie: Besprechung systematisch-theologischer Neuerscheinungen* GS V 300ff.
⁶⁶ DBWE 2, 32 (translation slightly altered - the German is *kirchlichen Denken*, translated here by Hans-Richard Reuter as 'ecclesiological thought' but at p90 as 'ecclesial thought'.
⁶⁷ DBWE 2, 33 note 1.
⁶⁸ cf. the discussion of the classifying tendencies of the human 'logos' in *Christology* esp. pp. 28-29.

We should note at this point that, although Bonhoeffer's antipathy towards metaphysics is well documented and deeply rooted,[69] Wayne Floyd is surely right when he dismisses as facile, suggestions that Bonhoeffer also rejects epistemology in favour of the social and ethical.[70] Floyd argues that *Act and Being* should be seen as 'a refusal to separate the moment of ethical responsibility before the thou ... from the need to find a form of rationality adequate to it.'[71] In *Sanctorum Communio*, Bonhoeffer writes of the limits of epistemology: 'How are we to reach the alien subject? There is no way there at all, through knowledge, just as there is no way to God through pure knowledge.'[72] However, we would argue that this assertion should be read in context, as a concern to preserve the integrity, or what Bonhoeffer calls the 'alien' nature of the other, against the tendency of the idealist subject to draw the other into itself, rather than as an assault on epistemology *per se*. Certainly by the time of writing *Act and Being*, Bonhoeffer sees his task in terms of a christological redefinition of epistemology in social and ethical terms, in order to make it usable for theology.

Indeed, at the opening of the discussion, Bonhoeffer suggests that the Kantian critique of reason, in its concern to delineate the limits of human knowledge, has affinities with Luther's theological critique of reason as *ratio in se ipsum incurva*,[73] and that Kant could well be termed 'the epistemologist *par excellence* of Protestantism.'[74] He finds that, in what he terms a 'pure transcendentalist' approach, (in his somewhat 'broad-brush' discussion, he is distinguishing between what he saw as Kant's intentions, from the idealist developments arising from and latent in his thought), thought is always 'with reference to' the transcendent. Being is suspended in thought and hence is not absorbed by it or at its disposal.[75] Kant's *Ding an sich*, acting as a limit to thought, had protected the integrity of the

---

[69] cf. the Tegel correspondence, where metaphysics regularly appears as a negative characteristic of 'religion'. (LPP 280, 286 etc.).
[70] Floyd W. W. *Theology and the Dialectics of Otherness* (op. cit.), 125.
[71] Ibid., 142.
[72] DBW 1 25; ET 28.
[73] cf. DBWE 2, 41, citing Luther's *Lectures on Romans* 291.
[74] DBWE 2, 34. As the editorial footnote indicates, the earlier English translation suggested erroneously that Bonhoeffer was denying such a title to Kant.
[75] Whether Bonhoeffer's attempted distinction is a valid one is not critical to his argument, that whilst most interpretations of the transcendentalist approach tend toward the totalising system and the hegemony of the thinking subject, this is not the inevitable outcome of the Kantian approach, which in its 'pure' form, has potential for the construction of an epistemology of revelation.

transcendent other, albeit rendering it unknowable in itself. Hence, whilst, on Bonhoeffer's terms, Kant's failure to give space for revelation is to be deplored, his reticence with regard to the scope of human reason is entirely proper and is, at least potentially, usable for theology.[76]

However, Bonhoeffer argues, the tendency is for the thinking I, in its search for autonomy, to fall into solipsism, setting itself up as the starting point rather than the limit of philosophy. In achieving its aim of freedom from the transcendent, it becomes trapped in itself. 'Thinking languishes in itself; precisely where it is free from the transcendent, from reality, there it is imprisoned in itself.'[77] Wayne Floyd, the editor of the new English edition comments 'for the proto-deconstructionist Bonhoeffer, an irony lies at the heart of all late modern and post-modern attempts to free the subject from any encumbrances of transcendence; for in attempting to free the subject from heteronomy, they actually leave the subject imprisoned with only itself, unable to allow the approach of that which is genuinely other.'[78] Whether Bonhoeffer, who shows relatively little interest in the structure of language, can be accurately described as a 'proto-deconstructionist' is doubtful, although Walter Lowe's more nuanced suggestion of an 'affinity' between Bonhoeffer and deconstructionist theory is more plausible.[79] Nevertheless, as we will see, the dissonance between expectation and achievement which Bonhoeffer sees as characteristic of the human condition apart from God, is an irony to which he returns repeatedly, for example in his understanding of the fall where humanity, striving to be like God, becomes in the process less than fully human, and his discussion of the legacy of the Enlightenment in *Ethics* where the technological advances which promised freedom in fact enslave humanity.

Bonhoeffer argues that the decision between a pure transcendentalism which respects the integrity of the other, and the Idealism in which the autonomous thinking subject draws the other into its control, is actually an ethical decision, a decision of 'practical reason' as to the use of freedom, rather than theoretical philosophy:

---

[76] For a recent critical analysis of Kant's legacy to theology cf. Wolterstorff N. 'Is it possible and desirable for theologians to recover from Kant?' in *Modern Theology* Vol. 14, Nr.1 January 1998, 1-18.

[77] DBWE 2, 39.

[78] Ibid., footnote 14.

[79] Lowe W. 'Bonhoeffer and Deconstruction: Towards a Theology of the Crucified Logos' in Floyd W. W. and Marsh C. ed. *Theology and the Practice of Responsibility: Essays on Dietrich Bonhoeffer* (Trinity Press International 1994).

Nothing can oblige thinking, precisely as free thinking, not to draw the unconditional into itself and take control of its I. But it is no less an act of free thinking when, precisely to remain free, it contents itself with the orientation towards transcendence and does not take control of its I, simply because it is always 'in reference to'.[80]

We will discuss the inherent connection between ethics and knowledge in more detail below. Here Bonhoeffer cites with approval Fichte's comment that 'the kind of philosophy one has depends on what kind of human being one is'.[81] In other words, the connection between freedom, knowledge and control is not intrinsic to the structural categories of thought, but a question of moral choice.

*The Critique of the Transcendental and Ontological Approaches*

Our concern in this chapter does not lie in a detailed exposition of Bonhoeffer's thesis and hence, whilst we must attend to Bonhoeffer's negative assessment of the transcendentalist and ontological attempts to address the problem of act and being, our discussion will be brief. Bonhoeffer conflates his discussion of Idealism and Neo-Kantianism under the heading of transcendentalist approaches, and it is to a review of these to which we will now turn.

*Transcendentalism* In its Neo-Kantian form, transcendentalism sought to maintain the freedom of God by refusing to say 'God is', in the belief that to do so would be to objectify him. Bonhoeffer argues that although 'In this way, to be sure, the Creator's integrity is honoured in principle, that is to the extent to which this is at all possible in philosophy',[82] the problem is that God remains ultimately unknowable and that in setting its own boundary in this way, reason becomes trapped in itself. '[It] sees only itself, even when it sees another, even when it wants to see God ... The I believes itself free and is captive; it has all power and has only itself as a vassal ...

---

[80] DBWE 2, 40; cf. Nicholas Lash's illuminating analogy of cognition as a bridge to the outside world and his comment that '[T]he Cartesian presents as *technical* questions (problems of engineering) what are, in fact, questions of *ethics*: of who, and what, and in what circumstances, might possibly be relied upon.' Lash N. *Easter in Ordinary* (SCM 1988), 69.
[81] Ibid., paraphrasing Fichte *Werke* 1, 434.
[82] DBWE 2, 44.

[this] is the ontic inversion into the self, the *cor curvum in se*.'[83] Here Bonhoeffer takes up Luther's definition of sin, (to which he will return repeatedly throughout his writings), but reinterprets it in the context of the deification of the thinking subject, the autonomous ego which constructs its own world, only to find itself imprisoned within it. Although the Neo-Kantian approach is usually viewed as tending toward dualism (an accusation often levelled at Barth's theology with its roots in Neo-Kantian philosophy), Bonhoeffer's concern here is with the way in which, despite the apparent cognitional modesty of the Neo-Kantian scheme, the thinking subject still constructs its own world, even in categorising knowledge of God as lying outside the limits of knowledge.[84] The duality between knower and known collapses into itself in monadic isolation.

In Idealism, which Bonhoeffer sees as an inevitable development from Kant's theory, the human spirit is the source of self-understanding, the universal reference point, Luther's '*ratio in se ipsum incurva*'.[85] Hegel's assertion that freedom was the predicate of knowledge was a clear case in point: 'The person is cradled in freedom. In freedom comes knowledge; in freedom alone can the existence of human beings apprehend itself and change. Act, meaning and freedom belong together. Thus, the essence of the person is freedom, autonomy, coming-to-itself or being-with-itself.'[86] It is in coming to itself that the I finds itself and in finding itself, finds God. In his seminar paper *The Theology of Crisis and its attitude towards Philosophy and Science*, Bonhoeffer writes of Idealism: 'Here the ego is found as not only the interpreting but even a creative ego; it creates its world itself. The ego stands in the centre of the world, which is created, ruled and overpowered by the ego.'[87] He continues: 'The ego knows reality, it knows itself, it is essentially autonomous.'[88] However, argues Bonhoeffer, that autonomy is illusory, since without Christ 'we live in our own overpowered and egocentric world, which is not the world of God.'[89] The I, in usurping the creator's role is trapped within its solipsist empire.

---

[83] Ibid., 45-6.
[84] As deconstructionist theory has indicated, monism and dualism are often inextricably connected.
[85] DBWE 2, 41 citing Luther's *Lectures on Romans* 291.
[86] Ibid., 48.
[87] *The Theology of Crisis and its attitude towards Philosophy and Science*, DBW 10, 443.
[88] Ibid., 444.
[89] Ibid., 449.

*Ontology* Bonhoeffer also assesses attempts to understand knowledge in ontological terms. As with his recognition that a pure transcendentalism could provide fruitful categories for theology, so he suggests that a pure ontological approach, in which thought would be suspended in being without being subsumed by it, could usefully assist the theological endeavour. However, as with the discussion of transcendentalist approaches, his assessment of the various attempts to delineate a being of knowledge, is that ultimately, they result in a totalising system. Husserl's human reason, despite its aim to preserve the freedom of being, actually subsumes being and falls into Idealism.[90] Scheler maintains God's freedom from absorption in consciousness, but only, in Bonhoeffer's assessment, at the expense of reducing him to an idea or value. 'Scheler's vision ... particularly in his last literary period, does violence to God, first ascending to God in love and then pulling God down to its level.'[91] As in Idealism, Bonhoeffer concludes, God is ultimately enclosed within the I, immanent within the system which phenomemology creates.

Heidegger's *Being and Time* had been published in 1927 and Bonhoeffer offers an appreciative assessment of his insistence on understanding being as unconditionally prior to thought. He suggests that in recognising that thought does not construct the world, but always finds itself already in the world, in history and sociality, Heidegger comes close to a solution to the problem of act and being. Nevertheless, because, in Bonhoeffer's assessment, Heidegger's philosophy is 'consciously atheistic',[92] ultimately human *Dasein* is enclosed within finitude, leaving no space for a concept of revelation. If, as revelation discloses, finitude is in fact characterised by creatureliness - which Bonhoeffer equates here with openness to God, rather than by 'enclosedness', Heidegger's approach becomes unusable for a theology which takes revelation seriously.

Theological attempts to conceive of a being of revelation are in his view equally flawed. Bonhoeffer applauds Przywara's attempt to take human creatureliness with due seriousness, but concludes that his schema tends to underplay both the rupture of sin and the contingency of grace. He finds the Thomist concept of the *analogia entis* unacceptable, in that it suggested that human being was always analogous to the being of God, whereas for Bonhoeffer, as he had argued in his first dissertation

---

[90] DBWE 2, 64.
[91] Ibid., 66.
[92] Ibid., 72.

*Sanctorum Communio*, humanity always existed either 'in Adam', or 'in Christ'.[93]

*The Inevitable Failure of Philosophy* Bonhoeffer concludes that '*Per se*, a philosophy can concede no room for revelation unless it knows revelation and confesses itself to be Christian philosophy in full recognition that the place it wanted to usurp *is* already occupied by another - namely, by Christ.'[94] Although in theory, an epistemology of revelation could make use of the pure transcendental concept of act as 'with reference to' being and pure ontology's 'suspension' of act in being, in practice, both positions tend towards a view of the human being as self-grounded and as capable of bringing itself into truth, with the result that they become unusable. Bonhoeffer concludes: 'Thinking is as little able as good works to deliver *the cor curvum in se* from itself.'[95] It is only from 'outside', that is through God's revelation, that humanity can be placed into truth.

## The Contingency of Revelation and the Freedom of God

Hence, as we have already argued, Bonhoeffer's concern is to find an epistemology of revelation which both preserves its character as the absolutely contingent act of a gracious God, and yet expresses its concrete nature as a real and apprehensible self-giving of God. In the section on 'The Contingency of Revelation', the focus sharpens and homes in on the question of divine freedom. Bonhoeffer asserts that theology must maintain 'the absolute freedom of revelation over against reason and hence over against all possibilities which could be developed, for example, from existence understood as potentiality.'[96] Revelation is never a human possibility, but must be seen as 'an event that has its basis in the freedom of God, positively as the self-giving and negatively as the self-withholding of God.'[97]

---

[93] DBW 1 71 note 1; cf. our discussion of Bonhoeffer's formula *analogia relationis* in Chapter 3.
[94] DBWE 2, 76-78.
[95] Ibid., 80.
[96] Ibid., 82 (translation slightly altered).
[97] Ibid.

## Potentiality and Actuality

However, before narrowing our focus to examine Bonhoeffer's understanding of God's freedom in revelation, we must first look briefly at questions of potentiality and actuality, which will prove foundational to our understanding of Bonhoeffer's view of divine freedom and in particular to his critique of the theology of the early Barth in *Act and Being*.[98] Bonhoeffer repeatedly makes negative reference to the concepts of possibility and potentiality in *Act and Being*, but without clearly defining them or their relationship to theology. However, the position is clarified on reading Bonhoeffer's Inaugural Lecture *Humanity in Contemporary Philosophy and Theology*, where he asserts trenchantly: '*the concept of possibility has no place in theology or therefore in theological anthropology*'.[99] In *Sanctorum Communio*, Bonhoeffer had distinguished the activity of Christ in the realisation (*Realisierung*) of the church, from that of the Spirit in the 'actualisation' (*Aktualisierung*) of it in time, but cautions that 'it must be clearly noted, that here the *actualisation through the Holy Spirit is not opposed to the potentiality in Christ, but to the reality in the revelation in Christ* ... We come very close here to applying the category of potentiality in Christ. But this category precisely destroys the character of reality (*Wirklichkeitscharakter*) of redemption.'[100]

Bonhoeffer argues that for humanity to understand itself from its possibilities means to understand oneself by reflection on oneself, rather than from revelation. He suggests that 'The concept of possibility rationalises reality. It defines any reality after the fashion of a logical entity. i.e. it holds it fast, makes it generally accessible. Human beings are thought of as having particular set possibilities with reference to God - either *capax* or *incapax infiniti*.'[101] Hence human being is defined as potentiality for being. However, for Bonhoeffer, to be human means either to be under revelation or outside it, in Christ or in Adam. Revelation is never a possibility. It is either a reality experienced in faith, or for those outside

---

[98] cf. especially pp 83, 90.

[99] DBW 10, 357ff at 373 (italics original).

[100] DBW 1 89; In the *Ethics* fragment 'Christ, Reality and Good', Bonhoeffer describes the relationship between Christ, and the Holy Spirit as the 'realisation of the real' (*Wirklichkeit /Wirklichwerden*).

[101] DBW 10, 373; In NRS 64 this sentence is mistranslated to suggest that Bonhoeffer opposes the concept of possibility because it views humanity as *capax infiniti* when he is actually *incapax infiniti*. In fact Bonhoeffer is refuting both *capax* and *incapax* as attempts to categorise human possibility apart from revelation.

faith, something entirely unknowable. He argues that the concept of possibility opens the door to a semi-Pelagianism in that both sin and faith are then seen to lie within a range of human possibilities with the result that 'the total incomprehensibility, inexcusability and infinity of the fall is rationalised as an explicable realisation of immanent possibilities.'[102] In such a scenario, even forgiveness becomes a human possibility, albeit one which comes from God. Although, in this way, possibility preserves human continuity, it does so only as an entity which fails to impinge on human existence. Bonhoeffer accepts that the concept of the limit (*Grenz*) implies possibility, and that this, at least at first sight, is problematic, in that theology wishes to affirm the boundary between God and humanity. However, he argues that the limit between God and humanity must be understood as a limit between persons, not entities, the content of which is defined by sin and holiness. '[T]he theme of theology is the crossing of this limit by God, namely the forgiveness of sins and sanctification.'[103] Hence in theology the limit is defined not by human possibility but by the reality of God.[104]

*Freedom, Formal and Substantial*

This concern to reckon with 'the reality of God' as the defining factor, informs Bonhoeffer's analysis of two different approaches to divine freedom.

*Formal Freedom* The first possible interpretation, which Bonhoeffer discusses at some length, is a formal concept of freedom, of which the primary thesis is that God is never at the disposal of humanity, but is always free to give or to withhold his presence. Bonhoeffer takes this approach to be the hallmark of the early Barth in *Römerbrief* and *Die Christliche Dogmatik*, where Barth emphatically affirms God's 'majestically free favour'.[105] 'God is free inasmuch as God is bound to nothing, not even the "existing", "historical" Word. The Word as truly

---

[102] DBW 10, 373-4.
[103] Ibid., 375.
[104] cf. also the discussion of 'vicarious action' (*Stellvertretung*) in DBW 1, 99, where Bonhoeffer argues that '[It] (vicarious action) is not an ethical possibility or norm, but solely the reality of the divine love towards the Christian community.' In other words, theology must concern itself with what is, in terms of the concrete revelation of God in Christ, rather than debating the ethical propriety of an abstract concept.
[105] *Die christliche Dogmatik*, 297 (1927) 297 cited at DBWE 2, 83.

God's is free ... it is God's glory that in relation to everything given and conditional, God remains utterly free, unconditioned.'[106] It is here that Bonhoeffer detects in Barth a lurking transcendentalism. 'God's freedom and the act of faith are essentially supratemporal', so that despite Barth's use of temporal language and his attempts to give historical meaning to his concept of act, human faith and obedience become references to God's activity, because no historical moment of time can bear the infinite.[107] 'God is understood as pure act. God's freedom is the possibility grasped in the concrete act - but just that: possibility'.[108] In this formal approach to divine freedom, Bonhoeffer suggests that theology impales itself on the transcendentalist dilemma. God can only be spoken of in reference to the knower, nothing can be said about God as he is in himself. The price of avoiding the objectification of God is to make God unknowable.

God's freedom was also understood in formal terms by the personalist philosopher Eberhard Grisebach and his theological counterparts Gogarten and Kittermeyer. However, unlike Barth, they interpreted the encounter between God and humanity in terms of the 'I-Thou' relationship. Although in *Sanctorum Communio*, Bonhoeffer had drawn enthusiastically upon the insights of personalist philosophy as exemplified by Grisebach, which saw the other or neighbour as an ethical rather than epistemological boundary to thought,[109] by the time of writing *Act and Being* his approach had become more christologically focused. He suggests that whilst Grisebach 'comes a long way to meet Christian thought, when he insists that human beings are directed into their reality only from outside',[110] in limiting 'the outside' to the claim of my neighbour, he falls into the opposite danger of absolutising the 'thou' and reducing the Gospel to ethics. God and revelation become unnecessary and humanity remains self-enclosed in the epistemic equivalent of the *cor curvum in se*, since even an ethically motivated concern for the integrity of the other remains self enclosed. Only the free

---

[106] DBWE 2, 82.

[107] Ibid. 84 Bonhoeffer suggests that the problem is Barth's espousal of the reformed *finitum non capax infiniti*, so that the human activity of faith could only be a reference back to, or a reflection on, the moment of revelation, not a real encounter with God in the historical moment. Bonhoeffer was later to argue for the formula *finitum non capax infiniti sed per infinitum*, which, whilst maintaining an assertion of the absolute contingency of revelation, placed the stress on God's freedom to choose to be less than free, or rather, to be free for rather than free from humanity.

[108] Ibid. 83.

[109] DBW 1, 25-32 passim esp. 25.

[110] DBWE 2, 89.

and contingent revelation of God, breaking in from outside can place human beings into reality and free them from self-enclosed isolation. As divine freedom and transcendence is understood relationally as freedom for the world, so human epistemological transcendence is a freedom in sociality and responsibility, a freedom for the other.[111]

*Substantial Freedom* Bonhoeffer concludes that 'the formalistic, actualistic understanding of the freedom and contingency of God in revelation',[112] whether as expounded by Barth, or as modified by personalism, remains inadequate as a foundation for theological thought, in that it admits no distinction between profane thought and the theological or ecclesial thought of the one placed in truth by revelation. He argues that Barth is addressing the abstract question of what might be possible for God, rather than engaging with the reality of the concrete revelation of God in Christ, and hence, is operating at least implicitly within the limits of a Kantian epistemology. For all his opposition to the anthropocentric theologies of nineteenth-century Liberalism, Barth is still working within human categories, whereas for Bonhoeffer, it is God's revelation of himself in Christ, which must subvert and define all our categories.[113] Barth is rightly concerned to affirm God's freedom, but what he in fact affirms is not the freedom which God demonstrates in his revelation in Christ, but a picture of divine freedom which is in fact a human epistemological construct. In a section which is deservedly well known and regularly quoted in part, but which merits citing again in full, Bonhoeffer claims:

> In revelation it is not so much a question of the freedom of God - eternally remaining in the divine self, aseity - on the other side of revelation, as it is of God's coming out of God's own self in revelation. It is a matter of God's *given* Word, the covenant in which God is bound by God's own action. It is a

---

[111] Writing later from prison, Bonhoeffer commented: 'Belief in the resurrection is *not* the 'solution' of the problem of death. God's 'beyond' is not the beyond of our cognitive faculties. The transcendence of epistemological theory has nothing to do with the transcendence of God. God is the beyond in the midst of our life.' (LPP 282) We would suggest that the statement should be read, not as dismissive of epistemology, but as rejecting the reductionist approach to theology which privileges the cognitive over the ethical and the social, a Christianity which provides answers to questions rather than affecting the whole of life.

[112] DBWE 2, 90.

[113] This approach is characteristic of Bonhoeffer's theology as a whole. The starting point must always be the concrete revelation of God in Christ, not an abstract notion which is then applied to him.

question of the freedom of God, which finds its strongest evidence precisely in that God freely chose to be bound to historical human beings and to be placed at the disposal of human beings. God is free not from human beings but for them. Christ is the word of God's freedom. God *is* present, that is, not in eternal non-objectivity but - to put it quite provisionally for now - 'haveable', graspable in the word within the church. Here the formal understanding of God's freedom is encountered by a substantial one. If the latter can be shown to be a true understanding of God's freedom, then we are guided towards concepts of being by the understanding of revelation as pure act.[114]

Bonhoeffer's suggestion that a substantial[115] understanding of freedom might offer the most constructive way forward is put forward quite tentatively at this stage of the argument in *Act and Being*. However, this is a crucial passage, both for the argument of this chapter and for our thesis as a whole, in that it informs and undergirds Bonhoeffer's understanding of both divine and human freedom. First, freedom is always to be understood christologically, in the light of the revelation of God in Christ, within the economy of redemption, not in terms of some abstract notion of God's freedom in himself. Even in an indubitably theocentric theology such as Barth's, the temptation is to view God's freedom as human freedom writ large. Instead, as indicated above, Bonhoeffer argues that divine freedom must be viewed as something which bursts through all human categories of meaning and can be defined only in Christ.

Second, as will be examined in greater detail in our discussion of the *imago Dei* in the next chapter, freedom is not individualistic, but relational. It is always freedom *for*, not freedom *from* the other, just as God is free *for* the world. However, that relationality is not merely between individuals, but is understood corporately, within the context of the church, as will be discussed in Chapter 4. Later, in our examination of the *Ethics* fragments, we will see how Bonhoeffer develops his understanding of human freedom as responsible action, indeed as vicarious action for the other.

---

[114] DBWE 2, 90-91.

[115] Bonhoeffer uses the word 'inhaltlich' in contrast to 'formal'. The comparison is between an understanding of freedom as an already existing category against which God's activity can be measured and an understanding of freedom which is given content by God's self-revelation in Christ. cf. *Creation and Fall* (DBW 3, 59; CF 37), where Bonhoeffer writes: 'Freedom cannot be conceived by any substantial or individualistic concept of freedom,' he uses the word 'substanziell' and is in fact making the same point, that a concept of freedom in which the content is already predetermined, without reference to the freedom of God in Christ, is false.

Third, and again this is a point which will be discussed in greater detail below, divine freedom 'finds its strongest evidence *precisely in that God freely chose to be bound* to historical human beings.'[116] Only the one who is truly free can freely give of him or her self. Bonhoeffer makes a similar point in his discussion of the church as the locus of revelation. In his critique of the Barthian attempt to preserve divine freedom by a dialectical understanding of knowing as 'not knowing', he argues that: 'What binds God to the church is God's freedom. Dialectically to leave open a freedom of God beyond the occurrence of salvation is to formalize, to *rationalize*, the contingent possibility of that occurrence.'[117] Human attempts at epistemic modesty are in fact disguised attempts by the human thinking subject to constrain God's freedom, even and indeed precisely in the very act of classifying and categorising him as ungraspable. For Bonhoeffer, the church is the place where there can be a knowing in faith which is not always negated by a 'not-knowing'. In surprisingly strong language he asserts: 'It is a fateful mistake on Barth's part to have substituted for the concept of creator and lord that of the subject.'[118] In Bonhoeffer's terms, the fundamental inadequacy in the concept of 'subject' is that it fails to understand God as person. It is to a discussion of this vitally important concept in Bonhoeffer's theology to which we must now turn.

## The Christian Concept of the Person

For Bonhoeffer, a correct understanding of the social category of 'person' is absolutely fundamental to the conceptual apparatus with which he addresses questions of freedom and of the relationship between God, humanity and community, and is a foundational concept in the 'ecclesial epistemology' which he seeks to develop in *Act and Being*. In Bonhoeffer's assessment, post-Enlightenment theology has been trapped within the dominant conceptuality of the Cartesian thinking subject. When God, humanity and the Christian community are re-conceptualised in personal terms rather than in terms of the monadic knowing I, the issues can be viewed from a new perspective.

---

[116] DBWE 2, 90 (my italics).
[117] Ibid., 124; cf. 112. As indicated above, Bonhoeffer's criticisms are largely answered by Barth in CD II/1.
[118] DBWE 2, 125.

It was in his earliest published work, *Sanctorum Communio*, that Bonhoeffer first introduced what he calls the 'Christian concept of the person'.[119] However, although he takes the human person as his starting point for a discussion of the church, Bonhoeffer immediately draws God into the equation by his assertion that:

> With an understanding of person and community, at the same time something definitive is said about the concept of God. Concept of person, concept of community and concept of God, stand in an indissoluble, essential, relationship. Where a concept of God is conceived, it will be conceived in relationship to the person and the personal community.[120]

Having made his claim about the intrinsic importance of the concept of person in theology, Bonhoeffer then makes a somewhat cursory examination of four standard philosophical schemes for understanding what he calls the 'basic ontic social relationships'.[121] As in his discussion of Idealism, Bonhoeffer's concern is not to produce a balanced appraisal of the different approaches, but to demonstrate how all four schemes fall short of the Christian understanding of personal relations, which for Bonhoeffer must be understood in terms of the I-Thou relationship.

*Personhood as Relational*

Whilst Bonhoeffer, if only for reasons of space, adopts a rather broad brush approach to these schemes, and could be accused of a failure to recognise nuances within the different systems, this does not detract from the basic point he wishes to emphasise, that none of these approaches define personhood in relational terms. In contrast, Bonhoeffer argues, there can be no 'person' in the Christian sense as he defines it, outside the context of relationship. In theological terms, he argues, this implies an understanding of personhood based not on the original pre-lapsarian state, but on fallen human beings who exist outside of unbroken communion with God, in knowledge of good and evil. Unlike the Idealist approach, such a Christian concept of person will, he suggests, preserve 'the concrete individual character of the person as definitive and willed by God.'[122] Only in a social

---

[119] DBW 1, 19.
[120] Ibid.
[121] DBW 1, 20 The approaches discussed are the Aristotelian, Stoic, Epicurean and the Idealist.
[122] DBW 1, 25.

or relational understanding of personhood is the integrity of identity, and hence the freedom of the other, recognised.

But the concept of person is also central to a right understanding of the relationship between God and humanity. Bonhoeffer writes: 'For Christian philosophy, the human person arises only in relation to the divine person who transcends it, is opposed to it and overpowers it.'[123] Only where human value is understood in terms of creatureliness, rather than the absolute autonomy of the knowing subject, can true Christian personhood exist. Again, Bonhoeffer asserts: 'The Christian person arises only out of the absolute distinction between God and humanity.'[124] It is because God is not humanity writ large, but because he is creator and lord, that human beings are free to become fully themselves. The implications for the relationship between divine and human freedom are clear. The two should not be viewed in competitive terms as if the price of God's freedom were humanity's bondage. Instead, God's freedom, as epitomised in Christ, operates as the catalyst for, and sustainer of human freedom.

Bonhoeffer emphasises that such an understanding of human personhood does not imply that the thou is necessary to make the other an I. 'A human being cannot of himself make the other into an I, into an ethical person, conscious of responsibility. God or the Holy Spirit comes to the concrete thou, only through his work does the other become for me a thou from which my I arises, in other words, every human thou is the image of the divine Thou.'[125] The other remains ultimately mysterious, impenetrable to our thought. Bonhoeffer makes the radical claim, which is of crucial importance to his argument, that:

> The other gives us the same problem of cognition as does God himself. My real relationship to the other is oriented on my relationship to God. *But just as I recognise God's I, only in the revelation of his love, so it is with the other human being; here the concept of the church finds its place.* Then it will become clear that the Christian person only achieves its true nature when God does not encounter him as a Thou, *but enters into him as an I.*[126]

---

[123] Ibid., 29.
[124] Ibid.; cf. the discussion of the distinction between God and humanity in Chapter 3.
[125] DBW 1, 33 The concept of 'responsibility' comes close to the heart of Bonhoeffer's understanding of Christian personhood. cf. Chapter 5.
[126] DBW 1, 34; (italics original).

In other words it is the presence of God, the Holy Spirit, in each Christian, within the community of the church, which brings into being the personhood of the other.

Bonhoeffer's approach to the question of personhood shares many features in common with other critiques of the idealist view of person. Like Kierkegaard, Bonhoeffer stresses the importance of the concrete moment of ethical decision in which human personhood arises. However, Bonhoeffer argues that in Kierkegaard's approach, there is no essential encounter with a concrete 'Thou' and hence it remains fundamentally individualistic and so fails to escape fully from the fetters of Idealism.[127] Bonhoeffer also draws heavily upon the personalism of Grisebach. However, where the latter focused narrowly on the I-Thou relationship between individuals,[128] for Bonhoeffer, the context was the wider community of the Christian church. In the eyes of God, the 'all-embracing Person',[129] individual and collective persons have the same structure. In theological terms, this shows that 'God does not desire a history of individuals, but the history of a community of human beings. But he does not want a community which absorbs the individual, but a community of human beings. In his eyes, the community and the individual are present at the same moment and rest in one another.'[130] We will discuss the relationship between freedom and community in more detail in Chapter 4.

*The Person in Act and Being*

It is in *Act and Being* that the importance of the concept of person, for epistemology, is spelled out most clearly. As we have seen, Bonhoeffer's diagnosis of the epistemological problem for theology is the apparent dilemma between the reduction of God to an entity, brought within the power of the knowing subject, and an agnosticism in which God can never be known. Bonhoeffer suggests that the Christian concept of the person can subvert and transcend this polarisation. He writes: 'There is no God who "is there" [Einen Gott den "es gibt", gibt es nicht]; God "is" in the relation of persons, and being is God's being-person [das Sein ist sein

---

[127] Ibid., note 12.
[128] cf. Martin Buber, although there is no evidence to suggest that Bonhoeffer had read Buber's work.
[129] DBW 1, 50.
[130] Ibid., 51.

Personsein.]'[131] Although Bonhoeffer never discusses the being of God' in terms of 'persons-in-relation' within the Trinity, but always focuses upon God's relationship to the world, within the economy of salvation, Charles Marsh's suggestion that 'Bonhoeffer pursues the enquiry of the secondary objectivity of revelation *within the presupposition of Barth's narration of God's primary trinitarian self identity*,' is surely correct.[132] Hunsinger in his review of Marsh argues that Marsh's attempt to re-contextualise Bonhoeffer's thought in Trinitarian terms, is not, as Marsh asserts 'an explication of what is implicitly there, but ... a corrective to what is not there.'[133] However, on the basis of Bonhoeffer's definition of personhood as constituted only in relationship, a less than Trinitarian account of God's aseity would suggest that relationship with the world is in some sense necessary to constitute God's personhood, an implication which would run entirely counter to all that Bonhoeffer says about the freedom and contingency of creation.

By using 'person' language of God, present in Christ in the Christian community, Bonhoeffer aims to re-conceive the parameters of the epistemological problem. The God who 'reveals the divine self in the church *as person*'[134] can give himself to be known, without being objectified as an entity or brought within the control of the knowing subject. As person, he is free to reveal *himself*, without overwhelming the humanity of the other. The concept of person recognises and preserves the ultimate mysteriousness of the other, whether God or my neighbour:

> The person is a unity over and above 'entity' and nonentity; it is objective, that is, knowable and recognisable. And yet on account of its true, qualified *objectivity*, and by virtue of its freedom from the knower and its freedom not to be, it never falls into the power of the knowing I. The person gives itself to the I through the word in the act of faith, which on its part acknowledges the freedom of the self-giving person, testifying thereby to its being absolutely 'from outside.[135]

As Bonhoeffer argues, 'The person "is" only in the act of self-giving. Yet the person "is" free from the one to whom it gives itself. It is through

---

[131] DBWE 2, 115 (square brackets original).
[132] Marsh C. *Reclaiming Dietrich Bonhoeffer* (Oxford OUP 1994), viii, (my italics).
[133] Op. cit. 123.
[134] DBWE 2, 112 (my italics).
[135] Ibid., 126.

the person of Christ that this understanding of person is won.'[136] By understanding Christ as person in this way, Bonhoeffer can affirm both that Christ fully gives himself to his church in revelation and that he always remains Lord over his church. What he gives of himself in revelation is real givenness, and yet the gift is always gracious, free and contingent:

> In faith Christ is the creator of my new being, a person and at the same time the Lord, 'in reference to whom' – εις αυτον – the person is created ... Christ, by being the one who creates in me the act of faith by granting me the Holy Spirit who hears and believes within me, thereby proves to be also the free Lord of my existence. Christ 'is' only in faith and yet 'is' Lord of my faith.[137]

Hans-Richard Reuter helpfully suggests that like the Hegelian concept of spirit, the category of person moves beyond the narrow constraints of the subject-object schema to a more adequate understanding of human being as social. And yet the concept maintains the boundary between the self and the external other, which is dissolved in the concept of spirit.[138]

*The Concept of Person in Other Writings*

In the seminar paper *Concerning the Christian Idea of God*, delivered at Union Theological Seminary in 1931, Bonhoeffer, writing in English, asserts the importance of understanding the transcendence of God in terms of 'personality', where the term is understood not, as in idealism, as the subjective realisation of absolute spirit, but as something other, something which limits me. 'God as the absolutely free personality is, therefore, absolutely transcendent.'[139] God always remains outside the possibilities of my thought. I can only attempt to 'make room for him'. Only God can reveal himself, in Jesus Christ.

Bonhoeffer argues that where 'idea' involves generality, the concept of person is particular: 'Personality exists in "oneness" because of its freedom. The only place where oneness might occur is history. Therefore, revelation of personality - that is to say, the self-revelation of God - must take place in history if at all.'[140] Such revelation in 'oneness' cannot be categorised or systematised in the way that an idea is incorporated into an

---

[136] Ibid., 128.
[137] Ibid.
[138] Ibid., 173-4 (Editor's Afterword).
[139] DBW 10, 427.
[140] Ibid., 428.

existing schema. 'That is the reason why God reveals himself in history: only so is the freedom of his personality guarded.'[141] Bonhoeffer claims that by reducing facts to bearers of ideas or values, Idealism fails to give due weight to the 'ontological category in history', which, he argues, is tantamount to failing to take history seriously. In God's self revelation, the personality of God encounters the human person. 'Here God transcends his transcendence, giving himself to man as Holy Spirit.'[142]

In the *Christology* lectures, Bonhoeffer again speaks of the human intellect or logos in terms of its propensity to classify and systematise. When it encounters Christ, the Counter-Logos, it attempts to assimilate it within itself. But Christ has appeared in history, not as an eternal idea, but as a person who himself questions humanity, dethroning the human logos. '[I]t is only from God that a human being knows who he is.'[143] Bachtell finds a discrepancy between Bonhoeffer's use of the word 'personality' in this seminar paper and his critique of the same term in the *Christology* lectures.[144] However, we would suggest that a reading of the two texts makes clear that the discrepancy arises not from any *volte face* between 1931 and 1933, but merely because in the Seminar Paper, Bonhoeffer is writing in English.[145]

*The Person and the Boundary*

In our next chapter, we will offer a detailed appraisal of the significance of the concept of the limit or boundary to an understanding of human freedom as creatureliness. However, this important concept first arises within the context of epistemology and personhood and so must receive some brief attention at this point. In his university dissertation, *Sanctorum Communio*, Bonhoeffer criticised idealist epistemology for relativising the other to the knowing I, reducing it to an object rather than a barrier or boundary to the mind of the knowing subject. Bonhoeffer argues that only in a social or relational understanding of personhood are the integrity and the discrete

---

[141] Ibid., 429.
[142] Ibid., 431.
[143] C 31.
[144] Bachtell D. S. *Freedom in the Theology of Dietrich Bonhoeffer* Unpublished PhD dissertation Drew University 1973 (Microfilm British Library) cf. C 44; GS III, 178.
[145] Bonhoeffer's usage of 'person' in *Christology* is entirely in line with earlier usage in DBW 1 and DBWE 2, whilst his definition of 'personality' in *Concerning the Christian Idea of God*, suggests that he has the same concept in mind, albeit that the English term 'person' or 'personhood' would have expressed this less ambiguously.

identity of the other recognised. As we saw earlier, in the Christian concept of person, as Bonhoeffer has defined it, the thou is one who confronts me as an I. Unlike Idealism where the thou is immanent in the mind of the subject, the thou 'sets a boundary to the subject, it acts out of a will with which the other comes into conflict so that this other will becomes a thou for the I.'[146] This transcendence of the thou is an ethical rather than an epistemological transcendence and can be understood only from within, by one who stands in the place of responsibility. The I can never be a boundary to itself, nor can it leap over the boundary which the thou presents to it in order to experience him or her as an I. Bonhoeffer argues that 'Psychology and epistemology both find their limits here, the ethical personal being of the other is neither a psychologically graspable fact, nor yet an epistemological necessity.'[147] He defines the I-thou relationship as the basic Christian relationship which leaves behind the subject-object paradigm intrinsic to the epistemological approach. However, as we have seen, by the time of *Act and Being*, Bonhoeffer takes a much less dismissive approach to epistemology. Although, he critiques the standard Cartesian understanding of the priority of the thinking subject which had led Kant, and to a degree Barth, to concern themselves with limits to human reason, he now accepts that revelation needs to 'yield an epistemology of its own'.[148] Bonhoeffer suggests that post-Enlightenment philosophy and theology have adopted an unduly reductionist approach to human being, as embodied mind, rather than as a unified person. He argues that it is not human reason which has bounds or limits because, as Hegel had shown, these could always be thought of and hence transcended as the thinking subject stood outside them. Instead, it is humanity as a whole which is limited. 'There is a boundary only for a concrete human being in its entirety, and this boundary is called *Christ*.'[149] This is because the human being is primarily person, not mind, and as such, only another person, in this case the person of Christ, can limit him. However, this limitation in fact frees humanity from the power of a boundless and meaningless selfhood.[150]

---

[146] DBW 1, 32.
[147] Ibid.
[148] DBWE 2, 31.
[149] Ibid., 45.
[150] cf. Sherman F. 'Act and Being', 91, in *The Place of Bonhoeffer* ed. Marty M. E. (SCM 1963).

## Freedom and Sociality, the Church as the Locus of Revelation

The concept of person is also critical to Bonhoeffer's understanding of the Christian community as the locus of revelation. As we noted above, it is in the church, where God gives himself to be known, that his freedom is truly revealed. The intrinsic connection between freedom and community within Bonhoeffer's work will be examined at length in Chapter 4. For the present, we will confine our discussion to Bonhoeffer's attempt to subvert the largely individualistic approach to knowing, which has been the legacy of Western Enlightenment thought, by locating revelation within the personal and corporate context of the Christian community. Hence our focus will be the relationship between freedom, knowledge and sociality.

If revelation is really to be revelation, asserts Bonhoeffer, it must somehow be knowable and indeed has become knowable in Christ. Bonhoeffer's solution to the apparent dilemma is, as he has already intimated, the church, not as institution, but, as he had argued in his earlier dissertation, *Sanctorum Communio*, 'Christ existing as [the Christian] community'. Bonhoeffer argues, 'Revelation should be thought of only in reference to the concept of church, where church is understood to be constituted by the present proclamation of Christ's death and resurrection - within, on the part of, and for the community of faith.'[151] Within the church Christ is 'the acting subject in the community of faith, proclaiming and believing'.[152] If God is not to be drawn into the thinking subject, then revelation cannot be conceived objectively. God must remain subject. However, because the church, in Bonhoeffer's definition, is 'Christ existing as community', the problems of continuity both of revelation and between the old and new existence, which he sees as inherent in the Barthian account, are resolved, or at least become far less acute when the receptive subject is understood christologically in terms of the corporate person of Christ. Because Christ is the corporate subject of the community of faith, human beings are encountered from outside themselves. '[O]ther persons themselves even become Christ for us in demand and promise, in the existential limits they place on us from outside; they become as such also the warrant for the continuity of revelation.'[153] Continuity is assured because revelation is both spoken and heard not by an individual but by a community of persons, the corporate person of Christ. God's freedom is not

---

[151] DBWE 2, 110.
[152] Ibid., 112.
[153] Ibid., 114.

thereby compromised, because he has freely bound himself to his word within the church.

Where philosophical attempts to define revelation were individualistic, focusing on the thinking subject in isolation, even when reconceived theologically, as in the early Barth's Neo-Kantian presuppositions, an ecclesial approach to revelation recognises that humanity is inherently social. 'Human beings... are always part of a community, "in Adam", or "in Christ"'.[154] Building on his earlier discussion, Bonhoeffer argues that within the church, the being of revelation is not some static entity at my disposal, nor is it free in the formal sense. Instead, it has its being in the community of persons constituted and formed by the person of Christ, and in which individuals already find themselves in their new existence. 'Hence, the Gospel is somehow *held fast* here. God's freedom has woven itself into this person-like community of faith, and *it is precisely this which manifests what God's freedom is: that God binds God's self to human beings*. The community of faith really does have the word of forgiveness at its disposal.'[155] God's freedom is here defined not abstractly in terms of what might be possible for God, but concretely, as encountered in his revelation in Christ, in the church. If, as Bonhoeffer maintains over against the early Barth, revelation is to be defined in personal and social terms, rather than individualistic terms, an appropriate epistemology will share these same characteristics: 'To the being of revelation, defined as the being of the person of Christ in the community of persons of the church - defined, that is, in terms of sociological categories - there must correspond a concept of knowledge that is also framed in sociological categories.'[156]

*Existential and Ecclesial Knowing*

Within the church, Bonhoeffer distinguishes three types of knowing: faith, preaching and theology. The three are to be carefully distinguished but are also intricately connected.

*Faith* The first type of knowledge, faith or believing, is categorised by Bonhoeffer as existential knowing, in that it does not reflect on itself, but is focused solely on Christ.[157] As with Barth's understanding of revelation in

---

[154] Ibid., 113.
[155] Ibid., 112 (my italics).
[156] Ibid., 125-6.
[157] Ibid., 133.

terms of Revealer, Revealed and Revealedness in the *Church Dogmatics*,[158] for Bonhoeffer, God is active as both revealing and receptive subjects, he is present in the church at both ends of cognitive equation. '[T]his cognition of revelation is called "believing", what is revealed is called Christ and the subject of understanding is God as Holy Spirit.'[159] Such knowledge is accessible only in faith. There is no neutral point to which the thinking subject can retreat to consider whether believing knowledge is possible. 'God is only in the act of believing. In "my" believing the Holy Spirit attests itself.'[160] Outside of Christ there can be no revelation, but in Christ, in the community of the church, this 'believing way of knowing means to know oneself overcome and pardoned by the person of Christ in the preached word.'[161] Faith is not an entity to be considered, but rather a perspective, a way of looking, not only at Christ, but at others and the world:

> Through the person of Christ other human beings, too, are moved out of the sphere of things ... and into the social sphere of person. Only through Christ does my neighbour meet me as one who claims me in an absolute way from a position outside my existence ... Without Christ, even my neighbour is for me no more than a possibility of self-assertion.[162]

In faith, even the external world appears in a different light. It is not viewed disinterestedly. 'Thus in faith is disclosed a new sphere of knowledge and objects, that of existence in social reference, which replaces other concepts of knowledge.'[163] The person of Christ, as the object of faith, resists attempts to subsume it into the thinking subject and attempts to reduce it to non-objectivity. 'In faith I "have" Christ in his personal objectivity, that is, as my Lord who has power over me, reconciles, and redeems me.'[164] The fact that the *actus directus* of the moment of faith, of being 'taken hold of by Christ' is only accessible as reflection upon it, is no reason to doubt the reality of the moment of faith.

---

[158] CD 1/1 295ff.
[159] DBWE 2, 92.
[160] Ibid.
[161] Ibid., 126.
[162] Ibid., 127.
[163] Ibid.
[164] Ibid., 128.

*Preaching* The second and third types of knowledge, preaching and theology respectively, which Bonhoeffer terms 'ecclesial knowing', are closely related, in that both are reflections upon the *actus directus* of faith. Preaching is to be distinguished both from existential confession and from theological reflection, because it involves speaking the word to be spoken *now*, to *this* community. Although it is not *actus directus* but reflection upon the word which witnesses to Christ, the preacher must 'know' what she proclaims. Bonhoeffer suggests: 'If the object of the believing way of knowing is the living word of Christ, then that of theological knowing is the word already spoken, and that of the preaching way of knowing is the word of proclamation to the community of faith.'[165] The preacher cannot qualify all his knowing with a not-knowing. '[I]n the sermon, which creates faith, Christ lets himself be proclaimed as "subject" of the words spoken. I preach, but I preach in the power of Christ, in the power of the faith of the community of faith, not in the power of my faith.'[166] The sermon exemplifies God's freedom to bind himself to humanity. In the *Christology* lectures Bonhoeffer writes: 'A human sermon is the word of God, because God has bound himself and is bound to human words.'[167] Although the preacher is an individual, his or her authority comes not from themselves but from their office. But if preachers are to preach faithfully, then there is the need for 'the theological scholarly discipline,'[168] preachers must be theologians,[169] which in turn means that the subject matter of the Christian faith must be knowable.

*Theology* Theology, the third type of knowing, in Bonhoeffer's categorisation, is 'the memory of the church.'[170]. The task of theology is 'to make the connection between past preaching and the real person of Christ, as Christ preaches in, and is preached by, the community of faith.'[171] Again, if it is to have validity, it must be knowledge.[172] Bonhoeffer argues that God's freedom is most appropriately acknowledged by an obedient recognition of his lordship, rather than by a particular theological method. As reflection on revelation, the difference between theology and 'profane

---

[165] Ibid., 133.
[166] Ibid., 129.
[167] C 52 (translation inclusivised).
[168] DBWE 2, 130.
[169] Ibid., 133.
[170] Ibid., 130.
[171] Ibid.
[172] Ibid.

thought is not primarily one of method, but of obedience, and, asserts Bonhoeffer, the dialectical method of negating all knowing with unknowing is no humbler than any other method.[173] Theology, if it is to be obedient theology, can and must reckon only with the revelation of God as given in Christ. It cannot withdraw to debate the possibility of such revelation, because to do so would be to seek to classify God and to fit him into a humanly constructed system in which certain things are or are not possible for him.[174] Yet, at the same time, it must constantly submit its understanding of and reflection on revelation to the scrutiny and critique of the living presence of Christ within the church, the arbiter before whom all theology must bow. Hence it is only in the church 'where the living person of Christ is itself present and can destroy this existing thing or acknowledge it', that true theology can take place.[175] All thought, including theological thought is subject to the human tendency to categorise and systematise. Only in the church 'which is the theologian's humility',[176] can such thought be subverted by the living presence of Christ. It is there that Christ is present to speak the word of forgiveness, which, asserts Bonhoeffer, is something utterly different from the theological truth that God forgives sin. By locating theology within the community of faith, the theologian is preserved from 'the lure of intellectual works-righteousness'[177] because theology is always confronted by its limitations, its inability to grasp the living person of Christ. However, where the theologian is also a believer, his theological knowing is rooted in faith, in a relationship of trust in the object of his faith, and so Bonhoeffer can reformulate Luther's *pecca fortiter* for theologians as '*Reflecte fortiter, sed fortius fide et gaude in Christo.*'[178] Bonhoeffer concludes this section with the statement :

> Christ, the crucified and risen one gives Christ's own self to be known by human beings who live to themselves. It is in being known by God that human beings know God. But to be known by God means to become a new person.[179]

---

[173] Bonhoeffer asserts: 'Dialectical theology takes its method more seriously than is consonant with its presuppositions, only because, in the final analysis, it thinks individualistically, that is, abstractly.' (DBWE 2, 132).
[174] cf. C 27ff.
[175] DBWE 2, 131.
[176] Ibid., 132.
[177] Ibid., 132.
[178] Ibid., 135.
[179] Ibid., 134.

The foundation of all theological knowledge, whether as faith, preaching or the scholarly discipline of theology, is our being known by God, being placed by him into truth, in the community of faith. Human beings are not primarily defined as 'knowers', but as those who, in Christ are known by God.[180]

## Being in Christ as Being in Freedom

By locating revelation within the Christian community, defined in christological and personal terms, Bonhoeffer launches an assault on the pervasive influence of Cartesian individualism in Western epistemology and asserts the intrinsic importance of social relationships and by implication, of ethics, to the understanding of knowledge. The 'I' can never place itself into truth, but in the community of the church, in the context of ethical encounter, the person of Christ places me into truth. It is only by participation in Christ, asserts Bonhoeffer, that human beings are freed from their compulsive introversion and know themselves no longer as creator but as creature. Such knowledge is accessible only by faith. In Adam, human beings, in their illusory autonomy, are separated from God and others. 'God has become a religious object, and human beings themselves have become their own creator and lord, belonging to themselves. It is only to be expected that they should now begin and end with themselves in their knowing, for they are only and utterly "with themselves" in the falsehood of naked self-glory.'[181] It is only in Christ that 'Dasein becomes free, not as if it could stand over against its being-how-it-is (Wiesein) as autonomous being, but in the sense of escaping from the power of the I into the power of Christ, where alone it recognises itself in original freedom as God's creature.'[182] In Chapter 3, we will encounter Bonhoeffer's understanding of freedom in terms of a recognition of creatureliness, a freedom from false aspirations towards divinity and a freedom for our true humanity. Here, in *Act and Being*, Bonhoeffer writes: 'Being in Christ, as being directed towards Christ, sets Dasein free. Human beings are "there" for and by means of Christ.'[183] Within the church, act and being are united without the one overwhelming the other. In the Christian community there can be unity without 'sameness', a non-

---

[180] cf. Galatians 4:9.
[181] DBWE 2, 137.
[182] Ibid., 150.
[183] Ibid., 153.

competitive freedom in Christ, the one in whom God freely binds himself to humanity.

In the powerful climax to *Act and Being*, Bonhoeffer defines being in Christ as the freedom to be a child once again. In lines suggestive of the parable of the prodigal son,[184] he writes:

> In contemplation of Christ, the tormented conscience of the I's tornness becomes the 'joyful conscience', confidence and courage. The servant becomes free. The one who became an adult in exile and misery becomes a child at home.[185]

The child is the one who allows himself to be defined by the future and so lives fully in the present, whereas the adult, in seeking to be defined by the present, finds himself captive to the past. In Christ, the human being is a new creation, she is by faith what she will become. The book closes with an eschatological vision of freedom in Christ. 'It is the new creation of those born from out of the world's confines into the wideness of heaven, becoming what they were, or never were, a creature of God, a child.'[186]

**Humanity Questioned**

As the editors of *Act and Being* note, this theme of the freedom of the child recurs in a sermon based on John 8:32 'The truth will make you free', preached in Berlin on 24th July 1932.[187] This sermon provides something of a bridge to the epistemological presuppositions which undergird the *Christology* lectures. As in *Act and Being*, Bonhoeffer argues that only Christ can place us into truth and set us free from the isolation of seeing ourselves as the centre of the world. It is Christ who sets me 'free from myself for the other. Only God's truth enables me to see the other. It directs my gaze, focused in on myself and points it outwards to the other.'[188] However, Bonhoeffer also introduces a new theme, that of the questionableness of human existence. To be human is not primarily to be the questioning subject, but the one whose very existence is brought into question by Christ. Bonhoeffer notes the irony that Pilate should ask Jesus,

---
[184] Ibid., 161 editorial footnote [66].
[185] Ibid.
[186] Ibid.
[187] DBW 11, 454.
[188] Ibid., 461.

the one who claims to be the truth, about truth and states 'It is not you who enquires about truth, but the truth which questions you.'[189] These ideas are further developed in the *Christology* lectures where Bonhoeffer speaks of Christ as the Counter-Logos, the one who, when questioned, turns the question back upon his questioner. Such a Christ cannot be assimilated or classified by the human mind. Instead, the Cartesian questioning subject is deposed, as his very existence is called into question. All that remains is 'the question of dethroned and distraught reason' which is also 'the question of faith: who are you?'[190] 'Who?' is the question of epistemological modesty and reticence, but this christological question, which is also the question of revelation, can only be answered in the church where the answer has already been given in Christ.[191] This picture of humanity as questioned, as addressed from outside itself, as creature before its creator, raises much wider issues of anthropology and these will be addressed in the next chapter. We will observe how in *Creation and Fall*, Bonhoeffer both widens his argument beyond epistemology and yet builds upon the foundations laid.

**Conclusion**

In this chapter, we have focused on the early thesis *Act and Being*, in order to show how Bonhoeffer's understanding of freedom challenges both the belief that knowledge is the key to freedom and the related assumption that a theology of revelation must side-step epistemology and retreat to the realm of ethics. In his critique of philosophical and theological attempts to understand revelation in transcendental or ontological terms, Bonhoeffer both affirms the precarious and provisional nature of all our knowing and puts forward a christologically centred epistemology of revelation, an ecclesial or churchly knowing which arises from God's free gift of himself to be known, rather than the autonomy of the human thinking subject. We noted a number of ideas which will prove foundational to subsequent chapters. Although Bonhoeffer's definition of freedom in terms of the divine self-revelation in Christ and the crucial distinction which he draws between formal and substantial freedom are developed within the context

---

[189] Ibid., 456.
[190] C, 30.
[191] Ibid., 31-2.

of epistemology, these Christ-shaped parameters of freedom will undergird all subsequent discussion of the relationship between divine and human freedom. Furthermore, Bonhoeffer's interpretation of the human person in relational terms provides a conceptuality which both subverts individualistic understandings of epistemology and will illuminate our subsequent discussions of creation and ecclesiology. We must now turn to the first of these issues, creation.

## Chapter Three
# Freedom in the Image of God

**Introduction**

It might be expected that a discussion of divine and human freedom would begin with an account of creation and of the relationship between the creator and the creature made in his image. However we took epistemology as our starting point, not merely because *Act and Being* is chronologically prior to *Creation and Fall*, but because there is a sense in which, methodologically, for Bonhoeffer, epistemology is prior to theology. This is not to privilege epistemology or to retreat into the sort of reductionist Cartesian view of the human person of which Bonhoeffer is rightly dismissive. But as we saw in the last chapter, for Bonhoeffer, theology cannot side-step the epistemological question by retreating into the realms of ethics or feeling. 'Knowing' matters, and so theology must find an 'ecclesial' way of knowing.

Hence, we would argue that, although after *Act and Being* and the writings which stem from that immediate period, Bonhoeffer never again discusses epistemology at any length, the conclusions which he has drawn concerning ecclesial knowing, inform his later theology both implicitly and explicitly. In addition, as we have already argued above, the christological, social and ethical understanding of freedom, which Bonhoeffer frames in epistemological terms in his early academic writings, is fundamental to his discussion of the issue in all his later writings. In this chapter, we will focus on *Creation and Fall*, the short book which began life as a series of lectures given by Bonhoeffer at Berlin University, during the Winter Term of 1932-3.[192] However, we will also give detailed attention to a number of the *Ethics* fragments, which take up the similar themes.

The central theological doctrines of creation, human sin and redemption, inevitably raise important questions about the relationship

---

[192] References throughout this chapter will be to the new English edition *Creation and Fall* ed. de Gruchy J. W. trans. Bax S. D. (Fortress 1997) (hereafter DBWE 3), translated from *Schöpfung und Fall* ed. Rüter M and Tödt I. (Chr. Kaiser Verlag 1989).

between divine and human freedom. However, what is striking about this brief lecture series and the later writings which develop its ideas, is the way in which, for Bonhoeffer, the concept of freedom lies at the very heart of such foundational theological themes as creation and preservation, sin, incarnation, redemption and indeed the doctrine of God itself. In creation, God is revealed as the one who creates in freedom. For Bonhoeffer creation itself is an expression of divine freedom. We will discuss Bonhoeffer's account of humanity as both created and free, giving particular attention to his understanding of creation in the image of God as creation in freedom. The relationship between creatureliness and freedom opens up a discussion of freedom within bounds, which in turn underlies Bonhoeffer's interpretation of the fall as a fall from freedom.

In the section on redemption we will look at the relationship between creation and incarnation as contingent acts of God's freedom, noting the parallels between Bonhoeffer's account of the original creation of humanity in the image as a creation in freedom and the restoration of that image in the redeemed freedom of new creation or re-creation. We will discuss the relative freedom of the preserved creation and will offer some brief reflections on the implications of these issues for the non-human creation.

## Creation and Fall - an Overview

In *Creation and Fall*, Bonhoeffer offered a christological reading of the first three chapters of Genesis. The lectures emerged against the political backdrop of the dramatic rise of the National Socialist Party within Germany, culminating in Hitler's installation as Reich Chancellor on 31st January 1933. Within theological circles, there was a rising ferment of interest in the so-called 'orders of creation', which were seen by many as the justification for national development and self-expression, as well as claims to racial superiority. As we will see in greater detail in our discussion of preservation below, Bonhoeffer coined the concept 'orders of preservation' to rebut this sort of theology. However, the book as a whole, with its forthright and unflattering portrait of human sinfulness, can also be seen as an implicit assault on the doctrine. *Creation and Fall* stands at the boundary between the earlier academic theology and the later writings which emerged from Bonhoeffer's involvement at the heart of the Church Struggle. Although it arose within the context of the academy, its prophetic content impels its hearers outside to engage with the growing menace of Nazism and the subtler attraction of the German Christians.

Donald Bachtell, in an unpublished thesis, devotes a section of his third chapter 'The theology of freedom', to a discussion of *Creation and Fall*, and, in view of the paucity of published secondary literature on this theme, we will engage with his argument at various points throughout this chapter. However, *Creation and Fall* has been largely neglected by many major interpreters. Ernst Feil makes only a passing reference, in the context of his discussion of the relationship between the centre and the boundary,[193] whilst John Godsey provides a précis of the content, but offers no critical reflection.[194] Edwin Robertson in his editorial comments in the first volume of the his selection from *Gesammelte Schriften, No Rusty Swords*, writes somewhat dismissively: 'There was little that was original in these lectures, but it gave [Bonhoeffer] the chance to deal with a biblical theme.'[195] John Phillips' concern is with the discrepancy which he traces between Bonhoeffer's endorsement of the critical historical approach to scripture in the *Christology* lectures, and his methodology in *Creation and Fall*.[196] Walter Harrelson raises similar concerns in his chapter on 'Bonhoeffer and the Bible', adjudging the christological references 'gratuitous'.[197]

However, although this short book has not received the scholarly attention devoted to the better known published works, it is our case that Bonhoeffer's treatment of his subject matter is striking, particularly in the context of Germany in 1932-3, and that the book as a whole is of pivotal importance to any discussion of Bonhoeffer's understanding of freedom. Furthermore, if, as I will argue, the motif of freedom provides, at the very least, an illuminating perspective on Bonhoeffer's life and work as a whole, the book plays a much more central role in the Bonhoeffer corpus than has generally been assumed.

Although this is not the place to attempt a detailed critique of Bonhoeffer's approach in *Creation and Fall*, we must comment briefly on Bonhoeffer's method and on the criticisms raised by Phillips and Harrelson. Without question this work is not an historical-critical study of the early chapters of Genesis, and in the 'Introduction' to the published

---

[193] Feil E. *The Theology of Dietrich Bonhoeffer* Trans. Martin Rumscheidt (Fortress 1985) 72-74.
[194] Godsey J. D. *The Theology of Dietrich Bonhoeffer* (SCM 1960), 119-143.
[195] NRS 89.
[196] Phillips J. A. *The Form of Christ in the World* op cit., 88.
[197] Harrelson W. in *The Place of Bonhoeffer* ed. Marty M. E. (SCM 1963), 121.

text, Bonhoeffer makes clear that this is not his intention. Instead, his professed aim is a 'theological interpretation' of the text from the standpoint of Christian theology. The methodological point, with regard to Bonhoeffer's approach to the scriptures, is made with greater clarity in the *Christology* lectures, where he argues that all Christian theology, and hence the theology of creation, begins with the person of the crucified, risen Christ, present in his church.[198] Such an approach is the inevitable and consistent outcome of Bonhoeffer's theological presupposition, expounded in those lectures, that Christ is present in his church, in the word of scripture.[199] Nevertheless, Bonhoeffer also affirms the insights of historical critical research, and indeed in *Christology*, is quite insistent on the necessity of rigorous critical study of the scriptures.[200] Although, as indicated above, some commentators have found these two positions incompatible, Bonhoeffer's Lutheran background, and in particular his understanding of the free condescension of God in Christ, enable him to affirm both Christ's presence in scripture and the flawed and essentially human nature of the text.[201] The one who takes on the likeness of fallen human flesh is precisely the one who freely chooses to witness to himself through the brokenness and ambiguity of the biblical text.[202]

From the standpoint of our study and in particular in view of our claim concerning epistemology, it is revealing that Bonhoeffer's comments on the opening verses of Genesis 1 begin with a discussion of the impossibility of 'the beginning' as a concept for human thought. Clearly a number of the concerns addressed by Bonhoeffer in *Act and Being* remain central to his thinking. Indeed *Creation and Fall* can be viewed as an attempt at 'ecclesial knowing', a Christ-centred theology which recognises the limitations of human thought. In language reminiscent of his Habilitation thesis, Bonhoeffer asserts: 'The Hegelian question how we are to make a beginning in philosophy can therefore only be answered by the bold and violent action of enthroning reason in the place of God.'[203] In its attempt to conceive the beginning, the human thinking subject puts itself in the place

---

[198] C, 43.
[199] Ibid., 49-52 For a more positive assessment of Bonhoeffer's use of scripture see Fowl S. E. and Jones L. G. *Reading in Communion:Scripture and Ethics in Christian Life* (SPCK 1991), esp. pp. 135-159.
[200] C, 73-4.
[201] Ibid., 74 '[I]t is through the Bible, with all its flaws that the risen one encounters us.'
[202] Ibid., 106.
[203] DBWE 3, 27.

of God, seeing itself as the beginning, rather than recognising it's position 'in the middle', between a beginning and an end which it cannot know. Only God, who was in the beginning, can truly speak of the beginning. Bonhoeffer contrasts his theological approach to that of autonomous reason when he states: 'We can *know* about the beginning in the true sense only by hearing of the beginning while we ourselves are in the middle between the beginning and the end.'[204] As the editors note, the contrast is between Hegel's concern to *know* the beginning, and Bonhoeffer's affirmation that we *hear* of it from the one who was in the beginning.[205]

## The Freedom of the Creator

As we indicated briefly above, the heart of Bonhoeffer's exposition of Genesis 1-3 can be encapsulated in the idea that God is the one who creates in freedom. This affirmation is expressed in two distinct but mutually complementary aspects. The first, which we will discuss at this point, stresses the divine side of the equation, that the act of creation is an entirely gratuitous and unconditioned expression of divine freedom. God *creates* in freedom. The second to which we will turn in detail below, affirms that that which God creates is gifted with and characterised by freedom; God creates *in freedom*.

### *Divine Freedom as Unconditioned*

In contrast to human freedom, as we will see below, divine freedom is entirely unconditioned, and it is that freedom which stands at the heart of Bonhoeffer's exposition of the opening verse of Genesis. The key to an understanding of creation as a totally gratuitous act of God is to see it as an expression of the uncreated freedom which characterises the divine activity. Bonhoeffer asserts '[T]he Bible begins with the free confirmation, attestation or revelation of God by God: In the beginning God created ...'[206] Hence, to speak of 'the beginning' is not to describe a temporal distinction, behind which the human mind can penetrate, as with other human beginnings, but to testify to ontological origins, the completely free and

---

[204] Ibid., 30; (italics original).
[205] Ibid., note 19.
[206] Ibid., 29; cf. Bachtell 110.

unrepeatable act in which the Creator creates the creature, unconditioned by anything except his freedom. Bonhoeffer is adamant that creation cannot be understood in causal terms, as if some logical connection between creator and creation could be demonstrated, but only as a 'quite unrepeatable, unique, free event in the beginning.'[207] For Bonhoeffer, there is no link between the freedom of the Creator and his creation, only 'nothingness'.[208] And that nothingness is not some primal possibility or causal connection between God and creation, but an impossibility, that which God has overcome in creating.[209] It is not an entity, even a negative entity, but 'the particular word that alone is able to define and express the relation between God's freedom and God's creation.'[210] Creation is not the actualisation of some already existing possibility, but God's impossible act in creating *ex nihilo*.

This stress on the sovereign freedom of God in creation is crucial to Bonhoeffer's discussion. In the Summer Term of 1933 Bonhoeffer gave a Seminar on Hegel's Philosophy of Religion and it seems probable that Hegel is an at times unnamed, conversation partner in the lectures on Genesis 3. For Hegel, creation was seen as a necessary aspect of the life of God, '[I]t belongs to his being, his essence, to be the creator; insofar as he is not the creator, he is grasped inadequately. His creative role is not an *actus* that happened once; [rather,] what takes place in the idea is an eternal moment, an eternal determination of the idea.'[211] Bonhoeffer differentiates himself sharply from this position. Hegel's use of the concept of *Geist* implied that there was no essential difference between human and divine freedom because the finite was a moment within the infinite, rather than something radically distinct. However, for Bonhoeffer, divine freedom can never be understood as a possibility inherent in humanity, as human freedom writ large. We have already noted Bonhoeffer's trenchant dismissal of the category of possibility as a useful concept for theology. Instead, one of his recurrent methodological concerns is to recognise the limits of theology, as a discipline which reflects upon the actuality of

---

[207] Ibid., 32.

[208] *das Nichts*.

[209] DBWE 3, 33; cf. also *The Theology of Crisis and its attitude towards Philosophy and Science*, (DBW 10, 434ff).

[210] DBWE 3, 34.

[211] *1827 Lectures on the Philosophy of Religion* ed. Hodgson P. C. Vol. III, 275 (These formed the basis of G. Lasson's Edition of 1925-9 used by Bonhoeffer).

the revelation of God in Christ, rather than a metaphysical science which attempts to go back behind that revelation.

## Divine Freedom as Christological

Hence, whilst Bonhoeffer emphasises the utter gratuity of divine freedom, any reflection upon this freedom must be earthed christologically. In Chapter 2 we noted the distinction which Bonhoeffer drew between formal and substantial freedom. God's freedom is expressed in his being free for the world in Christ. Here too, in *Creation and Fall*, the discussion of the divine freedom in creation is grounded christologically. We recognise God's freedom to create out of nothing, because we know him, through his gracious revelation, as the one who is free to raise the dead. For Bonhoeffer, the resurrection is the pivotal event between creation and new creation, and in epistemological terms, it is only from the resurrection, attested to by the living presence of Christ in his church, that creation can be understood. Hence, Bonhoeffer argues, the first *creatio ex nihilo* can be comprehended only in the light of Christ's resurrection, itself a 'creation out of nothing.' The resurrection, like the creation is an act of radical novelty. Just as there is no causal connection between the Creator and the creature, but only nothingness, so: 'There is absolutely no transition, no continuum between the dead Christ and the resurrected Christ, but the freedom of God that, in the beginning, created God's work out of nothing.'[212]

## Creation and the Word of God

As we have seen, creation is not then the act of some impersonal first cause, but comes into being when God speaks. The only continuity between God and his creation is his word. Bonhoeffer views this as further evidence of God's sovereign freedom in creation:

> That God creates by the word means that creation is God's order or command and that this command is free. God *says*, God *speaks*.[213] This means that God creates in complete freedom. Even in creating, God remains wholly free over

---

[212] DBWE 3, 35.

[213] The German reads 'Gott *spricht*'' but the translator suggests that both English words are necessary to bring out the full nuances of the German.

against what is created. God is not bound to what is created; instead God binds it to God.[214]

At first glance, this emphasis on the divine freedom from creation appears to be in conflict with Bonhoeffer's earlier affirmation in *Act and Being*, that in revelation, 'God freely chose to be bound to historical human beings'.[215] However, where in *Act and Being*, Bonhoeffer's aim was to contrast the early Barth's formal understanding of freedom with the 'haveability' and 'graspability' of God, constituted in Christ's presence as the word in the church, here his concern is to rebut a scholastic understanding of creation as revealing the creator through the threefold *via eminentiae, negationis* and *causalitatis*. He asserts that 'It is not "from" God's works, then, that we recognise the Creator,' but only in the word of creation.[216] In his use of the word as the agent of creation, God remains transcendent of his world,[217] and yet that transcendence is never remoteness, but a paradoxical unity of transcendence and immanence. 'God is, as the word, *in* the world, because God is the one who is utterly beyond, and God is utterly beyond the world, because God is in the world *in the word*.[218] Again Bonhoeffer reiterates that, although in human experience there is a causal connection between a command and the event commanded, this does not apply to God's creative word. What God commands is what is, his word is an inseparable unity with the event it commands. 'With God, the imperative is the indicative.'[219] By his word, God brings form to the formless void and light to the darkness, freeing creation to praise its creator.[220] He gives to the created order its own identity, a separateness of form and the capacity to create after its own kind. And yet creation knows itself to be created being, and hence obedient being, which 'never knows about its own being except by looking at the word of God, at the freedom with which God creates and upholds.'[221] As Bachtell rightly notes, for Bonhoeffer, God's word is never some

---

[214] DBWE 3, 41 (italics original).
[215] DBWE 2, 90.
[216] DBWE 3, 41.
[217] Ibid., cf. Bachtell 119.
[218] DBWE 3, 41.
[219] DBWE 3, 42.
[220] Ibid., 44.
[221] Ibid., 59.

impersonal creative power but always personal address.[222] In the *Christology* lectures, Bonhoeffer stresses that, unlike the concept of word as idea, 'Address requires response and responsibility ... the word lies wholly and freely at the disposal of the one who speaks'.[223] Human beings are those addressed by their creator and placed in a position of responsibility by him. We will be discussing the relationship between freedom and responsibility in Chapter 5, when we will focus particularly on *Ethics*. However, it is clear that the connection is in Bonhoeffer's mind, even in his earliest writings.

## The Freedom of the Creature - Human Freedom in the Image of God

As we noted above, the second part of the affirmation that God creates in freedom is that what divine freedom creates is characterised by its own freedom and integrity. The crucial concept in Bonhoeffer's exposition of created freedom and its relationship to uncreated freedom is the *imago dei*, human creation in the image of God. In view of the stress on sociality and on human personhood as relational in the early university theses *Sanctorum Communio* and *Act and Being*, we might expect that Bonhoeffer, like Barth, would ground his understanding of the image in the male/female relationship.[224] However, whilst the relational implications of human being are clearly never far from his thoughts, for Bonhoeffer, the key to the *imago Dei* is freedom. We have already noted Bonhoeffer's understanding of creation and incarnation as expressions of divine freedom and this conviction lies at the heart of his understanding of human creation in the image of God. He writes:

> Only in that which is itself free could the free Creator behold the Creator ... If the Creator wishes to create the Creator's own image, then the Creator must create it free. And only such an image, in its freedom would fully praise God, would fully proclaim God's glory as Creator.[225]

---

[222] Bachtell op. cit. 114.

[223] C, 50 The German plays on the cognate connection between *Wort*, *Antwort* and *Verantwortung*.

[224] CD III/1 (T&T Clark 1958) 184ff.

[225] DBWE 3, 61; cf. Bachtell 114. De Gruchy in his editorial introduction to DBWE 3 suggests that 'human sociality' is the 'central meaning' of the image. *Creation and Fall* ed. de Gruchy J. W. trans. Bax S. D. (Fortress 1997), 11, as does Robert Umidi in his *Imaging God Together: The Image of God as 'sociality' in the thought and life of*

God is free and because there is no separation between his being and his act, he always acts in freedom. But God's free action is never a freedom in and for himself, but a freedom for the world, demonstrated in creation and preservation and in re-creation through Christ's incarnation, cross and resurrection. In and through his action, God is recognised as the giver of freedom. A first cause creates effects, but cannot give freedom, but it is of the essence of the personal Creator God to create freedom.

*Human Freedom as Christ-shaped*

However, as with the concept of person, which played such a central role in Bonhoeffer's early academic theses, the way in which freedom is defined and understood is crucial here. Bonhoeffer's concern is never with some abstract concept of freedom. God alone, and specifically God in his activity in Christ in the economy of salvation, can define what freedom really means. Human beings are created to reflect that divine freedom, the 'substantial' freedom which Bonhoeffer had already defined in christological terms in *Act and Being* as freedom *for* the world, a freedom which found its fullest expression, not in divine aseity, but precisely in God's free choice to bind himself to human beings. Hence, he argues: '[I]n the language of the Bible, freedom is not something that people have for themselves but something they have for others.'[226] Human freedom is not to be reified as an attribute, something comparable to intelligence or musical gifting, a quality or commodity to be possessed. Freedom is a relationship and as such can never be understood in individualistic terms, as my isolated freedom to express myself or to make choices, but must always be understood in social, relational and hence ethical terms. Humanity's freedom for God is freedom to praise the Creator, freedom to be fully human, fully a creature, in relationship to the Creator. As Bonhoeffer expresses it: '[F]reedom is a relationship between two persons. Being free means "being-free-for-the-other" because I am bound to the other. Only by being in relation with the other am I free.'[227]

---

*Dietrich Bonhoeffer.* (Unpublished Ph.D. dissertation Drew University 1994). However, we would argue that it is clear from the text that when God sees the divine reflection in humanity, it is freedom not relationality which is mirrored, albeit that freedom can only be understood in relational terms.

[226] DBWE 3, 62.

[227] DBWE 3, 63.

Just as creation could only be fully understood in the light of the resurrection, so human beings can only know who they are, as those created in the image of God, in the light of Christ, and in particular, his resurrection.[228] The defining paradigm for human freedom is the revelation of God's freedom in the economy of salvation and, as we saw in our discussion of *Act and Being*, God's freedom is always a freedom for the other, a gracious self-giving of himself to the other, a Christ-shaped freedom:

> [I]t is the message of the gospel itself that God's freedom has bound itself to us, that God's free grace becomes real with us alone, that God wills not to be free for God's self but for humankind. Because God in Christ is free for humankind, because God does not keep God's freedom to God's self, we can think of freedom only as a 'being free for....' For us in the middle who exist through Christ and who know what it means to be human through Christ's resurrection, the fact that God is free means nothing else than that we are free for God. The freedom of the Creator demonstrates itself by allowing us to be free, free for the Creator. That however means nothing else than that the Creator's image is created on earth.[229]

Freedom can be defined only in relation to God and as we know God only in his free revelation of himself in Jesus Christ, we can only know freedom christologically, as a 'being free for' which involves a free acceptance of constraint. We will discuss the relationship between freedom and restriction in more detail below.

### *Freedom in Likeness and Difference - The Spirit as the Agent of Freedom*

Humanity is both created and free, reflecting the image of God and yet as creature also fundamentally unlike God. Where divine freedom is unconditioned, the very concept of 'image' implies dependence. Without the original, the image could have no existence. It is in this context that Bonhoeffer writes of 'The paradox of created freedom',[230] that in the creation of humanity God does not merely speak his word in order to create, but 'God enters into creation and so creates freedom.'[231] The original himself creates and maintains his image in human beings. Hence,

---

[228] Ibid.
[229] Ibid.
[230] Ibid.
[231] Ibid.

whilst created freedom is, by its very nature derivative, it is nonetheless real freedom, the key to which, as we shall see, is the work of the Holy Spirit.

Bonhoeffer has, with some justice, been criticised for an insufficiently Trinitarian theology and with somewhat less justice for an inadequate pneumatology.[232] It could perhaps be argued that a more explicit Trinitarian theology would save Bonhoeffer's account from any suspicion that the divine freedom as 'freedom for' operates only in the economy and is not inherent to the divine nature in itself. However, as we have already noted, unlike Barth, for whom an understanding of the perichoretic relationships within the immanent Trinity are foundational to his account, for Bonhoeffer, the key relationship is always that between God and the world. In the opening chapter of *Creation and Fall*, Bonhoeffer cites with evident approval, Luther's acerbic response to those who asked what God was doing before he created the world that 'God was cutting sticks to cane people who ask such idle questions.'[233] Bonhoeffer's approach to attempts to go behind God's self-revelation in Christ is similarly unsympathetic. However, whilst he does not take the explicitly Trinitarian starting point of Barth's *Church Dogmatics*, Bonhoeffer's theology is always orthodox in Trinitarian terms. Here, the discussion of human freedom as creation in the image of God, and as God himself entering into his creation, is clearly founded on an understanding of the Holy Spirit as the one who mediates freedom. Bonhoeffer writes:

> This is what the older dogmatic theologians meant when they spoke of the indwelling of the Trinity in Adam. In the free creature the Holy Spirit worships the Creator; uncreated freedom glorifies itself in view of created freedom. The

---

[232] Marsh C. in *The Modern Theologians* ed. Ford D. F. (Second Edition Blackwell 1996), 49, refers to perceived Trinitarian deficiencies in Bonhoeffer's theology and in his *Reclaiming Dietrich Bonhoeffer* (Oxford OUP 1994), uses Eberhard Jüngel's theology as a vehicle for exploring the Trinitarian possibilities in Bonhoeffer's thought. The alleged pneumatological deficiency, though often raised, is less firmly grounded. Bachtell op. cit. 296, refers to an absence of precise reference to the Holy Spirit except in *Sanctorum Communio*. However, in my view it is in that early work that the pneumatological inadequacies are most obvious, particularly in the concept of 'Christ existing as the church', where a greater role for the Spirit seems to be required. Bachtell also speaks of a 'conspicuous absence of any serious language regarding the Holy Spirit in [Bonhoeffer's] *Ethics* and prison correspondence', whereas it is in the *Ethics* fragment 'Christ, Reality and Good' that Bonhoeffer speaks most explicitly of the relationship between Christ and the Spirit in terms of the realisation of the real. *DBW 6,* 34; ET 190.

[233] DBWE 3, 31; Bonhoeffer is paraphrasing Luther's remarks in *Table Talk.*

creature loves the Creator, because the Creator loves the creature. Created *freedom* is freedom in the Holy Spirit, but as *created* freedom, it is humankind's own freedom.[234]

It is the Spirit who operates on both sides of the divine/human relationship, creating and sustaining a dynamic unity of difference between God and humanity, and enabling the fully human creation to relate in freedom to the Creator. To be truly free is to be truly human, but true humanity is humanity in the freedom of the Spirit. Human freedom is derived from and dependent upon divine freedom, it is the response of the image to the reality it reflects. However, Bonhoeffer is clear that God and his creation remain distinct in their freedom. Indeed, Rowan Williams suggests that this is Bonhoeffer's 'deep, perhaps deepest conviction'.[235] Williams asserts that the very grammar of talking about God is in danger of becoming meaningless once this distinction is no longer maintained, but submerged in some symbiotic union, as in process theology or more recently some approaches to feminist or ecological theology, which are distinctly uncomfortable with the concept of difference.[236] He comments provocatively, but perceptively: 'Isn't the difference of God and creature the mark of the freedom of the Creator's love and isn't that ultimately the only thing worth affirming about the grammar of God.'[237] In choosing both to create a world distinct from himself, a world with its own integrity, free to accept or reject his love, and in choosing not to be free from but free for that world, the Creator demonstrates the radical freedom of risk taking love. But Bonhoeffer is equally clear that difference does not imply separation. Human beings are free, but not self-constituting. Human freedom is not the freedom of autonomous, independent and unrelated beings - that is the *cor curvum in se*, the isolation of the self separated from God and others - but the free gift of participation in the divine freedom. By the Spirit, humanity participates in the freedom of God, so that, as Bonhoeffer says in his comments on the seventh day: 'God's rest is our rest (as God's freedom is our freedom, God's goodness our goodness).'[238]

---

[234] DBWE 3, 64.

[235] Williams R. *Bonhoeffer, the Sixties and After* op. cit., 5. In his discussion of the Christian concept of personhood in *Sanctorum Communio*, Bonhoeffer had maintained 'The Christian person arises solely from the absolute distinction between God and humanity.' (DBW 1, 29).

[236] Ibid.

[237] Ibid., 6.

[238] DBWE 3, 69.

## *The Image as Freedom 'for' - the 'Analogia Relationis'*

As we have seen, the defining characteristic of human being is its freedom in relationship, to God and to others. It is as Bonhoeffer goes on to discuss the relationship between the divine freedom of the Creator and the created freedom of the creature, and the way in which that freedom finds expression, that he develops his distinctive concept of *analogia relationis*. For Bonhoeffer, this is the key to holding in tension both the radical distinction and the continuity between divine and human existence. Humanity is free in relation to the other, free in creation as male and female, in interdependence. But the relationship between God and humanity can never be viewed in terms of a human capacity or potentiality, something within human control - as in the concept of the *analogia entis* - but only as a gift to be received, in Bonhoeffer's words, 'a given relation... a justitia passiva.'[239] The concept of *justitia passiva* had been of critical significance in Luther's discovery of the righteousness of God as a gift bestowed on humanity.[240] Bonhoeffer makes clear that such passivity is not to be seen as a constraint on human freedom to act, but as a theological statement about the standing of humanity before God as recipients of his gift:

> [T]he analogia or likeness must be understood very strictly in the sense that what is like derives its likeness *only* from the prototype, so that it always points us only to the prototype itself and is 'like' it *only* in pointing to it in this way. Analogia relationis is therefore the relation which God has established, and is analogia only in this relation which God has established. The relation of creature with creature is a relation established by God, because it consists of freedom and freedom comes from God.[241]

In his review of Charles Marsh's *Reclaiming Dietrich Bonhoeffer*, George Hunsinger suggests that, if, as Marsh claims, Bonhoeffer presupposed Barth's understanding of the Trinitarian relationality of God's being as it is in itself, he would have brought this concept into play in his discussion of the *analogia relationis*:

---

[239] Ibid., 65.
[240] cf. Bonhoeffer's use of this concept in *Sanctorum Communio*, (DBW 1, 128) in the context of the unity of the church as gift rather than as something to be established. cf. also DBWE 2, 134 and DBW 6, 340.
[241] DBWE 3, 65-61.

> Whereas the *analogatum* (the term to be compared) is humanity's being-in-relationship as male and female, the *analogans* (that to which it is compared) is tellingly, not at all God's inner-Trinitarian community, *but merely God's being-in-relation to the world.*[242]

However, in my view, that is precisely the point. In grounding the analogy in God's gracious, free and self-sacrificing relationship to the world in and through Christ, rather than in the inner-Trinitarian life of God's being in itself, the costliness of freedom in relationship is highlighted. Here is no cheap grace, but a relationship ultimately restored and sustained at the price of the cross. Because God is free for humanity, human beings who participate in God's freedom will be free for others, but the analogy or likeness is the gift of God and arises solely in and through relationship with God. Bachtell seems to come close to confusing the *analogia relationis* with the *analogia entis* when he suggests: 'The analogy then of man's likeness to God is the analogy of relation, the relationship *that he finds with other men* and with God.'[243] However, Bonhoeffer is clear that it is our participation through grace in relationship *with God*, and that alone which defines the analogy.

## *The Image as Freedom 'from'*

Human creation in the image of God is creation in the freedom of relatedness, or better perhaps, the relatedness which alone constitutes true freedom. However, where human freedom towards others is a freedom *for*, Bonhoeffer argues that humanity is free *from* the non-human creation. Humanity, created in the divine image is called to rule over creation as those commissioned by God. Nevertheless, as Bonhoeffer makes clear, this freedom *from* the created order is not to be conceived in idealist terms as the lordship of the spirit over nature. Humanity is not free from the world in the sense of being alienated or separate from it, but only in the light of his divinely given vocation to rule. He belongs fully to the earth, indeed it is precisely in his freedom from it, that he is bound to it.

However, in attempting to rule, humanity has lost sight of the corresponding call to care for the world as God's creation. Instead of seeing human sovereignty as a divinely given trust, the relationship has become

---

[242] *Modern Theology* 12.1, 1996, 121 at 122 (my italics). I would argue that, in fact, the analogy is one of freedom in relation rather than of relationality per se.

[243] Bachtell op. cit. 118 (my italics).

distorted into one of domination. Ironically in seeking to rule the created order, human beings find themselves enslaved. '[H]umankind is a prisoner, a slave of the world and its dominion is an illusion. Technology is the power with which the world seizes hold of humankind and masters it.'[244] Hence in seeking to be free *from* the earth, without being free for God and for his fellow human beings, humanity becomes alienated from the earth. Bonhoeffer's early reading of Nietzsche had convinced him of the intrinsic connectedness between humanity and the earth and he continues to maintain this, even in the face of the Nazis' deification of blood and soil. However, he stresses that a right relationship to the non-human creation is the fruit of a right relationship to the creator and to humanity. Care for creation arises not from deifying the created order, but results when humanity stands in right relationship to God and to others. This is what it means to live in the image of God. Although it would be anachronistic to read back current environmental concerns into Bonhoeffer's account, it is not difficult to trace the connection between the post-Enlightenment absolutising of human freedom, which Bonhoeffer addresses here and humanity's dislocation from creation.

*The Image as Bodily*

The alienation from the earth which underlies this dislocation from the non-human creation also finds expression within the Christian tradition in an ambivalence toward the human body. Although a dualistic polarising of soul and body may owe more to philosophy than to Christian scripture, the perception of the body as an encumbrance from which the mind, soul or spirit seeks to be freed lies not far below the surface in much theology, particularly within the Protestant tradition. For Bonhoeffer, however, the goal of the Christian is not freedom from the body, but freedom in it. Humanity is not a duality, but a unity of body and soul. Indeed to be bodily is part of what it means to be created in the image of God, because God himself took on human bodiliness. He writes:

> [Humanity] is the image of God not in spite of but precisely in its bodily nature. For in their bodily nature human beings are related to the earth and to other bodies; they are there for others, and are dependent on others. In their

---

[244] DBWE 3, 67.

bodily existence, human beings find their brothers and sisters and find the earth.[245]

Human bodiliness is not a prison. On the contrary, 'God ... is glorified in the body.'[246] For Bonhoeffer, personhood implies bodiliness and this remains the case even in the eschatological vision of the perfected body of Christ, because the resurrection of the saints is inherently corporeal.[247] As we have suggested, a denigration of bodiliness is often closely linked to a negative approach to the rest of the created order. However, Bonhoeffer's exposition of Genesis 2 focuses on the essential connectedness between humanity and the non-human creation. Where the first creation account stressed God's sovereignty and placed the creation of humanity as the crown of creation, the latter stresses God's closeness and puts the human creation in the centre of the account. Bonhoeffer asserts that the myth's anthropomorphic portrayal of God shaping humanity with his own hands, expresses profound truths about the divine/human relationship and the close ties between humanity and the non-human creation. The one created in God's image, in freedom, is also the one created out of the earth. Reflecting on Michelangelo's portrayal of creation in the Sistine Chapel,[248] Bonhoeffer speaks of Adam resting 'on the newly created earth'[249] to which he is so closely linked, and called from his sleep by bodily contact with the finger of God. He comments: 'God's hand no longer holds the human being in its grasp; instead it has *set the human being free*, and the creative power of that hand turns into the yearning love of the Creator towards the creature.'[250] Interestingly, Barth's reference to the same fresco in *The Epistle to the Romans*,[251] focuses on the conversation between Creator and creature, whereas Bonhoeffer's stress is on the physical connection between Adam, his Maker and the earth from which he came. As in his comments on the first creation account, Bonhoeffer notes that the creation

---

[245] Ibid., 79.

[246] Ibid., 79; cf. the distinction Bonhoeffer draws in *Christology* between incarnation, which is the glory of God, and the likeness of sinful flesh, which is the condescension of God.

[247] In *Ethics*, he writes: 'The human person is a bodily being and remains so even in eternity. Bodiliness and human life belong inseparably together.' DBW 6, 180; ET 156.

[248] cf. DBW 9, 81 at 105 where Bonhoeffer speaks of Michelangelo's portrayal of Adam as 'wholly earthly and yet wholly pure'.

[249] DBWE 3, 78.

[250] Ibid.; (my italics).

[251] Trans. Hoskyns E. C. (from the 6th German Edition 1928) (Oxford University Press 1968), 249.

of humanity is not, as with the rest of creation a calling into being by the word, but the gift of God's Spirit, of his own life. The human body is the form of existence of God's Spirit on earth. It is both distinct from other life-forms and yet continuous with them.

Bonhoeffer's thoughts on the inextricable connection between the body and personal existence and his affirmation of human physicality, continued to evolve and reached their most developed expression in the theology of the natural in *Ethics*. There, Bonhoeffer asserts that the human body, (like the *Gemeinde*, the body of Christ in *Sanctorum Communio)*, is willed by God to be an end in itself as well as a means to an end. To see it merely as the latter is unchristian. Hence bodiliness is to be celebrated:

> If the body is rightly to be understood as an end in itself, then there is a right to bodily joys, even though these are not necessarily subordinated to some higher purpose. It is inherent in the nature of joy itself that it is spoilt by any thought of purpose.[252]

In the letters from prison Bonhoeffer continues to celebrate bodiliness and physicality, arguing that the 'best christological exposition' of the Song of Songs is to read it as 'an ordinary love song'.[253] True humanity is the embodied freedom to live life to the full.

## Freedom within Limits

The idea of freedom as freedom from the body is only one example of the tendency to equate freedom with the absence or at least the minimising of limitation. However, throughout Bonhoeffer's discussion of freedom we encounter the paradox that true and authentic human freedom is never absolute, but is always freedom within limits. In the next two chapters we will see this expressed in terms of the dialectic between freedom and obedience and the intrinsic relatedness of freedom and responsibility. In *Creation and Fall*, however, this same dynamic is expressed in terms of creatureliness.

---

[252] DBW 6, 180 ; ET 157.
[253] LPP 315.

## Creatureliness and the Boundary

In early twenty-first-century theology, creatureliness remains a relatively neglected and unfashionable concept. However, its importance should not be underrated. Creatureliness is an inherently relational idea which sets humanity in the context of the primary relationship to the creator and the secondary relationship to other human creatures who share that same relationship to the creator. But the term also affirms humanity's relationship to all other created things and hence, as with our discussion of bodiliness, has ecological implications. For Bonhoeffer, original created freedom is freedom in creatureliness, freedom within bounds. In the creation story, Adam is called in his freedom to live within God given limits, portrayed in the paradise myth in terms of the tree of the knowledge of good and evil. Bonhoeffer writes:

> This singular interrelatedness, which is basically only the interrelatedness of freedom and creatureliness, is expressed here in the picture language of the Bible in that the tree of knowledge, the forbidden tree that denotes the human being's boundary, stands at the centre.[254]

In his original, God given freedom, Adam, in knowing God knows his limit, not as a restriction but as 'an expression of [his] creatureliness and freedom.'[255] In his relationship with God, the limit is not the boundary of his possibilities but the reality at the centre of his existence: 'The limit is grace, because it is the basis of creatureliness and freedom; the boundary is the centre.'[256] Eve's creation is a human expression of the limit which God places on humanity and for pre-lapsarian Adam, that limit is received as grace, as God's gift. Bonhoeffer argues that in the concrete prohibition concerning the tree of knowledge of good and evil, Adam is addressed both in his freedom and his creatureliness. It is, he writes, as if the Creator addresses him and says 'you are who you are because of me, your Creator; so now be what you are. You are a free creature, so now be that. You are free, so be free; you are a creature, so be a creature.'[257] Because freedom is not isolated autonomy but relationship, because it is not only gift but also

---

[254] DBWE 3, 86.
[255] Ibid.
[256] DBWE 3 87.
[257] Ibid., 85.

claim, humanity is both free and responsible, called to freedom but answerable in his freedom.

*The Boundary at the Centre*

If human freedom is derivative of and in the image of divine freedom, then true human freedom involves the free and willing limitation of the self by the other. It is precisely in his dependence on God, in recognising God as his limit, that humanity is free in relation to God. In other words, limitation or constraint is actually constitutive of Christian freedom. This, of course is entirely consistent with the 'Christ-shapedness' of divine and human freedom to which we have repeatedly referred. God in choosing to be free for the world, freely chooses to limit himself.

Although the concept of limit or boundary played an important role in the university dissertations,[258] as Feil has rightly shown, it was in *Creation and Fall* that Bonhoeffer first creatively explored the relationship between the boundary and the centre.[259] It is this understanding which undergirds the concept of Christ as the centre and mediator in the *Christology* lectures. There, Christ the Counter-logos is the limit or boundary to my existence who cannot be subsumed or transcended epistemologically by the human logos.[260] The boundary is not some limit to human possibility, a metaphorical mountain to be conquered, but is to be understood in personal terms, and more specifically, in terms of the person of Christ. Christ as person, the one who limits and constrains my existence 'is at one and the same time, my boundary and my rediscovered centre.'[261] The concept of the limit, which both enables and preserves freedom, also informs Bonhoeffer's understanding of the relationship between law and gospel. Although, in his Barcelona lecture on ethics, Bonhoeffer had argued that the Christian, bound only by the law of freedom, was free to create new decalogues,[262] this does not imply some facile polarisation between the divine commandment and the freedom of the Christian. As Bonhoeffer argues in

---

[258] Bonhoeffer had adopted Hegel's critique of Kant in arguing that an epistemological boundary was in fact no boundary at all because in the very act of conceiving it, the boundary was transcended. DBWE 2, 82; C, 29.

[259] Feil E. *The Theology of Dietrich Bonhoeffer* op. cit., 72-3.

[260] C, 29, 30; The same lectures expound Bonhoeffer's understanding of God's free self-limitation in Christ in his presence in word, sacrament and church. C, 49, 52, 53, 58.

[261] Ibid., 60.

[262] *Grundfragen einer christliche Ethik* DBW 10, 323ff at 331.

the *Ethics* fragment, the 'ethical' and the 'Christian', the divine commandments operate as limits which set free. Like the boundary in *Creation and Fall*, and the *Christology* lectures, they stand at the centre:

> God's commandment revealed in Jesus Christ, embraces the *whole of life*. Unlike the ethical, it does not only guard the untransgressible boundaries of life, but it is at the same time the centre and the *fullness of life*. It is not only obligation, but also permission. It does not only forbid but it sets free for *genuine life*; it sets free for unreflected action ... The commandment of God becomes the element "in" which one lives without being conscious of it.[263]

The relationship between the commandments and 'fullness of life' is particularly important. The commandment operates not to constrict, but as the controlling centre which brings freedom. Bonhoeffer makes a similar point in his paper '"Personal" and "Real" Ethos', where he discusses the relationship between Christian ethics and secular institutions:

> The Decalogue is the *law of life* revealed by God for *all of life* which stands under the lordship of Christ. It is the emancipation from alien lordship and autonomous arbitrariness ... The Decalogue is the framework, within which a free obedience becomes possible *in worldly life*. It emancipates for *free life* under the lordship of Christ.[264]

Later in the same section he writes that the lordship of Christ and the Decalogue 'set free for true worldliness'. The mandates, which in *Ethics* largely replace the term of 'orders of preservation', operate in a similar way, providing a structure or set of limits within which human beings can live freely without constant introspection. It is however, perhaps only in *Letters and Papers*, that for the first time Bonhoeffer discovers an adequate conceptuality to express this dynamic relationship of constraint and freedom, limit and creativity expressed in terms of the boundary at the centre, when he takes up the musical imagery of polyphony. Where visual imagery and spatial representations strain to conceptualise a boundary at

---

[263] DBW 6, 384; ET 280 (the English translation condenses the German text) (my italics).

[264] DBW 16, 559 (my italics). This paper was included in the English edition of *Ethics* at 320ff, but is now viewed as an occasional paper rather than part of the proposed book on ethics. On Bonhoeffer's use of the concept 'law of life' cf. Burtness J. *Shaping the Future: The Ethics of Dietrich Bonhoeffer* (Philadelphia Fortress Press 1985) pp. 97-98.

the centre, musical concepts offer new possibilities.[265] In polyphony, the *cantus firmus* is the limit at the centre around which the counterpoint is released in freedom.[266] A human life in which love for Christ is the 'limiting centre', is a life liberated for the freedom and fullness of life which is God's design for his creation.[267]

**The Fall**

The concept of limit, and in particular the limiting centre, is foundational to Bonhoeffer's understanding of human sin and alienation. The spiritual history of humanity is one of the displaced centre, in which, to use the language of the Tegel theology, instead of accepting the limiting centre as grace, human beings seek to be their own *cantus firmus*. The paradoxical union of freedom and limitation which was the gift of God in creation is broken, but in breaking free of the limit, humanity forfeits the authentic freedom which was its counterpart. In *Sanctorum Communio*, Bonhoeffer writes of humanity's fall from sociality into individualism and the deceptive freedom of self assertion, which is ultimately the self-absorption of the *cor curvum in se*. However, the most detailed treatment comes in *Creation and Fall* and *Ethics* fragments 'The Love of God and the Decay of the World' and 'Inheritance and Decay'. Despite the decade which separates these two works, they have much in common and we will discuss them together.[268]

*The Transgression of the Limit*

In *Creation and Fall*, Bonhoeffer argues that the fall was not some inevitable consequence of created freedom, but arose out of a wrong use of

---

[265] For the use of musical conceptuality in theology cf. Begbie J. *Theology, Music and Time* (CUP 2000).

[266] cf. Kemp W. H. 'The "Polyphony of Life" : References to Music in Bonhoeffer's *Letters and Papers from Prison*' in *Vita Laudanda Essays in Memory of Ulrich S Leopold* (Wilfred Laurier Univ. Press 1976), 145-146. Kemp speaks of the *cantus firmus* as 'the central thread of the sound structure', the 'controlling and cohesive force of the motet or Mass movement in which it appeared.'

[267] LPP 303.

[268] *Creation and Fall* was published in 1933, the fragment 'Inheritance and Decay' was probably written in the second half of 1941 and 'The Love of God and the Decay of the World' towards the end of 1942.

freedom.[269] The fall is a breaking through the limit, a grasping at uncreated freedom, a Promethean or Nietzschean assertion of the right to a freedom without bounds. Instead of knowing himself as free for God, free to obey in love, humanity seeks to be free from God. He violates the limits which God has placed upon him, whether these are expressed physically in the form of the other, epistemologically in the limits to human knowledge, or as a boundary to human possibilities in the form of revealed word of God. But the irony is that in seeking to become like God, to become self-grounding, humanity becomes less than human, less free. In seeking a self-constituted freedom, the freedom given by God is lost. The other, who had previously been acknowledged as gift, now becomes a physical and psychic boundary to my freedom and self-expression. 'Now he no longer sees the limit that the other person constitutes as grace but as God's wrath, God's hatred, God's begrudging.'[270] The other, whether God or my neighbour restricts my freedom and so must be overcome, but in fact loss of the other leads to loss of self. In seeking to be *sicut deus*, humanity transgresses the divine limit and in so doing, rejects the complementarity of freedom and constraint and severs the connection between creatureliness and freedom which had constituted human creation in the *imago dei*. He now stands in the middle, in the place of Christ; he has become his own limit.

This transgression of the limit is expressed secondly in epistemological terms as a grasping at the knowledge of good and evil, a desire to be free from God-imposed boundaries to knowledge. In Chapter 2 we discussed the close link between knowledge and freedom and the fallacious assumption that increased knowledge brings increased power. Here, in *Creation and Fall,* the fall is seen at least in part as an illegitimate quest for knowledge of good and evil which seems to promise a fulfilment of human possibility, a God-like freedom. A similar analysis appears in the discussion of the fall in the *Ethics* fragment 'God's Love and the Decay of the World'. There Bonhoeffer speaks of humanity's transition from his original state as God's chosen or elected one to his fallen state as the one who chooses.[271] Instead of living out of his centre in God as one who is constituted in and through God, who recognises his existence as a gift, humanity seeks to live out of his own centre, to be self constituting, the arbiter and agent of his own possibilities. In seeking knowledge of good

---

[269] DBWE 3, 104.
[270] Ibid., 122.
[271] DBW 6, 303; ET 19.

and evil 'He has become like God, but against God', and in the process has become less than fully human.[272] The image of God which humanity bears is now a stolen image and as a result, asserts Bonhoeffer, humanity lives in a state of fragmentation and conflict, paralysed by the burden of his illegitimate knowledge of good and evil, bewildered by the range of ethical possibilities.

The third over-reaching of the boundary is the attempt to go behind the revelation of God's word. The serpent's question, which Bonhoeffer dubs 'the pious question'[273] invites humanity to judge God's word, to test whether it fits with his idea of God. In Chapter 2 we examined Bonhoeffer's rejection of the concept of possibility in theology. Here in *Creation and Fall*, he views the fall in terms of an attempt to give expression to human possibility. Bonhoeffer asserts 'The possibility of Adam's own, "wanting-to-be-for-God", as Adam's own discovery, is the primal evil in the pious question of the serpent.'[274] Humanity exchanges the reality of relationship with God for the possibility of human divinisation. In the *Ethics* fragment 'God's Love and the Decay of the World' Bonhoeffer uses the language of choice rather than that of freedom. However the connection between the two is clearly a close one. Freedom is often understood in terms of freedom to choose, perhaps especially between ethical alternatives, but as in current thought within the Western world, the implications range across the whole sphere of personal, social and economic life. In 'Inheritance and Decay' Bonhoeffer again takes up the question of the fall in his discussion of the Enlightenment and the absolutising of human freedom which he saw as its legacy. He asserts: The French Revolution was the disclosure of emancipated humanity in his immense power and his most dreadful distortion. Emancipated humanity meant here emancipated reason, emancipated class, emancipated people.[275] It is in this section that we encounter for the first time the link between human autonomy and what Bonhoeffer in *Letters and Papers* will refer to as the 'world come of age'. He writes:

> The people considered themselves to have come of age, able to take their destiny into their own hands, both internally and externally. They demanded

---

[272] DBW 6, 303-4; ET 19.
[273] 'die fromme Frage' translated 'the religious question' in the earlier English translation. DBWE 3, 106-7.
[274] DBWE 3, 109.
[275] DBW 6, 105; ET 97.

their right to freedom and development as a nation, the right to a government based on the nation.[276]

Although Bonhoeffer is quite clear that there can be no return to a pre-Enlightenment world view, he argues that the effects of absolutising freedom were as dramatic as they were unforeseen, uncovering an apparent 'law of history' under which the quest for absolute freedom results in enslavement:

> The master of the machine becomes its slave, the machine becomes the enemy of humanity. The creature turns against its creator in a strange repetition of the fall! The emancipation of the masses leads to the reign of terror of the guillotine ... The liberation of humanity as an absolute ideal leads only to humanity's self-destruction.[277]

Bonhoeffer's image of a recapitulation of the fall is a particularly telling one. Humanity, in its search for absolute freedom from all constraint, becomes de-humanised. The result of the quest to become a creator *ex nihilo*, is humanity *sicut Deus,* separated from God, the giver of freedom and helplessly enslaved by the very works he has created.

## Preservation

Nevertheless, Bonhoeffer is clear that the fallen world is not abandoned by its Creator. When the gate to Eden is barred, 'The Creator is now the preserver'[278] and the fallen world is directed by means of what Bonhoeffer, in *Creation and Fall*, terms 'orders of preservation'. Preservation, like creation, is an act of God's gracious freedom. As we have already indicated, Bonhoeffer's use of this concept arose at a time when the idea of 'orders of creation' was being used to justify the excesses of the Nazi regime in the name of God-willed national self-expression. As a result many theologians became wary of engaging with a theology of creation. Bonhoeffer, however, whilst unequivocally rejecting the abuse of the concept of orders of creation, was concerned to affirm God's continuing care for his fallen world, in grace as well as judgement. In the light of Jesus

---

[276] DBW 6, 110; ET 100 The standard English translation reads 'history', rather than 'destiny', presumably a misreading of 'Geschicke' as 'Geschichte'.
[277] DBW 6, 112-113 cf. DBWE 3, 67.
[278] DBWE 3, 139.

Christ, creation is not forsaken, but stands under the preservation of God. However, because of human sinfulness, all orders of the world must be regarded as orders of preservation, obtaining value not from themselves, but only in so far as they are directed toward Christ.[279] By the time of the writing of *Ethics*, Bonhoeffer had developed the concept of the 'divine mandate' in the place of 'orders of preservation'. Burtness[280] suggests that the use of the latter expression by Paul Althaus, whose Nazi sympathies were well known, led Bonhoeffer to disassociate himself from the term.

## The Relative Freedom of Fallen Creation

Although in consequence of the fall of humanity, creation as a whole is alienated from its creator, it too stands under the preservation of God. As with fallen humanity, the concept of freedom is central to an understanding of the alienated state of nature. Among the early writings, this emerges most clearly from *Christology*, where Bonhoeffer argues that 'nature suffers from the loss of its meaning and freedom.'[281] However, where fallen humanity awaits reconciliation, 'Nature, unlike humanity and history, will not be reconciled, but it will be set free for a new freedom'.[282] Bonhoeffer re-writes the standard Protestant script, with its tendency to set grace and nature in opposition, by offering a Christ centred theology of nature rather than a natural theology. Christ stands at the centre of nature as the redeemer, the one who stands for creation before God and frees it from its bondage in fallenness. The sacraments witness proleptically to this reality, as eschatological signs of the redemption of the non-human creation in hope. Bonhoeffer writes: 'In the sacrament [Christ] breaks through the fallen creation at a defined point.'[283] Creation was created to praise the creator, but through the fall is rendered mute. In the sacraments the elements of the old fallen creation 'are set free from their dumbness and proclaim directly to the believer the new creative word of God.'[284]

The relationship between creation and preservation is again explored in detail in the *Ethics* fragments 'The Natural' and 'The Last and Penultimate

---

[279] *Towards a Theological Basis for the World Alliance* DBW 11, 317ff. cf. *Jüngste Theologie: Besprechung systematisch-theologischer Neuerscheinungen* GS V 305.
[280] Op.cit. 83.
[281] C, 66 cf. Bachtell op. cit. 207.
[282] Ibid., 64.
[283] Ibid., 57.
[284] Ibid., 65.

Things'. By 'the natural', Bonhoeffer means 'the form of life preserved by God for the fallen world and directed through Christ, towards justification, redemption and renewal.'[285] He argues that this is not a concept of which Protestant theology should be wary, out of fear of compromising the doctrine of grace, but constitutes the post-lapsarian equivalent of the creaturely. Again, freedom remains a crucial concept in the equation. Bonhoeffer writes:

> Through the fall, the 'creature' becomes 'nature'. The direct dependence on God of the true creature becomes the relative freedom of natural life. Within this freedom there are differences between the right and the mistaken use of freedom, and that means the difference between the natural and the unnatural, so there is a relative openness and a relative closedness for Christ.[286]

He argues that this relative freedom must be clearly distinguished from original pre-lapsarian freedom, the 'absolute freedom for God and for one's neighbour which only the coming of the word of God itself can create and give.'[287] Nevertheless, asserts Bonhoeffer, within the sphere of natural life, there remains a genuine, albeit fallen freedom. At Finkenwalde, Bonhoeffer had caused controversy by propounding the concept of 'the first step' in his discussion of the relationship between faith and obedience, arguing that humanity, though utterly dependent on grace alone for salvation, remained free to place him or herself in a position where that grace could be received. The step of obedience is not a work and does not in itself create faith, but it does place the one who takes it in a position to receive the grace of God:

> [The first step] is a step within everybody's capacity, for it lies within the limits of human freedom ... To take this step it is not necessary to surrender one's freedom. Come to church! You can do that of your own free will...If you will not, you are of your own free will excluding yourself from the place where faith is a possibility.[288]

---

[285] DBW 6, 166; ET 145.
[286] DBW 6, 165-6; ET 145. Bonhoeffer is clear that such openness cannot compel the coming of Christ, nor can such closedness prevent his activity.
[287] Ibid.
[288] CD 55; As we will see below, a similar dynamic arises in the concept of 'preparing the way' in 'The Last and the Penultimate things'.

*The Ultimate and the Penultimate*

The relationship between creation, preservation and redemption is powerfully encapsulated in Bonhoeffer's conception of the ultimate and the penultimate.[289] The concept of 'The last things' is normally treated in the context of eschatology. The church looks forward to the future in which the kingdom inaugurated by Christ in his incarnation will finally be consummated. In contrast, justification is often viewed, in temporal terms at least, as a past event accomplished through the incarnation and the cross, to which the believer in the present looks back. Both doctrines, the one focusing on the future, the other on the past, can tend towards a devaluation of the present and a polarisation between time and eternity, creation and redemption, the physical and the spiritual, ethics and doctrine. By his creative interpretation of 'the last things' in terms of justification, Bonhoeffer brings past and future into focus in the present, in the person of Christ. However, we are not directed to a timeless present moment, but a present suffused with the future and the past. In Christ, past, present and future are reconciled but never merged. In his understanding of the ultimate and penultimate, Bonhoeffer refuses the disjunction between creation and redemption, between compromise with the world or radical withdrawal and rejection. Christ is the one in whom 'those things which are here ranged in mutual hostility are one ... In him alone lies the solution for the problem of the relation between the ultimate and the penultimate.'[290] God is both Judge and Redeemer *and* Creator and Preserver. In an important christological statement he asserts: 'In Jesus Christ we believe in the incarnate, crucified, risen God. In the incarnation we learn of the love of God for his creation; in the crucifixion we learn of the judgement of God upon all flesh; and in the resurrection we learn of God's will for a new world. There could be no greater error than to tear these three elements apart; *for each of them comprises the whole.*'[291] Hence a theology or an ethics founded exclusively either on the incarnation or on the event of the cross and resurrection would inevitably be seriously distorted leading either to radical withdrawal from the world or uncritical compromise with it. Instead, the Christian is confronted with the subversive paradox of three wholes, three all-embracing truths to be affirmed, and lived.

---

[289] German 'die letzten und die vorletzten Dinge'.
[290] *Ethik* 148 ; ET 130.
[291] *Ethik* 148-9; ET 130-1 (my italics).

Although justification, as we will see below, is God's final word both in the temporal and qualitative senses, the penultimate, which Bonhoeffer defines as all that which precedes justification, is valued for the sake of Christ. Hence, there can be no disjunction between creation and redemption. A right understanding of the ultimate and penultimate provides the antidote both to an emphasis on faith at the expense of obedience, the 'cheap grace' which Bonhoeffer had so roundly condemned in *The Cost of Discipleship*, and to a view of the fallenness of creation which loses sight of the continuing grace of God in preserving his estranged world. Christ is the one in whom 'those things which are here ranged in mutual hostility are one ... . In him alone lies the solution for the problem of the relation between the ultimate and the penultimate.'[292]

The ultimate, God's last word of justification remains an entirely free and contingent act of his grace. However, because God chooses to act in freedom, all that which precedes the justifying word is given value as the recipient of both judgement and grace. The relationship between the ultimate and the penultimate helpfully illuminates the connection between divine and human freedom. Like the penultimate, human freedom is dependent and derivative, existing only in and through the ultimate of divine freedom. Nevertheless, as with the penultimate, it has its own integrity, it is not a cipher, but finds its authenticity in and through its relationship to divine freedom. In the paradox of divine and human freedom, God's gracious activity always remains free and contingent, and yet the church can 'prepare the way' for the Gospel by acts of social concern. God's action remains entirely within the sphere of his free grace, and yet humanity is also free, in the terminology of *Cost*, to take the 'first step'. Bonhoeffer's refusal to opt for an easy resolution of the paradox between divine grace and human responsibility, (all too frequently resolved to privilege one side of the equation at the expense of the other) seems to be entirely in accord with the tension evident within the New Testament, expressed with particular clarity in the Pauline exhortation in Philippians 2:12-13.[293] Divine freedom enables fallen human beings to exercise freedom, albeit in the limited and relative sense which we have described.

The detailed christological formulation in this section supports an eschatology which whilst giving primacy to the radical impact of the ultimate, takes the penultimate with all seriousness. Christ as a human

---

[292] DBW 6, 148, ET 130.
[293] 'Work out your own salvation with fear and trembling; for it is God who is at work in you, enabling you both to will and to work for his good pleasure.' (NRSV).

being, as the God who enters human reality, neither colludes with humanity, nor destroys it. He stands as a real human being and yet without sin amidst a world of sinners, as one who refuses to endorse worldly norms and value systems. Christ crucified condemns humanity, and passes judgement on the world and yet the world is not annihilated, or kept in existence only to await ultimate destruction, for there is also mercy in the cross. 'The ultimate has become real in the cross, as the judgement upon all that is penultimate, yet at the same time, as grace towards that penultimate which bows before the judgement of the ultimate.'[294] Humanity is both sentenced and pardoned in the cross. The risen Christ as the risen human being brings new life amid the old, the future into the present. 'Hence, even the resurrection does not annul the penultimate, so long as the earth continues, but the eternal life, the new life, breaks in with ever greater power into the earthly life and wins its space for itself within it.'[295] In the resurrection of Christ we see the breaking in of the new order, a foretaste of the ultimate.[296] 'In Christ the reality of God meets the reality of the world and allows us to share in this real encounter. It is an encounter beyond all radicalism and all compromise. Christian life is participation in Christ's encounter with the world.'[297] The Christian is called to a life lived fully in the world as one in whom the ultimate has already dawned. Because of the essential unity within diversity of the Christ event, the Christian is to live in the light of that three-fold unity. This 'means being human by virtue of the incarnation, being judged and forgiven by virtue of the cross, living a new life by virtue of the resurrection. There cannot be one of these without the others.'[298] Where for Luther, the Christian was always '*simul iustus et peccator*' in Bonhoeffer's reformulation, he or she is called to live before God in the world as one who is, at one and the same time, affirmed in humanity, judged and forgiven as a sinner and renewed in the Spirit. There can be no separation of these three aspects which are a unity in Christ.

---

[294] *Ethik* 150; ET 132.

[295] *Ethik* 150 ; ET 132.

[296] Earlier in the Christology lectures Bonhoeffer had asserted in similar vein 'In the sacrament, [Christ] breaks through fallen creation at a particular point. He is the new creature. He is the restored creation of our spiritual and bodily (geist-leiblichen) existence.' DBW 12, 305.

[297] *Ethik* 151 ; ET 133.

[298] *Ethik* 150-1; ET 132-3 cf. *Letters and Papers* 381 'Outline for a Book' where the three-fold aspect is taken up again as Bonhoeffer writes "Faith is participation in this being of Jesus (incarnation, cross and resurrection)."

## Redemption - the Image Restored

For Bonhoeffer, the God who creates and preserves is also the God who redeems, because God is both free and the giver of freedom. God's freedom is his freedom for the world, embodied in and through the reconciling love of Christ, who alone restores true freedom. In *Creation and Fall*, Bonhoeffer hints at the solution to the plight of fallen humanity, by pointing to the incarnation of Christ as the key to the restoration of the lost image:

> Imago dei, sicut deus, agnus dei - the human being who is God incarnate, who was sacrificed for humankind sicut deus, in true divinity slaying its false divinity and restoring the imago dei.[299]

In the final chapter of the study, Cain epitomising fallen humanity, *sicut deus*, becomes a murderer, a type of humanity who put Christ to death. But, asserts Bonhoeffer, in Christ, the story which begins with Cain, finds an ending in redemption as 'The trunk of the cross becomes the wood of life, and now in the midst of the world, on the accursed ground, life is raised up anew.'[300] What is lost in Adam is restored in Christ, the second Adam. Where the tree of life becomes a symbol of the fractured image and the fallen creation, the cross proclaims the Creator's love in redeeming his creation and restoring his image in humanity.

The incarnation, like creation, is an absolutely free and unconditioned act of God, indeed there are a number of striking parallels between Bonhoeffer's treatment of the two themes. As we have seen, in *Creation and Fall*, Bonhoeffer firmly rejects any concept of the necessity of creation. In *Christology*, in a trenchant dismissal of Hegel's view of incarnation as a necessary moment in the life of God, he argues 'The incarnation is the inconceivable, the impossible, belonging to the freedom of God, the coming of God which is totally unpredictable.'[301] The incarnation remains an entirely contingent act in which '*God freely binds himself* to the creature and freely glorifies himself in the incarnate one.'[302] In a series of lectures entitled *Recent Theology*, given during the same semester as *Creation and*

---

[299] DBWE 3, 113; cf. also Ibid., 79; 'where the original body in its created being has been destroyed, God enters it anew in Jesus Christ.'

[300] DBWE 3, 146.

[301] C, 81 cf. also 105.

[302] Ibid., 106 (my italics).

*Fall*, and which can therefore be seen as complementing and filling out the basic understanding of redemption hinted at in the lectures on Genesis, Bonhoeffer stresses the importance of holding together the doctrines of creation and redemption. He argues that to separate the two is to betray the uniqueness of Christ. 'There is only one revelation, because God is one, he creates and redeems. Therefore we must think of creation and redemption together in Christ.'[303] Hence, as we might expect, Bonhoeffer's treatment of redemption owes much to his understanding of creation, or rather, the two doctrines inform one another. In view of Bonhoeffer's understanding of freedom as the defining characteristic of human creation in the image of God, redemption must be characterised by a restoration of that freedom.

*Redemption as Freedom*

This understanding of redeemed humanity as characterised by a restoration of freedom, first emerges in one of Bonhoeffer's earliest writings, the lecture *Basic Questions for a Christian Ethic*, delivered in Barcelona in 1929. There Bonhoeffer asserts: 'In that Jesus places humanity directly under God, new and afresh in each moment, he restores to humanity the greatest gift which they had lost, freedom.'[304] Hence, Christian ethical action is 'action which arises out of freedom, out of the freedom of someone who has nothing in himself, but everything in God, who always allows his actions to be confirmed and ratified through eternity.' In a somewhat audacious exercise of 'clothes stealing' Bonhoeffer maintains that it is the Christian, rather than the Nietzschean *Übermensch* who is the one who truly lives in freedom. In fact, Bonhoeffer argues 'Nietzsche's Superhuman is really not, as he thought, the antitype of the Christian, but without knowing it, Nietzsche has here brought in many characteristics of the Christian made free, as Paul and Luther describe and know him.'[305] For the one set free in Christ, the only law which remains is the New Testament paradox, the law of freedom. In a seminar paper on *The Religious Experience of Grace and the Ethical Life*,[306] delivered during his time at

---

[303] *Jüngste Theologie: Besprechung systematisch-theologischer Neuerscheinungen* GS V 306.

[304] *Grundfragen einer christliche Ethik* DBW 10, 323ff at 330. Again we see the close connection between freedom and limit. Humanity finds genuine freedom in being placed 'directly under God'.

[305] Ibid., 330-1 cf. our discussion of Luther's 'The Freedom of the Christian' in Chapter 4.

[306] DBW 10, 416ff (written in English by Bonhoeffer).

Union Theological Seminary in 1931 and written in English, Bonhoeffer again discusses the restored freedom of the Christian in the context of ethics. In answer to the claim that too much emphasis on grace makes ethics irrelevant, he counters:

> Grace makes man free from himself (from his trust in his religion, in his ethical life etc. und (sic) free for God and for hearing his word. It points every moment to God himself and gives to man the only possible basis for being ethical - namely God himself. Man is free as long as he refers to God.[307]

True grace leads not to antinomianism but to genuine freedom from self, for God and for others and as such is the only authentic foundation for ethics. Bonhoeffer argues that grace is never a possession but always 'coming grace' which 'makes man free and responsible before God.'[308]

*Redemption in the Image - Conformation to Christ*

In our discussion of creation we considered the concept of the *imago dei* as a reflection of divine freedom. If redemption is a restoration of freedom, then it is also a restoration of the lost image and this is the approach taken by Bonhoeffer in the final chapter of *The Cost of Discipleship*. He discusses the incarnation of Christ in terms of the revelation and recreation on earth of the true image of God lost in the fall, and writes: 'Because human beings can no longer be like the image of God, God must become like the image of humanity.'[309] Redemption is the restoration of freedom in the image of God, a restoration understood christologically, in terms of conformation to Christ. Christ conforms himself to the world, in order that the world might be conformed to him. Bonhoeffer claims:

> Either the human being models himself on the god of his own invention, or the true and living God moulds the human form into his image. There must be a complete transformation, a 'metamorphosis' (Rom. 12:2; 2 Cor 3:18) if humanity is to be restored to the image of God.[310]

---

[307] DBW 10, 422 cf. Ibid., 423 'Only the christian conception of grace makes man before God free und (sic) gives so the only possible basis for ethical life.'
[308] DBW 10, 422.
[309] DBW 4, 298; CD, 270.
[310] DBW 4, 299; CD, 270-1.

In Christ, the second Adam, God has again entered into his creation in order to create freedom. The incarnation can be seen as a non-identical repetition of creation, the *re-creation* of humanity in God's image, through the life death and resurrection of Christ.[311] Bonhoeffer asserts that 'To be conformed to the image of Christ is not an ideal to be striven after ... We cannot transform ourselves into his image; it is rather the form of Christ which seeks to be formed in us.'[312] Christians are to be conformed to the three-fold form of Christ, incarnate, crucified and risen. In *Ethics*, Bonhoeffer again uses this same concept to express his understanding of the outworking of justification and sanctification within the Christian. As in *Cost*, he emphasises that conformation is the free initiative and work of God, not the effort of human beings and is to the threefold form of Christ. '[F]ormation comes only by being drawn into the form of Jesus Christ. It comes only as formation in his likeness, as *conformation* with the unique form of him who was made human, was crucified and rose again.'[313] Humanity is not divinised, but becomes fully human, recovering both the freedom and the creatureliness of the primal state. 'The real human being can freely be his creator's creature. To be conformed to the incarnate means to have the right to be who one truly is.'[314] In being conformed to the crucified Christ, the Christian is called to share his sufferings, dying to sin and living only by the grace of God. Bonhoeffer quotes with approval from a poem by K. F. Harttmann: 'In suffering the Master imprints his all-valid image upon our hearts and minds.'[315] To be conformed to the risen Christ is to be a new human being before God, living in the redeemed freedom.

*Justification*

In the section on 'The Last and the Penultimate Things', Bonhoeffer looks specifically at the doctrine of justification. Like the word, which brought creation to being, justification 'is God's own free word, which is subject to

---

[311] I owe the concept of non-identical repetition, which attempts to express both the absolute consistency and the rich and radical newness of God's action, to Dr. Catherine Pickstock of Cambridge University in 'Necrophilia: The Middle of Modernity', *Modern Theology* 12:4, 429.

[312] CD 272.

[313] DBW 6, 80; ET 80.

[314] Ibid., 81-2; ET 81; Bachtell (op. cit. 199) makes a similar point.

[315] Ibid., 82; ET 82 cf. Chapter 6 for a discussion of the *theologia crucis*.

no compulsion.'³¹⁶ As with creation, there is no necessity or causal connection with what has gone before. In *Act and Being*, Bonhoeffer had first summed up the plight of humanity in Adam, using Luther's concept of the *cor curvum in se*, the fallen human being trapped in self-enclosed isolation. In striking contrast, justification is a reorientation outwards to Christ, in which the unity of freedom and creatureliness is rediscovered:

> Dasein becomes free, not as if it could stand over against its being-how-it-is (Wiesein) as autonomous being, but in the sense of escaping from the power of the I into the power of Christ, where alone it recognises itself in original freedom as God's creature.³¹⁷

In *Ethics*, Bonhoeffer describes justification as an entirely new life, a life turned outwards, to God and to others, lived out of a centre in Christ:

> Faith means founding my life upon a foundation which is outside myself, upon an eternal and holy foundation, upon Christ. Faith means being held captive by the sight of Jesus Christ, no longer seeing anything but him, being wrested from my imprisonment in my own self, being set free by Jesus Christ.³¹⁸

Again we encounter the intrinsic connectedness between freedom and constraint, the paradox of created freedom, as the Christian is freed from the self-absorption of the *cor curvum in se*, to a life captivated by Christ, the restoration of true creatureliness. Once again we see redeemed freedom expressed in terms of a restoration of original freedom for God and for the other as in *Creation and Fall*. Through their participation in freedom in Christ, redeemed human beings are called release others into freedom. The liberated become liberators. However, echoing Bonhoeffer's earlier insistence on a social understanding of Christian doctrines,³¹⁹ this is not merely a transaction between the individual and his or her God but is inherently social, setting the individual in right relationship to God and to his neighbour. 'Humanity is free for God *and for his brothers.*'³²⁰

---

³¹⁶ Ibid., 140; ET 123.
³¹⁷ DBWE 2, 150.
³¹⁸ DBW 6, 138 ; ET 121.
³¹⁹ cf. *Sanctorum Communio* passim.
³²⁰ DBW 6, 137; ET 120.

## Conclusion

In this chapter we set out to show how the concept of freedom was fundamental to Bonhoeffer's understanding of the central Christian doctrines of creation, sin and redemption and indeed the doctrine of God himself. We focused on *Creation and Fall,* a book often overlooked by Bonhoeffer interpreters, but in which all of these themes emerge, and suggested that a reading of Bonhoeffer, informed by a discussion of freedom should lead to a reassessment of this work's significance within the Bonhoeffer corpus. We saw that the concept of freedom lies at the heart of Bonhoeffer's understanding of God in creation, both from the standpoint of divine agency and in terms of the defining characteristic of the creature made in his image. Where divine freedom is gracious and freely given, human freedom is gift. We noted the way in which Bonhoeffer expresses the relationship between divine and human freedom both christologically and pneumatologically. Christologically, because both uncreated and created freedom are given definition and content by the person of Christ, the one who is free for others, and pneumatologically in the light of the Holy Spirit's role as the agent of created freedom in likeness and difference.

Within our discussion of human creation in the image of God, we explored Bonhoeffer's emphasis on the intrinsic connectedness both between the Creator and his creation and between human beings and the non-human creation. We saw how Bonhoeffer's conviction that a right relationship to the earth is possible only through being rightly related to God and to others, opened the way both to a celebration of bodiliness and to a Christ-centred theology of nature. In the context of our discussion of the fall, we introduced a theme which will recur throughout our study, that of freedom within limits. In particular, we suggested that Bonhoeffer's christological re-configuration of the concept of boundary in terms of 'the limiting centre', offered a fruitful way of reconceiving the limit as facilitating freedom rather than as a barrier to be overcome. Similarly, Bonhoeffer's discussion of the ultimate and penultimate in *Ethics* offers a way beyond the dualisms of creation and redemption and affords a useful conceptuality for an understanding of the relationship between divine and human freedom. Throughout our discussion, we noted the essentially social and relational context of both original and redeemed freedom and this will be the focus of our next chapter.

## Chapter Four
# Freedom in Community

**Introduction**

In modernity, the image of freedom created and evoked by the convergence of the Cartesian emphasis on the individual thinking subject and the Nietzschean concept of the Übermensch bestriding the world, is the autonomous individual, free *for* him or herself, free *from* external interference and constraints. Bonhoeffer, however, sets his understanding of freedom firmly within the context of community and, as a result, the equation is precisely reversed. Authentic freedom is freedom *from* self, *for* God and *for* others. From his earliest writings, Bonhoeffer demonstrated a concern to resist the focus on the individual, in isolation from the social and historical context, which had become prevalent in much Protestant theology. In the Preface to his doctoral dissertation, *Sanctorum Communio*, he had asserted, 'The longer attention has been focused on the meaning of sociological categories for theology, the more clearly *the social intention of all basic Christian concepts* has emerged.'[321] Clifford Green, the first Bonhoeffer interpreter to give serious attention to the issue of sociality within Bonhoeffer's writings, maintains that this statement should be seen as 'programmatic' for the whole of the early writings.[322] Whilst this suggestion would seem to owe more to hindsight than to any systematic intent on Bonhoeffer's part, it is certainly the case that, although detailed analysis of the relationship between sociology and theology is confined to this early dissertation, the whole of Bonhoeffer's theology, including the prison writings, is pervaded by the conviction that the Christian life is inherently corporate and personal, rather than individual. Human being is by definition social being, with inevitable consequences for theology, and theological concepts can never be abstracted from their social and historical context. As we have already noted, for Bonhoeffer, both divine and human

---

[321] DBW 1, 15 (my italics).
[322] Green C.J. *Bonhoeffer:The Sociality of Christ and Humanity* op. cit., 1.

freedom are to be understood in relational, rather than individualistic terms. However, unlike personalist philosophers such as Buber and Grisebach who stressed the basic I-Thou relationship of one individual with another, for Bonhoeffer the locus of freedom is the complex web of inter-personal relationships within society, and specifically within the Christian community. In this chapter we will focus on Bonhoeffer's understanding of the Christian community as the historical and social context in which God's freedom is most clearly demonstrated, and yet where human beings also find themselves most free. We will argue that for Bonhoeffer, it is the concrete reality of the Christian community which prevents his understanding of human freedom as freedom *for* God and *for* others from becoming an abstraction, by giving it a social and an ethical groundedness.

We begin by focusing on the two early academic theses *Sanctorum Communio* and *Act and Being*, and the lecture series *The Nature of the Church*, in order to trace the role which freedom plays in Bonhoeffer's ecclesiology. We will then discuss the period at Finkenwalde, which can be seen as a practical outworking of many of the principles outlined in the university dissertations, before considering the two books which arose out of the Finkenwalde experiment, *The Cost of Discipleship* and *Life Together*. We aim to show the inadequacy of individualistic interpretations of *Cost* and to suggest a new reading which both illuminates and is illuminated by our discussion of freedom. *Life Together*, despite being Bonhoeffer's best selling book, has received relatively little scholarly attention. We hope to begin to redress this imbalance and to establish the importance of this short volume within the Bonhoeffer corpus. Clifford Green, to whose work we have already referred, will be an important conversation partner at various points in this chapter. However, his original study confined itself to the period from 1927-33, with a final chapter on *Letters and Papers*, and although the revised edition includes a new chapter on *Ethics*, there is no discussion of *Life Together*, which, as a reflection on the lived experience of Christian community is perhaps the most significant of Bonhoeffer's writings in this area.

## Ecclesiology in *Sanctorum Communio* and *Act and Being*

*Sanctorum Communio* was Bonhoeffer's doctoral thesis, supervised by Reinhold Seeberg and presented to the theological faculty at Berlin University in 1927. In it, he sought to present a dogmatic understanding of the structure of the church by bringing a theology of revelation into dialogue with current sociological insights. Probably the enduring value of this early work lies in the discussion of the church in the fifth chapter (which in fact comprises more than half the book), and it is this section which will be the focus of our discussion in this chapter.[323] In *Act and Being*, Bonhoeffer takes up the claim made in his Introduction to *Sanctorum Communio*, that theological concepts such as revelation 'can only be fully grasped in relation to sociality.'[324] He asserts that the church emerges as the solution to the problem posed by revelation as 'the place where human existence is understood'[325] and the starting point for the development of an 'ecclesial epistemology'.

*The Christian Community*

For Bonhoeffer, to speak of community, is to speak not primarily of structures or institutions, but of persons. Indeed, the concept of person is fundamental to Bonhoeffer's conceptualisation of Christian community. In *Sanctorum Communio*, he asserts:

> With an understanding of person and community, at the same time something definitive is said about the concept of God. Concept of person, concept of community and concept of God, stand in an indissoluble, essential, relationship. Where a concept of God is conceived, it will be conceived in relationship to the person and the personal community.[326]

Unlike the modern Trinitarian ecclesiologies of Zizioulas and others, Bonhoeffer is not attempting to draw any sort of parallel between human communal relationships and the intra-Trinitarian life of God. For Bonhoeffer, it is the concept of person as essentially relational and ethical which illuminates the essential relationship between God as person, the human person and the personlike community of the church.[327] As person, the ultimate mystery of the other, whether God or my neighbour is preserved. I can never fully know him or draw him into my consciousness, and yet as person, both God and my neighbour can freely choose to reveal themselves to me. As person, the individual is never dissolved into the

---

[323] Richard Roberts offers a positive evaluation of Bonhoeffer's method in 'Theology and the Social Sciences' in *The Modern Theologians* ed. Ford D. F. (Second Edition Blackwell 1996), 700 at 706-7 and 714-715.
[324] DBW 1, 13.
[325] DBWE 2, 109.
[326] Ibid.
[327] DBW 1, 19; ET 22.

community or indeed into Christ, but exists within a unity of diversity, a community of difference.

*The Community as the Locus of Divine and Human Freedom*

The church is both the community in which God chooses to express his freedom in Christ, and in which the individual becomes more fully him or herself, not in isolation or self-preservation, but in and through relationship with God and the other. God's free self giving of himself in Christ does not overwhelm humanity or restrict his freedom, but enables human beings to give themselves to God and to others. It is God's decision to be 'free *for* humanity', which enables human beings to give themselves freely to God and to the other within the community, without being absorbed into God or the other. It is that sacrificial Christ-shaped divine freedom which enables true human freedom:

> That a human being can surrender himself radically to God, is [due to] God's radical self-giving to humanity ... [God's] will seeks communion and the human will surrendering itself completely stands in communion, precisely because this surrender is only possible through God's surrender.[328]

Divine freedom is demonstrated in love which willingly gives itself for the other and this self-giving love is the source of human self-giving. As we saw in the last chapter, for fallen humanity, the other had become a burden and a barrier to freedom. But in the redeemed community of the church, it is precisely in relationship with the other, mediated through Christ, that I find freedom from myself, and in so doing am free to become more fully myself, within the community in which I know myself to be loved and accepted. The community of the church, where God demonstrates his freedom in the gift of himself is the place where:

> The one who lives in the communion of I-thou relationships receives the certainty that he is loved and through faith in Christ receives the power to be able to love ... The others within the church are for him no longer essentially claim, but gift, the revelation of his love, that is the love of God . The fact that my claim is fulfilled for me by the other I who loves me, that is of course by Christ, humbles me, *releases me from my bondage to the I and lets me love the other, lets me give and reveal myself wholly to him* - again of course only in the power of faith in Christ.[329]

---

[328] DBW 1, 113.
[329] DBW 1, 107; (italics mine).

As we have already indicated, in *Act and Being*, Bonhoeffer's critique of the early Barth centred on the latter's formal understanding of divine freedom, which he felt was in danger of equating God with the autonomous human subject, writ large. For Bonhoeffer, God's freedom was to be conceptualised in material or substantial terms, as a freedom which, in Christ, freely and graciously bound itself to humanity, in word, sacrament and the Christian community.[330] To quote Green once again, Christ is 'the free and liberating God who restores a person to true being in community with others; in Christ, God is free for humanity, setting people free to participate in the community of the new humanity of which he is the prototype and personification.'[331]

Hence, whilst carefully distancing himself from a Roman Catholic position which would identify revelation with the church, Bonhoeffer argues that although God's self revelation always remains at God's disposal, in the church, it is somehow 'held fast'.[332] 'God's freedom has woven itself into this personlike community of faith,[333] and *it is precisely this which manifests what God's freedom is*, that God binds God's self to human beings.'[334] Again we encounter the relationship between freedom and freely chosen constraint, which characterises divine freedom. Divine freedom is not a pre-existing construct against which God's activity can be measured, but is defined and shaped by God's revelation in Christ, the one who in freedom gives himself to be known within his church.

*The Community as the Place of Freedom for Others*

As we have already noted, for Bonhoeffer, divine freedom, as embodied in Christ, is essentially freedom for others. Hence, the Christian community established and indwelt by Christ, is characterised not only by a being 'with-one-another' (*Miteinander*), but also by a being 'for-one-another'(*Füreinander)*. Furthermore, this 'being-with-one-another', is not merely a question of gathering together around the word and sacraments, but, argues Bonhoeffer, it affirms the more profound truth that the individual is never separated from the communion of saints, because Christ who is head of the church, first gives himself to his church. However, as we have seen, this unity does not imply a mystical union or the merging of

---

[330] C, 49-58.
[331] Green op. cit., 100.
[332] DBWE 2, 112;
[333] Ibid., 'in die personhafte Gemeinde'.
[334] DBWE 2, 112; (my italics).

boundaries between the concrete I and the thou, or a denial of personal responsibility before God.[335] Furthermore, the unity of the Christian community is not an abstract concept but is actualised in ethical terms in the community's 'being-for-one-another', in acts of love. As members of Christ's body, each Christian is set free from self-absorption and called to live for others in acts of costly self-renunciation, intercession and the forgiveness of sin. Bonhoeffer quotes with approval Luther's words: 'You must take the need and infirmities of others to heart as if they were your own, and offer your means as if they were theirs, just as Christ does for you in the sacrament.'[336] Indeed, he asserts: 'The one standing in love is Christ in relation to his neighbour - of course only in this respect.'[337] Christ, the one who exists as community, is both the example and measure of Christian conduct and the one who equips and enables the Christian to love in this way.[338]

*Christ Existing as Community*

This concept of 'Christ existing as the (Christian) community', which recurs repeatedly throughout *Sanctorum Communio*,[339] is almost certainly an adaptation of Hegel's phrase in *The Absolute Religion* 'God existing as community.'[340] Hegel had seen the Christian community as the place where the Holy Spirit existed in the form of absolute spirit. Bonhoeffer's aim was to re-think the concept christologically as a way of holding together God's genuine transcendence and his real self-giving to the world, his radical distance and his radical closeness. Charles Marsh writes:

> "Christ existing as community" is....taken to be the source of both the *difference* of the unique person and the *continuity* of their basic relations in the church ... The isolation of the monadic I - the *cor curvum in se* - is broken such that the person is restored to the source of its genuine meaning in community.[341]

---

[335] Bonhoeffer seeks to hold in balance Luther's statements about the responsibility of the individual before God and the ontological reality of being in Christ. DBW 1, 119-120.
[336] Sermon *von dem Hochwürdigen Sakrament des heiligen wahren Leichnams Christi* quoted at DBW 1, 117. The concept of 'vicarious action' within the church is discussed in detail in the next chapter.
[337] DBW 1, 117.
[338] DBW 1, 120-121.
[339] DBW 1, 126, 133 etc. (Christus als Gemeinde existierend).
[340] DBW 1, 133 ft. 68; cf. also DB, 59.
[341] Marsh C. *Reclaiming Dietrich Bonhoeffer* op. cit., 74.

Marsh, rightly in my view, sees this understanding of the community in terms of God's 'I' becoming concrete in Christ, as the most important insight in *Sanctorum Communio*. This christological reconstruction of the Hegelian concept is closely related to Bonhoeffer's understanding of the collective person.[342] For Bonhoeffer, as we have seen, humanity is inherently social. He exists either in Adam, that is in solidarity with fallen humanity, or in Christ, that is as a member of the new community of the church, formed and actualised in Christ. In Adam the relationship with God and with other human beings is distorted through sin which turns the individual in upon herself, in Christ humanity is set free to live for God and for others. Clifford Green's analysis is helpful here. He argues that the ecclesiological formula 'Christ existing as the church' can only be understood in the light of Bonhoeffer's prior claim that *'Christ is the Kollektivperson of the new humanity.'*[343] As this collective person Christ 'embodies and inaugurates a new social basic-relation between God and humanity, and therefore among human beings.'[344] Hence the unity of the church is not posited on shared aims or beliefs, nor as an ideal to be achieved, but as an already existing reality, given in Christ, the collective person of the church in whom individual Christians participate.[345] Furthermore, it is in and through Christ, as the collective person of the new humanity, that God as the divine Thou continues to encounter the collective human 'I' in Adam. Hence Christ, as and in the personal community of the church, is always in relationship to the world, indeed, as Bonhoeffer asserts 'The history of the church is the hidden centre of world history.'[346]

---

[342] The editors of DBW 1 state that Bonhoeffer's concept of *Kollektivperson* arises from Max Scheler's *Gesamtperson*. (DBW 1, 229 note 48), and Bonhoeffer's own footnotes tend to confirm this.

[343] Green, op. cit. 52 (italics original); In a footnote (op.cit. 52 note 92), Green refers his readers to Bonhoeffer's theses in support of his doctoral graduation in Berlin, where he holds these two concepts together in the statement 'Die Kirche ist Christus "als Gemeinde existierend" und als Kollektivperson zu verstehen.' (GS III 47).

[344] Green op. cit. 53.

[345] Ibid., 133. Bonhoeffer acknowledges the eschatological tension between the unity that is in Christ and its far from perfect expression in the historical church.

[346] DBW 1, 142 cf. C, 63; Green (op. cit. 53) comments 'when Bonhoeffer describes Christ in the social form of the church as the Kollektivperson of the new humanity, this is a deliberate way of relating Christ and the church to humanity as a whole; it is not a way of confining Christ to the church, or of sanctifying any complacent and self-righteous ecclesiastical self-preoccupation.'

*Ecclesiology in Other Early Writings 'The Nature of the Church' and 'Christology'*

Many of the themes which emerged in Bonhoeffer's university dissertations are taken up again in a set of lectures which he delivered in Berlin in Summer Term 1932, under the title *The Nature of the Church*. Once again, Bonhoeffer stresses the corporate nature of the church over against the standard Protestant understanding of the church as a gathering of individual Christians. He argues that where Luther had begun with the Christian community (*Gemeinde*), modern Protestantism, exemplified in its different forms by Troeltsch and Barth, begins with the individual, an approach which has profound implications for an understanding of the place of theology.[347] Bonhoeffer argues that the church must be recognised as the presumption for Christian theology, not merely one aspect of it, because the church is the place where God reveals himself.[348] He insists, perhaps even more clearly than in his university dissertation, that 'The church is person, it is the form of the presence of the second person of the Trinity.'[349] However, he continues to affirm the 'eschatological gap', that Christ also stands over against his church and will only be fully present in it at the eschaton.

An important new theme within this lecture series is Bonhoeffer's exposition of the church's call to renounce purity for the sake of solidarity with the sinful world. It is, he writes, in her 'courageous confession that she is the world that the church is free from the world.'[350] But this freedom comes only as a result of a renunciation of the claim to purity. In the light of interpretations of Bonhoeffer which seek to restrict a concern for engagement with the world to the later writings, it is striking that in such an early work, Bonhoeffer should write in these terms. Here we can trace an early articulation, in corporate terms, of the ideas which would later find expression in *Ethics*, where Bonhoeffer was to write of Christian responsibility in terms of the freedom to incur guilt. The image of a church free to concern herself not with her own purity but with others, anticipates much of what Bonhoeffer will write about the church in *Letters and Papers from Prison*.[351] In the *Christology* lectures, delivered a year later,

---

[347] Ibid., 259. Bonhoeffer of course refers to the Barth of *Römerbrief* and *Christliche Dogmatik*.
[348] DBW 11, 242-3.
[349] *Die Wesen der Kirche* DBW 11, 271.
[350] Ibid. 299.
[351] cf. 'Thoughts on the Day of the Baptism of Dietrich Wilhelm Rüdiger Bethge' LPP 300.

Bonhoeffer, discusses the presence of Christ *pro me* in word, sacrament and Christian community. Although the reference to Christ's presence in and as the community is an addition to the traditional Lutheran formulation of word and sacrament, Bonhoeffer's understanding of Christ's presence as word and sacrament is also intrinsically relational and corporate. In the word, Christ encounters humanity not in the form of concepts or ideas about God, but as personal address, which as such, requires response and the taking of responsibility. In the sacraments, Christ's presence is not a static entity but a dynamic giving of himself *pro me* within the community of the church. Again Bonhoeffer maintains both that there is no question of God renouncing his freedom and sovereignty or putting himself 'at the disposal of the community', and yet that there is a genuine gift of himself. Christ is the one who 'has really bound himself in the freedom of his existence to me. And he is the one who has preserved his contingency in being there for me.'[352] In other words, it is precisely in the Christ-shaped giving of himself to humanity that the divine aseity and contingency are expressed.

## Ecclesiology in Practice

In his involvement in what was to become the Confessing Church, Bonhoeffer repeatedly found himself on the radical edge of opposition to the National Socialist agenda, for example in his advocacy of an interdict, which older clergy dismissed as an over-dramatisation of the situation. This increasing isolation was one reason behind a decision to move to London in October 1933, to be pastor to two German speaking churches. He wrote from London to Karl Barth, explaining that 'there seemed no particular reason why my own view in these matters should be any better, any more right, than the views of many really able pastors whom I sincerely respect - and so I thought it was about time to go into the wilderness for a spell.'[353] However, he continued to keep in touch with the situation in Germany and in September 1934 the leaders of the Confessing Church invited him to return to Germany to establish a seminary for trainee ministers.

---

[352] C, 48.
[353] DBW 13, 13.

## Finkenwalde

Bonhoeffer returned to Germany in April 1935 and the Seminary began life in Zingst, but within two months moved to Finkenwalde. Bethge paints an attractive picture of what he terms 'a community of friendship',[354] characterised by both discipline and freedom. Bonhoeffer, who implemented an ordered regime and abhorred indiscipline, would nevertheless on occasion abandon classes and take his ordinands to the beach. Bethge writes of Bonhoeffer's 'infectious joie de vivre',[355] expressed in music, literature and sporting activities. At the end of the first course at Finkenwalde, Bonhoeffer obtained permission from the Confessing Church leadership to establish a community house within the seminary. This became known as the 'House of Brothers', and was made up of six or so young ministers who had completed the course at Finkenwalde, who could commit themselves to the seminary for a longer period and were willing to submit to a simple rule of community life. The role of community was both to provide a measure of continuity for the ordinands who attended the standard six month course, and more importantly to offer a model of community life which would give ordinands a vision for 'the strength and liberation to be found in brotherly service and communal life in a Christian community.'[356] A compelling and inspiring account of the dynamics of life at Finkenwalde is given in Bonhoeffer's short book *Life Together* which we will discuss in detail below. However, we turn first to an appraisal of *The Cost of Discipleship*, a book which emerged from a course of lectures on the theme of 'Discipleship' delivered during the Finkenwalde period.

## The Cost of Discipleship

The Finkenwalde experiment came to an end in September 1937 when the seminary was finally closed by the Gestapo. Bonhoeffer had recently completed the manuscript of *The Cost of Discipleship*, which was published in November 1937 and encapsulated the heart of what he had taught at the seminary. However, despite its origins within the context of community, *Cost* has often been interpreted in terms of individualistic piety, and viewed as a retreat from the world into the monastic ghetto. Eberhard Bethge, who was himself a student at Finkenwalde and a member

---

[354] Conversation with the writer 20th Feb. 1997.
[355] DB 450.
[356] Bonhoeffer to W. Staemler 17.6.36 cited by Bethge DB 385.

of the House of Brothers, trenchantly rejects such an interpretation. He writes:

> *The Cost of Discipleship* is not the peaceful backwater of the Pietists, nor is it the other-worldliness of the Enthusiasts, neither of which remain in touch with reality. It is, rather, the summons to battle, it is concentration and hence also restriction, so that the whole of this earth might be conquered by the illimitable message.[357]

In Bethge's assessment, in *Cost,* we again encounter the dynamic relationship between constraint and freedom which had become a recurrent motif throughout Bonhoeffer's writings. We can perhaps also trace a foreshadowing of the *Arkandisziplin*, the discipline of prayer and worship which frees the Christian from self, for righteous action in the world, of which Bonhoeffer will write in *Letters and Papers*.[358]

*The Myth of Individualism* Nevertheless, assessments of *Cost* as individualistic and pietistic continue to be propounded and we must address this issue in some detail before offering our own interpretation of the book. The approach of David Hopper, one of the few Bonhoeffer interpreters to examine Bonhoeffer's use of Kierkegaard, highlights the issues.[359] Freedom was of course a significant concept in Kierkegaard's understanding of the three stages of human existence, the aesthetic, the ethical and the religious, in which the illusory search for autonomy of the 'aesthetic stage' contrasts with the true freedom of spiritual dependence which characterises 'the religious stage'. Hopper, in a paper delivered at the American Academy of Religion in 1989,[360] structures his argument around an attempt to give content to the reservations which Bonhoeffer himself expressed about *Cost* in an oft cited letter to Bethge from Tegel, in which he commented: 'I thought I could acquire faith by trying to lead a holy life. I suppose I wrote *The Cost of Discipleship* as the end of that path. Today I can see the

---

[357] DB 378.
[358] LPP 281, 286, 300.
[359] Amongst the few studies which attempt a discussion of Kierkegaard's influence on Bonhoeffer are Rades J. *Kierkegaard and Bonhoeffer* (unpublished draft) and Kelly G. 'The Influence of Kierkegaard on Bonhoeffer's Concept of Discipleship' *Irish Theological Quarterly* April 1974, 148ff (which limits itself to a discussion of Kierkegaardian influence in *Cost*).
[360] Hopper D. *Bonhoeffer's 'Love of the World', 'The Dangers of that Book' and the Kierkegaard Question* Unpublished Paper American Academy of Religion 1989 (Bonhoeffer Society Archive, Union Theological Seminary New York).

dangers of that book, though I still stand by what I wrote.'[361] One of the 'dangers' to which Hopper suggests Bonhoeffer refers, is what he views as a reversion to individualism in *Cost*, something he attributes to a misguided but short-lived fascination with Kierkegaard. For Kierkegaard, the freedom of the Gospel could be received only by taking a 'leap' of faith,[362] and hence must always be seen in individualistic rather than corporate terms.[363] Indeed, some of his later writings were particularly vitriolic in their condemnation of the church and what he perceived as its cultural accommodation, which obscured and softened the demands of the Gospel to make it acceptable.

In building his case, Hopper makes much of the fact that in his preparations for the writing of *Cost*, Bonhoeffer clearly used the Kütemeyer edition of Kierkegaard's Journals, published in 1934 under the title 'The Individual and the Church',[364] which places greater stress on the later Kierkegaard and his criticisms of the Danish Lutheran Church.[365] However, whilst the influence of Kierkegaardian thought on *Cost* is almost certainly beyond dispute, there are a number of flaws in Hopper's argument. First, ideas which Hopper attributes to Kütemeyer's Kierkegaard can be found in Bonhoeffer's own writings well prior to the publication of the Kütemeyer edition in 1934. For example, references to 'cheap' and 'costly' grace, which Hopper ascribes to Kütemeyer's influence, appear as early as 1932, where in an address to an ecumenical youth assembly Bonhoeffer states 'we make grace cheap, and with the justification of the sinner through the cross, we overlook the cry of the Lord who never justifies sin.'[366] Hence,

---

[361] Letter 21st July 1944 (LPP 369).
[362] Discussed in *Fear and Trembling* and in *A Concluding Unscientific Postscript*.
[363] Although in *Works of Love* (1847) trans. Hong H. V and E. H. (Princeton University Press 1995) Kierkegaard writes of an I-thou relationship with one's neighbour as well as with God, the neighbour remains a somewhat shadowy figure.
[364] *Kierkegaard Søren: Der Einzelne und die Kirche. Über Luther und den Protestantismus*, Übersetzung und Vorwort von W. Kütemeyer (Berlin 1934).
[365] The suggestion that Bonhoeffer worked from the Kütemeyer edition was first mooted by Traugott Vogel in 1968 in his thesis *Christus als Vorbild und Versöhner, eine kritische Studie zum Problem des Verhaltnisses von Gesetz und Evangelium im Werke Søren Kierkegaard* (Berlin Humbolt 1968) and was later proven to be the case when Bonhoeffer's own copy of Kütemeyer, with copious underlinings, was discovered. This book, which was in the possession of Eberhard Bethge is now in the Berlin Stadtbibliotek.
[366] *Christus und der Friede* DBW 12, 232 at 234 For a catalogue of citations of Kierkegaard in Bonhoeffer's writings prior to 1934, see Rades J *Kierkegaard and Bonhoeffer* op. cit.

whilst Kierkegaard may well be Bonhoeffer's source for the phrase, it is clearly not Kütemeyer's Kierkegaard.[367]

Second, although there are few direct quotations of the Dane in the early academic treatises and published writings, it is difficult to deny Bonhoeffer's familiarity with Kierkegaard prior the publication of the Kütemeyer edition. In *Sanctorum Communio*, Bonhoeffer makes use of the Kierkegaardian critique of idealism, but is also clear in his criticism of Kierkegaard precisely on the question of individualism.[368] He also makes several references to *Fear and Trembling*, the text which presumably underlies his discussion of Abraham and Isaac in *Cost*.[369] In his essays *Concerning the Christian Idea of God* and *The Theology of Crisis and its Attitude towards Philosophy and Science*, both written during his period at Union Theological Seminary in 1930-31, Bonhoeffer lists Kierkegaard with Paul, Luther and Barth as someone standing 'in the tradition of genuine Christian thinking'.[370] A year later, in a seminar series in Berlin entitled *The Problems of a Theological Anthropology*, Bonhoeffer devoted a section to the 'The Individual and Individualism' which included a section on Kierkegaard and the individual.[371] The *Christology* lectures, delivered in 1933, open with a quotation from the Dane and Bonhoeffer's account of the relationship between the resurrection and history suggests a familiarity with Kierkegaard's discussion of Lessing's 'great ugly ditch' in *A Concluding Unscientific Postscript*.[372]

Third, Hopper's argument lacks internal consistency. He claims, on the one hand that Bonhoeffer was subject to a brief infatuation with Kierkegaard, to which he attributes the reversion to individualism which he finds in *Cost*. However, he also argues that Bonhoeffer makes cavalier use of his sources, so that for him 'theology is not dialogue and commentary

---

[367] Bonhoeffer's source for the phrase may well be the young Luther who wrote of 'cheap grace' in *Rationis Latominae Confutatio* 1521. Geoffrey Kelly makes this connection in his article 'The Influence of Kierkegaard on Bonhoeffer's Concept of Discipleship' *Irish Theological Quarterly* April 1974 148ff at 150 citing WA 8; 54:30 'it is within your power and on very easy terms to acquire grace from good works performed... by doing so they both make Christ's grace cheap and God's mercy of little worth.'

[368] DBW 1, 34 note 12 and 104 note 20 where Bonhoeffer attributes Kierkegaard's rejection of the church to his understanding of the aloneness of the individual.

[369] DBW 1, 104 ft. 20; 179 ft. 130.

[370] DBW 10, 435 cf. Ibid. 432 where Augustine also features in the list.

[371] GS V 342; Unfortunately no notes from the seminar have survived.

[372] C 72; cf. *A Concluding Unscientific Postscript* (1992 Princeton University Press) trans. Hong H. V. and E. H. 93-105. cf. also Bonhoeffer's use of the term 'God-man' which appears in Kierkegaard's *Sickness Unto Death*.

but soliloquy',[373] in which Kierkegaard, Luther and others are not engaged with but made to speak in Bonhoefferian tones. This suggestion that Bonhoeffer distorts and manipulates his sources to his own ends surely undermines his argument that in *Cost*, Bonhoeffer imbibes Kierkegaard uncritically. Furthermore, whilst this claim is striking rhetoric,[374] it is not supported by the evidence. We have already made brief reference to Bonhoeffer's critical use of Kierkegaard in *Sanctorum Communio*. If we compare Bonhoeffer's use of other non-biblical sources, for example the work of Nietzsche, it is clear that Bonhoeffer could use the latter's critique of the German Lutheran church of his day to good effect, without either endorsing the nihilistic or individualistic presuppositions of Nietzsche's thought, or turning Nietzsche into a Christian. Similarly in his use of Hegel, Bonhoeffer could robustly defend Hegel against his detractors, and reformulate Hegelian concepts christologically, but still clearly distance himself from Hegelian notions of the necessity of incarnation as a moment within the life of God.

Finally, I would suggest that Hopper's analysis of Bonhoeffer's comments in the letter from Tegel, lacks balance, in that it focuses on the phrase 'the dangers of that book', without giving due weight to Bonhoeffer's affirmation that 'I still stand by what I wrote'. When this latter phrase is also taken into consideration, it might well suggest that Bonhoeffer's unease with his earlier work lies less with the content, ('I still stand by what I wrote'), than with its potential for misinterpretation in individualistic, pietistic terms. Certainly, from his perspective in Tegel, Bonhoeffer felt that the Confessing Church had settled for a narrow personal piety and perhaps recognised that his own writings could be misunderstood in such a way.[375] However, such a narrow reading of *Cost* overlooks the context of community life out of which the book arose and the sections which focus quite specifically on the visible community of the church. Furthermore, it fails to pay sufficient attention to the distinction between individualism, and the call and responsibility of the individual, which for Bonhoeffer always arises within the concrete historical situation - and hence in relationship and in community. Even in the most overtly individualistic section on 'Discipleship and the Individual', after his discussion of the lonely decision of Abraham, Bonhoeffer writes 'the same Mediator who makes us individuals is also the ground of a wholly new community. He stands in the centre between my neighbour and myself. He

---

[373] Hopper op. cit. 43.
[374] Ibid. 'We read Bonhoeffer and we meet Bonhoeffer - and his struggle for faith.'
[375] cf. Bonhoeffer's remarks in *Outline for a Book* LPP 381.

divides but he also unites.'[376] The call to take up the cross of Christ is a call not to solitary self-flagellation, but to bear the burdens of others.[377]

*A Corporate Interpretation of 'Cost'* Eberhard Bethge, rightly in my view, sees *The Cost of Discipleship* in terms of an attempt to unite the reformed articles of faith, justification and sanctification, in the one concept, discipleship. Such an interpretation is in line with Bonhoeffer's own comments on the work in a letter to Karl Barth, where he wrote: 'The most important questions are those of the interpretation of the Sermon on the Mount and the Pauline doctrine of justification and sanctification. I am engaged in a work on the subject.'[378] Bonhoeffer's concern was to counter the propensity within the German Lutheran Church to set the epistles in opposition to the Gospels, thereby suggesting that the radical call to discipleship was applicable only to the first disciples, not to the contemporary Christian. He aimed to demonstrate that although Paul does not use the language of discipleship, his understanding of baptism as a clear breach with the old life and a participation in the death of Christ, evokes the same summons to radical commitment to Christ, so that the Gospels and the Epistles are a unity in their call to follow Christ.[379] The original German edition of *Cost,* was composed of two distinct sections, the first expounding the picture of discipleship given in the Gospels and focusing on the Sermon on the Mount, and the second, headed 'The Church of Jesus Christ and Discipleship', concentrating on the Pauline understanding of the church. Unfortunately, this arrangement was not reflected in the standard English edition, which divides the text into four parts, and so unhelpfully obscures Bonhoeffer's deliberate bi-partite structuring of the work and perhaps encourages an interpretation in terms of individualistic pietism.[380] In particular, the early chapters of *Cost* which contain an extended exegesis of the Sermon on the Mount, tend to fall prey to the traditionally individualistic interpretation of this section of Jesus' teaching. Hence Bonhoeffer's understanding of the Sermon on the Mount is critical to our case.

---

[376] CD 90.
[377] Ibid., 80.
[378] Letter 19th Sept. 1936, GS II 283 at 284, TF 116.
[379] See especially CD 205ff.
[380] This error was corrected in *Discipleship* the English translation of the new German critical edition (Fortress 2000).

*Bonhoeffer and the Sermon on the Mount* It was during his year at Union Theological Seminary that Bonhoeffer's traditional Lutheran approach to the Sermon on the Mount first came under challenge through his friendship with Jean Lasserre, whose commitment to pacifism on this basis, eventually won Bonhoeffer's respect.[381] On his return to Germany, Bonhoeffer began to study the Sermon on the Mount afresh. An early indication of this change in attitude can be seen in the draft catechism prepared with Franz Hildebrandt in the summer of 1931,[382] and by 1932 the Sermon on the Mount had assumed major importance in his thinking. In a letter to Elizabeth Zinn written from Finkenwalde at the beginning from 1936, but relecting back on an earlier period, he gives a rare insight into his own Christian development, referring to the impact of his engagement with the Bible and above all the Sermon on the Mount and reflects: 'It was a great liberation. It became clear to me that the life of a servant of Jesus Christ must belong to the church and step by step it became clearer how far that must be.'[383] Correspondence dating from the period in London shows that Bonhoeffer continued to wrestle with the implications of this teaching.[384] In a letter dated 11th September 1934, written from London to his friend Erwin Sutz, Bonhoeffer referred to his proposed return to Germany to set up a seminary and commented: 'The whole training of the rising generation of theologians belongs today in church run monastic-like schools in which sound doctrine, the Sermon on the Mount and worship are taken seriously.'[385] A few months later in January 1935, Bonhoeffer's annual birthday letter to his brother Karl Friedrich included the reflection that the Sermon on the Mount was 'the only source of power which could one day blow up the whole glamour and glitter so that only a few burned out remnants remain from the fireworks.'[386] He adds:

---

[381] Earlier references during the pastorate in Barcelona in 1928 reveal a conventional Lutheran approach which stressed the dangers of legalism in applying the Sermon on the Mount. Lasserre is the 'French pastor' referred to in the letter to Bethge of 21/7/97 (LPP 369).

[382] DBW 11 228 at 234 'Today, the church knows more than ever, how little it listens to the Sermon on the Mount'. Bonhoeffer remained critical of attempts to found a 'social Gospel' on the *Bergpredigt* cf. 'Memorandum' headed 'Das 'Sozial gospel' (soziale Evangelium) (DBW 12, 203 at 208) written during the Winter Semester in Berlin 1932-3.

[383] GS VI, 368. The content of the letter makes it clear that Bonhoeffer is speaking of a time before 'the crisis of 1933'.

[384] Bethge indicates that Bonhoeffer preached several sermons on sections of the *Bergpredigt*, but unfortunately these have not survived. (DB 259).

[385] DBW 13, 204.

[386] DBW 13, 272. The reference is to the superficial success of the Third Reich.

The restoration of the church will certainly come from a new type of monasticism, which has in common with the old only the uncompromising attitude of a life lived according to the Sermon on the Mount in the discipleship of Christ. I believe that now is the time to gather people together for this purpose.[387]

Hence, for Bonhoeffer the Sermon on the Mount was not primarily a call to individual piety, (although, as we have seen, for him the individual is never negated or subsumed by the corporate), but a blueprint for a counter-cultural community which would breathe fresh life into a weak and compromised church and provide an effective challenge in word and lifestyle to the seductive attractions of National Socialism. In particular, it seems clear that at this stage, Bonhoeffer saw the teaching of the *Bergpredigt* as the inspiration for non-violent resistance to Hitler. In our opening chapter we noted the Nazi policy of *Gleichschaltung*, in which communities or social groupings were systematically broken down and either absorbed into the mass or fragmented and atomised. It is against this backdrop that Bonhoeffer envisioned the establishment of communities of freedom, based on the Sermon on the Mount.[388]

In the second half of *Cost*, (which as we have already indicated, focuses on the Pauline epistles), the corporate implications are even more apparent. This section of the book, opens with a chapter on baptism and is followed by chapters headed 'The Body of Christ' and 'The Visible Community' in which Bonhoeffer attempts to spell out the implications of baptism into the community of Jesus Christ. Here, once again, we encounter the key concepts used by Bonhoeffer in his early dissertations to explain the relationship between the individual believer, the community and Christ. Bonhoeffer again draws upon the idea of Christ as the collective person, the one who, as the second Adam, is both an individual and representative of the whole human race, the one in whom the new humanity is created.[389] 'The incarnate Son of God existed, so to speak in two capacities - in his own person, and as the representative of the new humanity.'[390] Christians participate in the body of Christ through the sacraments, baptism the sacrament of incorporation and the Lord's Supper, the sacrament which

---

[387] Ibid. I am grateful to the late Professor Bethge for pointing me to this annual correspondence (Conversation with the writer February 20th 1997).
[388] Bonhoeffer had been deeply influenced by the effectiveness of Ghandi's non-violent opposition to the British Raj. However plans to visit Ghandi's ashram were eventually shelved in order to set up the Finkenwalde seminary. (DB 330-332).
[389] CD 213-214, cf. also 247.
[390] Ibid., 214.

sustains our communion (koinonia) in the body. The crucial concept of 'Christ existing as community' which, as we have seen, was foundational to the ecclesiology of *Sanctorum Communio* and the christology of *Act and Being*, emerges again here, although now, the role of the Spirit is spelled out explicitly in a way which unlocks what could otherwise be seen as a somewhat static notion. Bonhoeffer writes: 'The crucified and risen Lord exists, through the Holy Spirit, as community (*Gemeinde*), and as the 'new humanity'; as truly as he is the incarnate one and dwells in eternity, so truly is his body the new humanity'.[391] Here too, Bonhoeffer utilises the concept of person in order to illuminate the presence of Christ as and in the community of the church when he asserts: 'We are accustomed to think of the church as an institution. But the church should rather be thought of as a living *person*, though of course a person in a wholly unique sense.'[392] Nevertheless, as in his earlier work, the eschatological tension is maintained. Bonhoeffer clearly distinguishes Christ from his body; the one present in his church is also the one who is to come.

In the chapter headed 'The Visible Community', Bonhoeffer expounds the picture of the early church in Acts. He argues that the church is made visible through the congregation gathered around the preaching of the word and the administration the sacraments. 'The whole common life of the Christian fellowship oscillates between word and sacrament. It begins and ends in worship.'[393] As we will see below, this picture of life lived between word and sacrament aptly encapsulates the community life of the Finkenwalde seminary. Bonhoeffer maintains that a community which finds the source of its fellowship in the word and the culmination of its life together in the eucharist, will overflow in generosity and care for one another: 'In freedom, joy and the power of the Holy Spirit, a pattern of common life is produced where: 'there was no one among them who lacked anything', where 'no one said that any of the things he possessed was his own.'[394] Here, writes Bonhoeffer, 'In the everyday quality of these events, was a perfect picture of evangelical freedom where there is no need of compulsion'.[395]

---

[391] DBW 4, 234 (my translation) cf. CD 218 where the reference to 'Gemeinde' and to the Holy Spirit is obscured. In *Sanctorum Communio*, Bonhoeffer sees the role of the Spirit in terms of God's presence and work in bringing individuals together in the church, a function which he distinguishes from that of the Spirit of Christ, which is present in and as the community. DBW 1, 86, 99.
[392] DBW 4, 232; (my translation) CD 217.
[393] DBW 4, 249; CD 229.
[394] Ibid. The reference is to Acts 4:32.
[395] Ibid.

*'Cost' and Freedom* It is this 'perfect picture of evangelical freedom', which, we suggest, offers the key to a full understanding of *Cost*. Indeed, we would submit that *The Cost of Discipleship* as a whole, can and should be read as an attempt to rediscover and express the integrity of Luther's understanding of the freedom of the Christian, which current Lutheran thought had reduced to a vapid anti-nomianism.[396] Luther had expressed the position in these terms: 'A Christian is a perfectly free Lord of all, subject to none. A Christian is a perfectly dutiful servant of all, subject to all.'[397] Although the Christian is free from the law and from the demands of works righteousness, 'he ought in this liberty to empty himself ... and in every way deal with his neighbour as he sees that God through Christ has dealt and still deals with him.'[398] The Christian is set free, to serve others, even to 'submit his will to that of others in the freedom of love'.[399] For Bonhoeffer too, freedom and obedience are inseparable and complementary. In the introduction to *Cost*, Bonhoeffer asserts that 'The full emancipation of humanity into the community of Jesus is possible only where the whole command of Jesus, the call to unconditional discipleship remains in force.'[400] If we push the connection a little further, we can see how, in seeking to hold together justification and sanctification, Bonhoeffer is redefining the Christian life of faith and discipleship, as life lived in the contradictory unity of freedom and obedience which was constitutive of humanity's original creation in the image of God. If justification can be seen, as we have already argued, as freedom from the isolation of the self-enclosed ego, the *cor curvum in se*, sanctification is the outworking of freedom, in service of God and others.

The 'cheap grace' which Bonhoeffer so roundly condemns in the opening chapter of *Cost*, is 'Grace as a principle, *pecca fortiter* as a principle, cheap grace is ultimately only a new law which does not help and does not set free.'[401] Luther's 'Sin boldly, but all the more boldly believe

---

[396] Bonhoeffer makes specific reference to Luther's *The Freedom of a Christian* at DBW 4, 88 and there are several oblique references.

[397] Luther M. 'The Freedom of a Christian' 1520 in Dillenberger J ed. *Martin Luther A Selection from his Writings*, 53; LW 31 333-377. cf. *Grundfragen einer christliche Ethik* DBW 10 323ff at 331 where Bonhoeffer commented 'Nietzsche's Superhuman is really not, as he thought, the antitype of the Christian, but *without knowing it*, Nietzsche has here brought in many characteristics of the Christian made free, as Paul and Luther describe and know him.' (my italics).

[398] Luther op. cit., 75.

[399] Ibid., 78.

[400] DBW 4, 23 (my translation); CD 31.

[401] DBW 4, 39; CD 44.

and rejoice in Christ', which had been intended to set free from the burden of guilt those who could not believe themselves forgiven, had become a licence for a life of disobedience. In such a situation, Bonhoeffer asserts, in words which foreshadow the famous question in *Letters and Papers*, 'The predicament of our church is increasingly to be summed up in the one question, how we can live today as Christians.'[402] The remaining chapters of *Cost* can be seen as an attempt to answer that question in terms of costly discipleship, of freedom in Christ, lived out in obedience to Christ. Bonhoeffer's insistence on the inseparability of faith and obedience in the oft quoted couplet 'Only the one who obeys believes' and yet 'Only the one who believes obeys'[403] would bear out such an interpretation. In a paper on 'Freedom and Obedience in Bonhoeffer', Bethge suggests that this formula is 'the most radical expression of that relational character which Bonhoeffer saw in the concept of freedom.'[404] He argues that the couplet could with equal validity be expressed as 'Only the free (believing one) is obedient and only the obedient is free (believes).'[405] Certainly the link between faith and freedom is clearly established in Bonhoeffer's earlier writings where justification is seen in terms of freedom from the self-centredness of the *cor curvum in se*. This theme recurs again in the climactic closing section of *The Cost of Discipleship*, 'The Image of Christ', where Bonhoeffer speaks of the recovery of the true image of God as a liberation from self-centredness and the restoration of lost community:

> In communion with the incarnate one, we recover our true humanity, and at the same time we are delivered from that individualism which is the consequence of sin, and recover our solidarity with the whole human race ... In so far as we participate in Christ the incarnate one, we participate in the whole humanity which he bore....The 'philanthropy' of God (Titus 3.4) which was revealed in the incarnation of Christ is the ground of Christian love towards all on earth that bears the name of humanity.[406]

It is in the church, the body of Christ, and by extension in the members of the church, that the image of Christ, incarnate, crucified and glorified, is revealed. This was the sort of community life which Bonhoeffer had sought

---

[402] DBW 4, 42; CD 47 The English translation renders *heute* as 'in the modern world', but Bonhoeffer's focus is the witness of the church amid the growth of National Socialism.
[403] CD 54, 60.
[404] Bethge E. 'Freiheit und Gehorsam bei Bonhoeffer' in *Am gegebenen Ort: Aufsätze und Reden* (Chr Kaiser Verlag 1979), 71.
[405] Ibid.
[406] DBW 4, 301 (my translation); CD 272.

to build at Finkenwalde and to which Bonhoeffer's short book *Life Together* bears witness.

## Life Together

It was the closure of the Finkenwalde Seminary, and with it the end to the experiment in community living, which led Bonhoeffer to write *Life Together* in September 1938. If our assessment of *Cost* as an attempt to restore the paradoxical unity of the freedom and obedience, constitutive of redeemed human existence, is correct, *Life Together* can be seen as a focusing in on the daily life of a community characterised by this unsynthesised dialectic of freedom and obedience, a 'fleshing out' of the redeemed Christian life in the tensions and pressures of everydayness.[407] We have already indicated the comparative paucity of scholarly interest in this short book and our concern to redress this balance. Certainly Bonhoeffer seems to have been convinced that the community experiment contained valuable lessons for the church at a crisis point in its history.[408] As we have seen in our survey of *The Cost of Discipleship*, many of the ideas first expressed in *Sanctorum Communio* are still present in Bonhoeffer's ecclesiology during the Finkenwalde period, and hence must inform our discussion of *Life Together*. In *Cost*, Bonhoeffer had spoken of the common life of the Christian community as oscillating between word and sacrament, and it is significant that *Life Together* opens with an exposition of life 'under the word of God',[409] and comes to a climax with the words 'The life together of Christians under the word has reached its fulfilment in the sacrament.'[410]

### *The Community of Freedom*

For Bonhoeffer, the Christian community is not primarily a goal to be achieved, but a gift of God's grace. The one who took our flesh in incarnation, who gives himself to us bodily in the sacrament, knows our

---

[407] Earlier in his Berlin Seminar *The Problems of a Theological Anthropology*, in a discussion of the formation of 'Christian character', Bonhoeffer had written 'The Christian lives in the tension between asceticism and freedom.' (GS V 340 at 358).

[408] The fact that the book was completed in just four weeks, at his twin sister Sabine's house in Göttingen suggests the urgency with which Bonhoeffer viewed his task.

[409] *Life Together* (hereafter DBWE 5) English Edition ed. Kelly G. B., trans. Bloesch D. (Fortress 1996), 27.

[410] DBWE 5, 118.

human need for the physical presence of other Christians. The Christian community is a foretaste and anticipation of the eschatological community in which all God's people will share at the end of time.[411] It is not some human vision or ideal to be realised, but is founded, formed and focused christologically. 'We belong to one another only through and in Jesus Christ.'[412] In his conclusion to *Sanctorum Communio,* Bonhoeffer had asserted that 'Our age is not poor in experiences, but in faith'.[413] Here, in *Life Together,* more than ten years later, he contrasts the community based on human emotion, the search for the experience of community, with the Christ-centred Christian community. Where the former is ultimately self-centred and accentuates the human desire to draw the other under its influence, rather than to recognise his or her integrity and freedom, in the latter, all relationships are mediated through Christ and so affirm the free and unique personhood of the other and encourage its flourishing.[414] Bonhoeffer comments incisively that much that passes under the name of Christian love, in fact merely feeds the self's need to dominate and control the other, to create dependency, to love them on its own terms. Instead, he argues:

> In their freedom from me, other people want to be loved for who they are, as those for whom Christ became a human being, died and rose again, as those for whom Christ has won the forgiveness of sins and won eternal life. As Christ has long since acted decisively for other Christians, before I could begin to act, I must allow them the freedom to be Christ's.[415]

For fallen humanity, God and my neighbour are seen not as gift, but as boundaries to my freedom to be overcome. However, within the community of the church, the place of redeemed freedom in the image of God, the Christian, in being free for others, is called to recognise and respect the freedom of the other from him. True relationships are always mediated through Christ, who stands as the boundary between us. Where self-centred love leads to 'human enslavement, bondage, rigidity', spiritual love 'creates the *freedom* of Christians under the word.'[416] To be free for others, means to respect the personhood of the other, their formation in the image of Christ, which is the sanctifying work of the Spirit. It does not seek

---

[411] Ibid., 28-30.
[412] Ibid., 31; cf. CD 259.
[413] DBW 1, 192.
[414] DBWE 5, 38-47 passim.
[415] Ibid., 44.
[416] Ibid. Italics original.

to manipulate, even for what might seem to be their best interests, but frees them to be fully themselves in Christ.

*Freedom and Worship*

As is clear from *Life Together*, this life of freedom for others is structured and undergirded by worship. Bethge informs us that prior to setting up the seminary at Finkenwalde in 1935, Bonhoeffer had visited a number of communities and training colleges in the UK, including the Community of the Resurrection at Mirfield, the Cowley Fathers in Oxford and the Society of the Sacred Mission at Kelham, all three of which followed the daily discipline of the monastic offices. Julius Rieger, another German pastor to an expatriate congregation in London, accompanied Bonhoeffer on these visits and comments: 'There was a freedom in their community life which we could not help noticing during our visits.'[417] Although Bonhoeffer did not seek to impose a monastic discipline on his Finkenwalde students, he clearly saw the worshipping community as a fundamental key to the formation of his seminarians, and his indebtedness to that tradition is clear. Daily life at Finkenwalde was marked by a rhythm of prayer (both the systematic praying of the Psalms and extemporaneous prayer), scripture reading and meditation, and community singing. Individually and together these were to provide a structure and discipline within which the members were freed from themselves, for God and for others, and true community was free to grow and develop. In each aspect of the life of worship we encounter the recurrent theme that it is by participation in and submission to the corporate act of worship that the individual finds true freedom from self.

The high priority which Bonhoeffer placed on the regular corporate praying of the Psalter arises from his conviction that to pray the Psalms is to participate in the prayer of the ascended Christ.[418] Bonhoeffer maintains that the Psalms, like the prayer Jesus taught his disciples, enable true prayer, not the 'empty phrases' of the Gentiles:[419]

---

[417] Rieger J. 'Contacts with London' in IKDB, 98.
[418] Like Luther, to whose commentary he refers repeatedly, Bonhoeffer interprets the Psalms christologically and links them closely to the Lord's Prayer, as an answer to the early disciples' plea: 'Teach us to pray'. cf. *Prayerbook of the Bible: An Introduction to the Psalms* trans. Burtness J. H. (Minneapolis: Fortress Press 1996) (Included in DBWE 5) and *Christus in den Psalmen* DBW 14, 369-377; GS III, 294-302, a lecture delivered at Finkenwalde on 31/7/35.
[419] cf. Matt. 6.7ff.

In all our praying there remains only the prayer of Jesus Christ, which has the promise of fulfilment and frees us from the vain repetition of the heathen. The more deeply we grow into the Psalms and the more often we ourselves have prayed them, the more simple and rewarding will our praying become.[420]

The Psalter becomes the vehicle for prayer which is truly corporate rather than individualistic, as the believer is freed from an exclusive focus on his own needs, concerns and perspectives, to pray as the body of Christ, and the prayer of Christ both indwells and is indwelt by his church.

In addition to the daily praying of the Psalms, Bonhoeffer stresses the value of prayer for specific community needs. Such prayer is not to be 'the chaotic outburst of a human heart, but the prayer of an internally ordered community.'[421] He suggests that linking extemporary prayer to the daily scripture readings, frees it from subjectivity and arbitrariness.[422] Again we encounter the same principle in operation, that discipline and structure actually enable true freedom and authentic community. Bonhoeffer maintains that the apparent constriction of disciplined extemporary prayer, is the very thing which brings freedom. He advises:

At first there may be some monotony in the daily repetition of the same petitions that are entrusted to us as a community, but later freedom from an all to individualistic form of prayer will surely be found.[423]

We find the same focus on corporate discipline in Bonhoeffer's discussion of the role of the scriptures within the life of the community. As we noted above, for Bonhoeffer, freedom in community is 'freedom under the word'. In *Life Together*, which closely reflects the Finkenwalde practice, Bonhoeffer argues for the systematic and consecutive reading of scripture as a whole, in addition to meditation on verses and shorter sections. The church, as a community, the body of Christ, not only reads, but participates in the salvation narrative.[424] In this way, he argues, it is not primarily a question of applying the Bible to our own individual situation, but of recognising ourselves as part of the history of God with his people. 'What is important', maintains Bonhoeffer, 'is not that God is a spectator and participant in our life today, but that we are attentive listeners and participants in God's action in the sacred story, the story of Christ on

---

[420] DBWE 5, 58.
[421] Ibid., 70.
[422] Ibid.
[423] Ibid.
[424] Ibid., 61-2.

earth.'[425] Our salvation is *extra nos*, in the story of Christ, not in our own life story.[426]

In communal praise and worship, the church is called to join in the new song of the heavenly community and again the sense is of participation in something much more than the sum of individual voices. Bonhoeffer discloses a suspicion of elaborate musical settings, which focus on the particular gift of an individual, and instead, recommends the discipline of unison singing. This, he asserts, frees the participants to sing from the heart, in unity with others, rather than concentrating on their own musical contribution: 'It is the voice of the church that is heard in singing together. It is not I who sing, but the church.'[427] As is well known, in his letters from Tegel prison, Bonhoeffer makes repeated use of the musical imagery of polyphony, in contrast to the emphasis here on unison singing. However it would seem unwise to take this contrast as the basis for any rigid conclusions which set the Finkenwalde period and the years in prison in opposition. As ever, context is vital. Bonhoeffer's focus in *Life Together* is on the discipline which he sees as necessary for the formation of a community of freedom. His concern is not with the passing judgement on particular choral styles, but with the question of what will form and conform the community to Christ, in whom alone true freedom is found.[428]

*Freedom and Discipline*

In all these areas of worship, it is the discipline of structured prayer, scripture reading and community singing which brings freedom and this ordered life of worship forms the structure which enables and sustains the whole of community life. As we noted above, in *Sanctorum Communio*, Bonhoeffer had written of a community life characterised by sacrificial service, intercessory prayer and the forgiveness of sins, and as already indicated, this had become a framework for life at Finkenwalde. If the university dissertation could at times read like an 'ecclesiology for angels',[429] *Life Together*, is resonant with much more earthly melodies, in

---

[425] Ibid., 62.
[426] Ibid.
[427] Ibid., 68.
[428] In a sermon for 'Cantate' Sunday, 22/4/34, Bonhoeffer had preached on the danger of focusing on the creature (music) rather than the Creator, to whom the music points us. DBW 13 351-356; GS V 510-515.
[429] In *Act and Being*, Bonhoeffer had complained that Hegel had written 'a philosophy of angels, not of human existence' (DBWE 2, 42) and Franklin Sherman in his chapter 'Act

which the practical implications of ecclesiological concepts are spelled out with admirable simplicity. Bethge records that the one rule to which Bonhoeffer asked the seminarians to commit themselves was the resolve never to speak about another ordinand in his absence.[430] Here too, we encounter the creative relationship between discipline and freedom, but the emphasis is different. Here it is my discipline, my voluntary constriction, which enables the freedom of the other. Again, the parallel with the freedom of God emerges. God in his relation to the world constricts himself, to enable the freedom of the other. If human freedom is derivative of and in the image of divine freedom, then true human freedom involves the free and willing limitation of the self by the other, which enables the other to be free in Christ:

> They can now allow other Christians to live freely, just as God has brought them face to face with each other ... Now other people, in the freedom with which they were created, become an occasion for me to rejoice, whereas before they were only a nuisance and a trouble for me. God does not want me to mould others into the image that seems good for me, that is, into my own image. Instead in their freedom from me, God made other people in God's own image.[431]

Again we see the strong connection between creation in the image of God and freedom, which we first encountered in *Creation and Fall*. Human fallenness, which Bonhoeffer had diagnosed in *Act and Being* in epistemological terms, as the overwhelming and objectification of the other by the knowing subject, is now expressed theologically in the language of Genesis, as the illicit attempt to usurp the place of God as the image to which humanity is to be conformed. With clear-sighted realism Bonhoeffer recognises the continuing temptation to turn others into a reflection of ourselves:

> The freedom of the other goes against Christians' high opinions of themselves, and yet they must recognise it. Christians could rid themselves of this burden by not giving other persons their freedom, thus doing violence to the personhood of others and stamping their own image on others. *But when Christians allow God to create God's own image in others, they allow others their own freedom.*[432]

---

and Being' in *The Place of Bonhoeffer* op. cit., 103 suggested that Bonhoeffer's ecclesiology could be subject to the same critique.
[430] DB 349.
[431] DBWE 5, 95.
[432] Ibid. 101, (my italics).

Where fallen humanity, *sicut deus*, but tragically no longer in *imago dei*, tends towards the dehumanising of the other, violating the integrity of the other by 'stamping their own image' on him or her, for the Christian, to be free for the other is to allow them to be free to be themselves. Hence to be free for others is not to be free to control others, imposing a vision or agenda upon them, even where we convince ourselves that our concern is their best interests. And yet, as we shall see in more detail in the next chapter, respect for the freedom of the other does not allow an abdication of responsibility. Respect for the freedom and integrity of the other does not preclude an obligation to rebuke or warn another, with gentleness and humility and yet with firmness.[433]

*Confession as the Pathway to Freedom in Community*

However, for Bonhoeffer, such a life of freedom for others is only possible within the context of another discipline, one which within the Protestant church of his day, was traditionally understood as a 'Catholic' practice, the personal confession of sins. It is this, asserts Bonhoeffer, which brings the final breakthrough to real community, rather than community founded on the pious image we each project. In 1932, Bonhoeffer had preached passionately on the text from John's Gospel 'The truth will make you free.'[434] Now he writes of the Gospel as a message of 'liberation through truth', in which we recognise our sinfulness and yet also encounter the graciousness of God. In confession to another Christian, I am freed from the power of sin, because the root of sin is the pride which makes me hide my faults from others, the *cor curvum in se* which isolates me from others.[435] I am freed from the self-deception of forgiving myself rather than truly receiving God's forgiveness. I am freed into a new life of assurance, because the other, on behalf of God, ministers words of forgiveness to me.[436] Bethge writes of the initial consternation within the community when Bonhoeffer first broached the subject of confession, prior to the occasion of the first community celebration of Holy Communion, whilst the Seminary was still in Zingst.[437] Another Finkenwalde student Wolf-Dieter Zimmermann records:

---

[433] Ibid. 104.
[434] DBW 11, 454.
[435] DBWE 5, 111. Bonhoeffer follows Augustine and Aquinas in seeing *superbia* (pride) as the root sin.
[436] Ibid. 113 cf. CD 260 'Confession is the God-given remedy for self-deception and self-indulgence.'
[437] DB 383.

*Freedom in Community* 111

In deep earnest, he spoke to us, stressing the urgency of it, but leaving us the freedom of personal decision. He said if we wished to be free we would have to make a clean breast of the grudges we bore one another.... [afterwards] The atmosphere was pure again, we could go to communion together without bearing a grudge against anyone among us.[438]

Bonhoeffer had in fact already outlined his understanding of the practice and value of oral confession in a series of lectures given to the Finkenwalde students on the pastoral role of the minister, published in English as *Spiritual Care*. In the section 'Confession as the heart of spiritual care', he expands upon his conviction as to the close connection between the liberating impact of this discipline on the individual and its role in the establishing of true community:

Complete self-surrender to the grace, help and judgement of God occurs in confession ... Thus we become free of ourselves...In absolution God receives us once again in order to reign over our whole lives and to set us completely free ... *Genuine community is not established before confession takes place.*[439]

True community is only possible among those who are set free from themselves. However, because Christians live with the permanent eschatological tension of those who are redeemed and yet sinful, the receiving of divine grace and forgiveness needs to be repeatedly actualised and made concrete.

As we have already seen, Bonhoeffer analyses the soteriological problem in terms of Luther's *cor curvum in se*, humanity trapped and isolated within himself, alienated from others. In redemption and forgiveness, the Christian recognises himself in original freedom as God's creature and as a new creature. He finds himself 'in Christ', and therefore in the new community. Later, in the *Ethics* fragment 'The Ultimate and the Penultimate', Bonhoeffer speaks of justification by grace through faith, in terms of the setting free of humanity for God and for others. In justification, God breaks into the prison of isolation in which fallen humanity is trapped. This is the transforming event which encapsulates the whole of life. Now, '[h]umanity is free for God *and for his brothers.*'[440] In the light of justification, human life is transformed. '[It] now knows that it is held in

---

[438] Zimmermann W-D. 'Finkenwalde' in IKDB op. cit., 109. As in other respects, Bonhoeffer led by example, on one occasion making his own confession to Bethge.

[439] *Seelsorge* DBW 14, 591; Eng. Trans. Rochelle J. as *Spiritual Care* (Fortress 1985), 63, (my italics).

[440] DBW 6, 137; ET 120, (my italics).

tension between the two poles of eternity, that it extends from the choice made before the time of the world to the everlasting salvation. It knows itself to be a member of a church and a creation which sings the praise of the triune God.'[441] Redeemed freedom, like pre-lapsarian freedom is essentially relational. It is a freeing from a life lived out of self, out of one's own resources and potential, to the reorientation of a life before God from a centre in Christ. It is this understanding of sin and redemption which provides the rationale for Bonhoeffer's advocacy of oral confession.[442] Only those freed from the isolation of sin can live in freedom for others within community.

Although, as we have seen, most Protestant theologians of his time viewed confession with suspicion as an alien 'Catholic' practice, Bonhoeffer finds strong support for its use in Luther's writings. In *The Cost of Discipleship* he quotes with approval from Luther's *Greater Catechism*: 'So, when I exhort people to confession, I am doing nothing other than exhorting them to be Christians.'[443] Although Luther had deplored the abuses of this 'third sacrament', which turned it into a weapon of oppression and subjugation against the laity by the clergy, he had asserted 'I would not wish it to cease; rather I rejoice that it exists in the church of Christ for it is a singular medicine for afflicted consciences.'[444] His concern had been to democratise the practice so that the forgiveness of sins became the province of the priesthood of all believers, not of the priestly hierarchy. Confession was to be the sacrament of emancipation, not one which kept the laity in bondage and fear. It is on this basis that Bonhoeffer grounds his advocacy of confession in *Spiritual Care*. Like Luther, he sees confession as grace, and argues that although personal confession to another should never be obligatory, it should be commended by pastors as 'a liberation from that which destroys my very life, not along the lines of a self transformation, but through the forgiving means God has given.'[445] In confession to another the isolation of the self-enclosing grip of sin is broken open and 'we gain freedom from pride of flesh or reason'.[446] To

---

[441] Ibid., 138 ; ET 121.
[442] It seems that Bonhoeffer first encountered the practice on his visit to Rome in 1924. He commented: 'To many of these people confession is not an externally imposed 'must', but has become an inner need. Confession does not necessarily lead to scrupulous living: often however, that may occur and always will with the most serious people.' DB 39.
[443] DBW 4, 287 , also *Seelsorge* DBW 14, 591.
[444] Luther M. 'The Pagan Servitude of the Church' 1520 in Dillenberger J. ed. *Martin Luther A Selection from his Writings*, 319.
[445] *Spiritual Care* op. cit. 62.
[446] Ibid., 63.

confess is an act of conversion and discipleship, the putting of oneself in the place where grace can be received. Just as the Christian cannot manufacture faith, so she cannot free herself from sin, but in coming before another Christian who will pronounce forgiveness in the name of Christ, she can freely choose to put herself in the place where, instead of the false delusion of self-forgiveness, the costly grace of true forgiveness and freedom, is available 'from outside'.

Bonhoeffer discusses the practice of confession again in the *Ethics* section on 'The Commandment of God in the Church'. There he argues that the loss of confession as a discipline within the Protestant church, in the name of what he sees as a 'fallacious call to Christian freedom',[447] has resulted in an inability to proclaim the commandment of God in concrete form. He suggests that the church has confused authentic and inauthentic freedom, forfeiting the true freedom from self which is the gift of God, the concretising of the reconciling work of Christ in the social and historical setting of the here and now, in the name of an illusory freedom.

*The Freedom of the Eucharist*

For Bonhoeffer, confession is particularly important and appropriate as preparation for Holy Communion. In *Cost*, Bonhoeffer had spoken of the common life of the Christian community as oscillating between word and sacrament. Hence it is fitting that the climax to *Life Together* is the Eucharist, the sacrament through which the life of the community is renewed and strengthened. If confession is the starting point for true community, 'The community of the holy Lord's Supper is above all the fulfilment of Christian community.'[448]

Although it is clear from *Life Together* that Bonhoeffer sees the eucharist as the climax of community life, we must turn to his earlier writings for any detailed consideration of the meaning of the sacrament. In *Sanctorum Communio*, Bonhoeffer had written 'Holy Communion is first God's gift to every individual ... [but] secondly and to a much greater extent, a gift to the church.'[449] Here again we encounter the shift in emphasis from the individual in isolation to the community of persons which is the church. The eucharist is not primarily about my individual communion with Christ but about Christ's gift of himself to his body. In the sacrament, Bonhoeffer writes: '*Christ gives himself* ... that is he gives me

---

[447] DBW 6, 399; ET 292.
[448] DBWE 5, 118.
[449] DBW 1, 166; ET 168.

the benefits of his vicarious passion', but he also 'gives to each the rights and duties of priestly action toward our neighbour ... Christ's priestly action is the basis for ours'.[450] Hence the sacrament is both gift and task, gracious invitation and ethical imperative. Christ's gift of himself in bringing the freedom of forgiveness both calls and enables the eucharistic community to live vicariously for others. In *The Cost of Discipleship*, Bonhoeffer writes that baptism and eucharist both 'flow from the true humanity of our Lord Jesus Christ. In both he encounters us *bodily* and makes us partakers in the communion of his body.'[451] He maintains that because the sacraments are God's exclusive gift to the church 'the Christian community is in a particular sense a baptismal and eucharistic community and only secondly a preaching community.'[452] Participation in the sacraments brings ethical consequences. Those who receive the body and blood of Christ must live lives which reflect their participation in Christ. In a barely veiled attack on the German Christians' approach to Jewish believers, Bonhoeffer writes 'Where the Holy Spirit has spoken and we listen instead to the call of blood and nature, or to our personal sympathies, we are profaning the sacrament.'[453]

## Conclusion

Throughout this chapter, we have focused on Bonhoeffer's understanding of freedom in sociality. In a brief discussion of the ecclesiology of the early academic dissertations we saw how for Bonhoeffer, the church operates as place where divine freedom is expressed and true human freedom from self, for God and others, is realised. The central section focused on *The Cost of Discipleship*, offering a rebuttal of individualistic interpretations and suggesting a fresh approach which sees *Cost* as an exposition of true Christian freedom, which consists not in anti-nomianism but in obedience to Christ. We suggested that *The Cost of Discipleship,* can best be seen as an exploration of the theme of freedom and obedience, an outworking of Luther's *The Freedom of the Christian*, over against the tendency of contemporary Lutheranism to cut Luther's insistence on the primacy of grace and faith free from its rootedness in costly discipleship. As we will see, this lays the foundation for the understanding of freedom which we

---

[450] Ibid., 166-7; ET 166, (italics original).
[451] CD 226.
[452] CD 226; DBW 4 245.
[453] Ibid., 231; DBW 4, 250.

encounter in the prison correspondence and which we will expound in our penultimate chapter.

In our discussion of *Life Together,* we saw how, for Bonhoeffer, corporate worship is the primary context within which Christians are formed in discipline and freedom, from self, for God and for others. We focused on the importance of confession as the foundation for genuine community in true freedom from self for God and for others and concluded with a discussion of the eucharist, as the sacrament of gift and of ethical demand. Right worship is to be lived out in right practice; the community founded on the word and renewed and strengthened through the sacrament, is called to live in sacrificial love for others. It is this ethical content of redeemed freedom and its concrete outworking in Bonhoeffer's own life in the closing years of the Third Reich, to which we must now turn.

# Chapter Five
# Freedom and Responsibility

**Introduction**

As we have seen throughout our discussion, for Bonhoeffer, doctrine and ethics, faith and life are inextricably related. The ethical implications of freedom, as freedom from self, for God and for others, emerge both implicitly and explicitly throughout his work. In the last chapter we discussed the outworking of freedom for others in corporate terms, focusing on the Christian community as the place where God freely chooses to give himself to his people, and where human beings are freed to become most fully themselves. However, although any discussion of human relationships and community life inevitably raises questions of ethics, we touched only briefly on the ethical implications of freedom and the relationship between freedom and responsibility. It is to this question that we must now turn.

All ethics, by its very definition, makes assumptions about human freedom. If human beings are automata, human freedom is illusory, and ethical theory becomes at best an academic exercise and at worst a cruel deception. However, where much ethical theory has understood freedom in terms of the individual's capacity to chose the good from among an array of ethical alternatives, free from external constraint, for Bonhoeffer the issue is rather one of freedom from self, constrained by obedience to the will of Christ. Hence, for Bonhoeffer, the concept of absolute freedom, of freedom without boundaries, is meaningless. Human freedom is always freedom within limits, whether the limitation is seen in terms of creatureliness, as in *Creation and Fall*, or in terms of obedience, as in *The Cost of Discipleship*. Indeed, it is those very limitations which enable authentic freedom from self, for God and for others. The discussion of the relationship between freedom and responsibility, which is the focus of this chapter, can be seen as an improvisation upon the same theme. The concept of responsibility has already appeared at various points in Bonhoeffer's writings. Freedom is both gracious gift and call to responsibility. However, as we shall see, it is in *Ethics*, and in particular in 'History and Good', the fragmentary text which will be the main focus of this chapter, that the question of the relationship between freedom and responsibility is brought into sharpest focus and receives its most developed treatment.

## Freedom and Responsibility

In this chapter we will briefly rehearse the background to the new critical edition of *Ethics*, the text of which will be the focus of much of our discussion. We cannot hope to do justice to the whole of Bonhoeffer's ethical thinking within the confines of one chapter and we have therefore chosen to focus on the issue of responsibility, which, we will argue, goes to the heart of Bonhoeffer's attempt to construct a genuine Christian ethic. We will trace the development of Bonhoeffer's understanding of freedom in the context of the specific political circumstances of the Third Reich, in order to assess whether his ethic of free responsibility should be viewed purely in terms of a response to a very particular set of circumstances, a situation ethic, or whether it emerges as a natural progression and elaboration of the understanding of freedom which we have discussed in the previous chapters. We will examine the relationship between the pacifism of *The Cost of Discipleship* and the responsible action of *Ethics*, discussing in some detail the developments in Bonhoeffer's thinking between the two editions of the fragment 'History and Good', and suggesting a possible explanation for the changes. In the body of the chapter we will examine Bonhoeffer's writings on freedom and responsibility, beginning with a brief appraisal of two papers written on his return to Germany in July 1939. In our discussion of *Ethics*, our major focus will be upon the second edition of 'History and Good'. We will consider Bonhoeffer's understanding of the relationship between freedom and responsibility giving particular attention to three components of the responsible life: vicarious action, correspondence with reality and the acceptance of guilt. The first of these, vicarious action or deputyship, has proved one of the most controversial aspects of Bonhoeffer's ethics and we will engage with some of his major critics on this question. However, we will suggest that it is the third component, acceptance of guilt, which most radically and effectively subverts traditional ethical theory. We will also examine the relationship between responsibility and obedience, before offering some concluding observations assessing Bonhoeffer's contribution to an understanding of freedom in the context of ethics.

### The Background to the Revised Edition of Ethics

The first edition of *Ethics* was published in 1948, under the editorship of Eberhard Bethge. Bethge arranged the various fragments on the basis of an outline found in 'Zettel 38'.[454] However, as this sketch did not refer to all

---

[454] The 'Zettel' are the notes made in preparation for the writing of the *Ethics* manuscripts, found with Bonhoeffer's papers and preserved by Eberhard Bethge. In 1985, they were

the extant manuscripts, Bethge admitted that the ordering of the rest was 'guesswork'.[455] Bethge's guiding principle was thematic rather than chronological and his 'Forward' included the caveat: 'This book is not the *Ethics* which Dietrich Bonhoeffer intended to be published.'[456] A major revision took place at the time of the sixth edition in 1963. The publication of the prison correspondence between Bonhoeffer and Bethge had aroused interest in Bonhoeffer's theological development, culminating in the Tegel correspondence. Against this background, the new edition attempted to re-order the manuscripts chronologically, on the assumption that Bonhoeffer's writings could be characterised in terms of a gradual movement, 'From the church to the world.'[457]

In contrast to, and perhaps as a result of the huge interest generated by the prison correspondence, *Ethics* did not initially excite significant scholarly attention and as late as 1975, Bethge could refer to it as a neglected work in Bonhoeffer studies.[458] However, the position began to change in the wake of the Third International Bonhoeffer Conference held in Oxford in 1980, which focused on questions of ethics and personal responsibility.[459] Of particular significance was a paper by Clifford Green. Green presented the results of a careful analysis of the *Ethics* manuscripts which concluded both that the standard ordering of the volume was unsatisfactory and that, contrary to previous assumptions, the writing of *Ethics* could not have begun before March 1940, given Bonhoeffer's apparent familiarity with a book by Dilschneider published in 1940.[460] Green's paper acted as something of a catalyst for a decade of further research on the *Ethics* manuscripts, a reappraisal which resulted in the publication in 1992 of a significantly re-ordered edition, Band 6 of the *Dietrich Bonhoeffer Werke*. Ilse Tödt, on behalf of the editorial team, sets

---

re-deciphered by Bethge, Ilse Tödt and Herbert Anzinger, synchronised with the *Ethics* manuscripts, re-numbered and placed on microfiche. In 1993 they were published as *Zettelnotizen für ein 'Ethik'* (DBW 6 (Ergänzungsband) *Zettelnotizen für eine 'Ethik'* ed. Tödt I. (1993)).

[455] 'Vermutungen'. DBW 6, 10.
[456] *Ethics* (SCM 1955), 7. Cited in DBW 6 at 10.
[457] The title of one of the earliest studies of Bonhoeffer's work by Hanfried Müller, (Op. cit.).
[458] Bethge in *Bonhoeffer: Exile and Martyr* (New York Seabury Press 1975), 20; cited by Peck W. J. in Preface to *New studies in Bonhoeffer's Ethics* ed. Peck W. J. (New York Edwin Mellen Press 1987).
[459] A number of papers from the conference were published as *Ethical Responsibility: Bonhoeffer's Legacy to the Church* ed. Godsey J. D. and Kelly G. B. (New York Edwin Mellen Press 1981).
[460] Dilschneider O. *Die evangelische Tat. Grundlagen und Grundzüge der evangelischen Ethik*, (Gütersloh, 1940).

out a detailed history of the revised volume in the 'Editors' Preface' to the new edition and it is not necessary to rehearse that here.[461] For our purposes it is sufficient to note that by far the most important change from earlier editions is the relocation of the fragment 'Christ, Reality and Good' as the opening chapter of the volume. We take the view that this decision is of crucial importance in determining the thrust and focus of *Ethics*, which now opens with Bonhoeffer's revolutionary reconstruction of the ethical question:

> There is an unprecedented demand which must be confronted by everyone who wishes to take up the problem of a Christian ethic. The demand is that he must from the outset discard as irrelevant the two questions which generally lead him to pursue the problem of ethics 'How can I be good?' and 'How can I do good?'. Instead of these he must pose a question wholly other and totally different from these two, a question about the will of God.[462]

In earlier editions, the force of this radical challenge, which defines Bonhoeffer's ethical agenda with startling clarity, had been softened by its placement midway through the volume. Its re-positioning at the beginning of the revised edition means that it inevitably informs all later discussion. We would suggest that it becomes clear from the rest of this opening section that Bonhoeffer sees his task as nothing less than a radical re-formulation of the entire basis of Christian ethics in christological terms. Just as the concrete incarnation of God in Christ, rather than abstract metaphysical speculation set the parameters for Bonhoeffer's theology, so a Christian ethics must be shaped and focused, not by universal norms or abstract theories of good, but by the reality of the reconciliation of God and humanity brought about through the life, death and resurrection of Christ.

## Political and Theological Background

However, before looking in detail at Bonhoeffer's ethical agenda, we must make some comments regarding the political and theological background against which these writings emerged. In the last chapter we took issue with David Hopper's assessment of Bonhoeffer's theology as no more than 'soliloquy', a reflection upon his own theological and ethical struggles. However, to deny the influence of the historical and personal context on Bonhoeffer's writing would be equally misguided. In 'History and Good'

---

[461] DBW 6, 7-28.
[462] Ibid., 31.

Bonhoeffer is deeply critical of an ethics abstracted from the particularity and concreteness of life and writes: 'Whether an isolated individual, detached from his historical situation and his historical connections can be viewed as at all ethically relevant is at least very questionable and in view of its unreality is in any event an uninteresting theoretical borderline case.'[463] Hence, whilst we will argue that *Ethics* is much more than an autobiographical account of Bonhoeffer's existential struggle to come to terms with his role as a double agent and as a Christian plotting the downfall of his country, the importance of the historical and personal circumstances amid which he was writing must not be underestimated. In a context in which church had been paralysed by its internal divisions over how far resistance should be taken, Bethge's suggestion that Bonhoeffer's aim was 'not only to argue logically, but also to *free people for action*,'[464] is convincing. Bethge continues: '[A]nyone who looks in his *Ethics* for a direct justification of a *coup d'état* ... will be disappointed. It is a question of *liberation and of awakening responsibility*, not of offering ready-made safeguards that could serve as justification for timid souls.'[465] If, as we are convinced, Bethge is right in his assessment, then *Ethics* constitutes a call to step out from the passivity which colludes with evil, a call to the risk of responsible action. Ironically, for Bonhoeffer, as a theologian in the Lutheran tradition, one of the major constraints to such freedom of action came in the shape of Lutheran history and practice. Two separate issues arise. The first relates to Christian involvement in the political sphere and seems to have been clearly resolved by the time of the writing of *Ethics*. The second, the far more controversial question of the use of violence, was, we will suggest, only finally resolved with the writing of the second edition of 'History and Good' in the first half of 1942. We will address these issues in turn arguing that at the root of Bonhoeffer's response in both cases lies in his reaction to the Nazi persecution of the Jews.

*The Christian and Political Involvement*

In Germany in the 1930s, Luther's doctrine of the two kingdoms had developed into a rigid polarisation between the church and the so-called secular world.[466] In such 'thinking in two spheres', Christ and the world

---

[463] Ibid., 246; ET 215.
[464] DB 625 (my italics) cf. also 529-30. This was also the purpose of the paper *After Ten Years*.
[465] Ibid., 625-6 (second set of italics mine).
[466] Luther's *Sermon for Advent Sunday 1532* WA 36, 385, speaks of worldly government in terms of the kingdom of God's left hand (*das Reich mit der linken Hand*).

were conceived in terms of 'two opposing and mutually repellent zones'[467] and concepts such as Christian and secular, sacred and profane, supernatural and natural were viewed as total antitheses. Within this context, the calling and responsibility of the Christian was very clearly confined to the realm of the church, a position which was implicitly accepted even in the Barmen declaration, which defended the rights of Jews within the church but made no protest against the wider implications of the so-called 'Aryan Clause' which prohibited those of Jewish origin from holding office in church or state.[468] Bonhoeffer was not present at Barmen, but welcomed the declaration enthusiastically as a major step forward in the struggle against Nazism. Nevertheless, in his own writings, he had already moved, at least implicitly, beyond the approach of Barmen. A year previously, as one of the first theologians to reflect on the implications of the Aryan Clause and the growing tide of anti-semitism, Bonhoeffer had written a paper entitled *The Church and the Jewish Question*. There he had envisaged the possibility that the State might overstep its mandate to the point that the church would be called to take direct political action by putting 'a spoke in the wheel'.[469] Although the phrase is ambiguous, it seems unlikely that Bonhoeffer at that early stage envisaged that such action would involve the use of violence. Indeed, as we saw in the last chapter, in this period leading up to the writing of *The Cost of Discipleship*, Bonhoeffer had become convinced that the appropriate response to Hitler was one of non-violent resistance, modelled on the Sermon on the Mount. In his exposition of that text in *Cost*, Bonhoeffer clearly has the question of the Jews in mind when he reiterates the call of the Christian to assist those who suffer and to suffer with them. In the section on 'The Visible Community', he writes:

> [W]here the world oppresses, [the Christian] will stoop down and raise up the oppressed. If the world refuses justice, the Christian will pursue mercy, and if the world takes refuge in lies, he will open his mouth for the dumb,[470] and bear testimony to the truth. For the sake of the brother, *be he Jew or Greek* ... he will renounce all fellowship with the world.[471]

---

[467] DBW 6, 43; ET 197.

[468] cf. Bethge E. 'Christologisches Bekenntnis und Antijudaismus: Zum Defizit von Barmen I' in *Bekennen und Widerstehen* (Chr. Kaiser Verlag München 1984), 113ff.

[469] *The Church and the Jewish Question* NRS 221, GS II 44ff. 'The third possibility is not just to bandage the victims under the wheel, but to put a spoke in the wheel itself'. cf. DBW 16, 550.

[470] The reference is to Proverbs 31:8. The footnote to the revised edition states that the verse is firmly underlined in Bonhoeffer's Luther Bible. DBW 4, 253. cf. also DBW 13, 204-5.

[471] CD 232 (my italics).

In the closing chapter of the book, he broadens the scope of his argument beyond the church, making implicit reference to the persecution of the Jews, when he asserts that 'any attack on the least of humanity is an attack on Christ who took human form and in his own person restored the image of God in all that bears the human form.'[472] However, *Cost* stopped short of advocating active resistance to the political regime; the focus was still on 'bandaging the victims'. A year later, however, the horrific events of 'Kristallnacht' seem to have convinced Bonhoeffer that such a response was no longer adequate. In Bonhoeffer's personal Bible the words of Psalm 74 'they have burned all the houses of God in the land' are underlined and the date of Kristallnacht written in the margin.[473] He also added a sentence to the circular letter which he had already drafted to send to his former Finkenwalde students, now in isolated parishes: 'In recent days I have been thinking very much about Psalm 74, Zech. 2:8 and Rom 9:4 and 11:11-15. That leads us into very earnest prayer.'[474] Bethge recalls that a year or so previously, Bonhoeffer had preached on the text from Zechariah ('The one who touches you touches the apple of his eye'), applying it to the Confessing Church, and comments that for Bonhoeffer 'to relate it to the Jews was something totally new.'[475] However, although by this stage Bonhoeffer had met some of those involved in the conspiracy through his brother-in-law, Hans Dohnyani, the question of his own involvement remained unclear. The invitation in 1939 to spend a further period in the USA initially seemed to offer a way forward. However, although, as is well known, Bonhoeffer almost immediately decided to return to Germany, this brief visit would seem to have been catalytic in the evolution of his understanding of the relationship between freedom and responsible action, a development to which the papers and articles written on his return to Germany in 1939 provide a fascinating testimony.

*The Call to Action*

Of particular interest is the paper *Protestantism Without Reformation*, written in August 1939. There Bonhoeffer reflects upon his encounter with America and American theology in terms which suggest a strong

---

[472] Ibid. 272 (translation inclusivised).
[473] DB 511.
[474] GS II 544. Bethge states that this sentence was added to the letter after Kristallnacht. (interview with the writer 20th February 1997).
[475] Writer's interview with Bethge as above. cf. 'Dietrich Bonhoeffer unter den Verstummten?' in *Erst Gebot und Zeitgeschichte: Aufsätze und Reden 1980-1990* (Chr. Kaiser Verlag München 1991), 106; and Bonhoeffer's insistence on the indissoluble link between Christians and the Jewish people in DBW 6, 95, ET 89-90.

connection between his decision to return to Germany and his reflections upon the true meaning of freedom. In a lengthy section headed 'Freedom', Bonhoeffer criticises the American understanding of the concept for confusing true freedom with a superficial independence. He writes: 'America calls herself the land of freedom. Under this term today she understands the right of the individual to independent thought, speech and action. In this setting, religious freedom is for the American, a self-evident possession.'[476] However, it is this very freedom in terms of 'independent thought, speech and freedom' which Bonhoeffer consciously and freely renounces by his decision to return to Germany. As in his earlier writings, Bonhoeffer is strongly critical of an understanding of freedom as a possibility to be realised rather than as a gift of God. He argues:

> So it can happen that a church which prides itself in its freedom as a possibility offered to it by the world, slips back into the world in a singular way, that it is precisely a church which is free in this sense that becomes secularised more quickly than a church which does not possess freedom as a possibility.[477]

As in *Creation and Fall*, Bonhoeffer draws a sharp distinction between freedom as a possession and what he terms 'essential freedom'(*wesentliche Freiheit*). In a passage which merits citing at length he argues:

> Freedom as an institutional possession is not an essential attribute of the church. It can be a gracious gift granted to the church by the providence of God; but it can also be the great temptation to which the church succumbs in that it sacrifices its essential freedom to institutional freedom. Whether the churches of America are really free, only the actual preaching of the word of God can determine. Only where this word can be preached concretely, in judgement, command, forgiveness of sinners and liberation from all human statutes, in the midst of historical reality, is there freedom of the church. But where thanks for institutional freedom must be rendered by a sacrifice of the freedom of preaching, the church is in chains, even when it believes itself to be free.[478]

At one level, Bonhoeffer's words offer a critical assessment of the American church, where freedom had become reified as an end in itself, a principle to be defended and preserved above all else, even at the price of sacrificing its responsibility to proclaim the Gospel. Such freedom, he argues is illusory. However at a deeper level lies an unstated but surely implied indictment on much of the church in Germany. The *Deutsche*

---

[476] DBW 15, 443.
[477] Ibid., 444.
[478] Ibid., 445.

*Christen* and even sections of the Confessing Church, had failed to preach God's word concretely 'in the midst of historical reality', they had succumbed to that 'great temptation' and made precisely that compromise of sacrificing the essential freedom to preach the Gospel, in exchange for a limited institutional freedom.

Another of Bonhoeffer's occasional writings of this period, a preliminary sketch reflecting upon William Paton's 'The church and the new order', prepared for Visser't Hooft, General Secretary of the World Council of Churches in September 1941,[479] takes up many of the points made in *Protestantism without Reformation*. Again, it gives insight into Bonhoeffer's developing thinking on the contrast between the freedom for self, retained at the price of passivity and collusion with the status quo, and the freedom for others which constitutes true responsibility. In words which were to find more developed expression in *Ethics* he writes 'Freedom is not in the first place an individual *right* but a *responsibility*.'[480] It was this costly freedom which Bonhoeffer chose in his decision to return to Germany, as Europe stood on the brink of war, and it is against this background that the discussion of freedom and responsibility in *Ethics* is to be understood. However, before addressing the issue of responsibility in detail we must first examine the final development in Bonhoeffer's break with the pacifism of his Lutheran tradition.

*Pacifism and Beyond*

Throughout *The Cost of Discipleship*, Bonhoeffer had resolutely refused to countenance violence as an option for the Christian. Whilst non-violence must not be turned into a principle, Christians who proclaim the victory of divine love over evil in the cross, are called to participate in that suffering love.[481] However, Bethge is clear that by the time Bonhoeffer travelled to Norway with Helmuth von Moltke in April 1942, he was committed to the use of violence if necessary, and indeed this commitment provided a major area of disagreement with von Moltke. Von Moltke's biographers write 'One might have expected them to become fast friends. But in fact there were a number of reasons why this didn't happen. They certainly differed on the question of whether it was wise and consistent with Christian

---

[479] DBW 16 at 536ff. The document prepared by Visser't Hooft is included in DBW 16 at 541ff. It was forwarded to SCM press with a message to Paton requesting that 'some of these considerations ... be brought before responsible people in Britain' as evidence of the existence of a significant opposition movement in Germany. (GS I 361).

[480] DBW 16, 540.

[481] Ibid. 130.

principles to work for the assassination of Hitler'.[482] Bethge himself recalls Bonhoeffer's comment that although the meeting with Moltke had been stimulating, 'we are not of the same opinion.'[483]

As we saw in the last chapter, the way in which the Sermon on the Mount became central to Bonhoeffer's vision for a non-violent offensive against National Socialism is well documented in his correspondence with friends and family. However there is no comparable documentation to explain what was clearly a major change of heart on this issue. There are however a number of clues in the political developments and in Bonhoeffer's own writings. We have already seen the way in which *Kristallnacht* operated as a watershed in Bonhoeffer's thinking. A survey of events in the months prior to the Norway visit does not suggest one isolated incident, but rather a general trend of developments which might account for Bonhoeffer's stance. First, although Hitler's military victories made the possibility of a bloodless coup initiated by the generals increasingly unlikely, it was only in December 1941 when Hitler appointed himself as commander in chief of the army, that all hope of such an outcome was clearly lost. Second, October 1941 had seen the first mass deportations of Jews from Berlin. Bonhoeffer and a colleague in the *Abwehr*, F. J. Perels were commissioned to prepare a report on these events and so were fully informed as to what took place.[484] Bonhoeffer's statement in the *Ethics* fragment 'Inheritance and Decay' (probably written in autumn 1941), that 'The expulsion of the Jews from the West must necessarily bring with it the expulsion of Christ; for Jesus Christ was a Jew', may well reflect this knowledge.[485] The beginning of 1942 was marked by the infamous conference at Wannsee which agreed the so-called 'Final Solution' to the Jewish question, and it would appear that rumours of this soon circulated within the *Abwehr*. Christine-Ruth Müller suggests that the news may have come direct from State Secretary Ernst von Weizsäcker with whom Dohnanyi was in regular contact.[486] Matthias Schrieber suggests that Perels, with whom Bonhoeffer had been working closely, would also have been

---

[482] Balfour M. and Frisby J. in *Helmuth von Moltke* (London: Macmillan 1972), 187.
[483] DB 659.
[484] DBW 16, 212-217; DB 649-50.
[485] DBW 6 95, ET 90. Bethge, in Dietrich Bonhoeffer and the Jews' in Godsey J. D. and Kelly G. B. (eds.) *Ethical Responsibility: Bonhoeffer's Legacy to the Church* (New York: Edwin Mellen Press 1981), 78, assumes the reference is to deportations of Jews from Stettin in 1940. However, he is writing prior to the revised edition of *Ethics* and on the assumption that 'Inheritance and Decay' was written in 1940.
[486] Müller C-R. *Dietrich Bonhoeffers Kampf gegen die nationalsozialistische Verfolgung und Vernichtung der Juden* (München: Chr Kaiser Verlag 1990), 248.

informed of these developments.[487] It seems likely that this combination of the dashing of any lingering hopes of a peaceful overthrow of Hitler, coupled with the escalation of the persecution of the Jews, combined to convince Bonhoeffer that this was an extraordinary situation in which called for exceptional action.

From the standpoint of Bonhoeffer's own writing, we would suggest that the key texts are the two versions of the fragment 'History and Good'[488] and the various 'Zettel' written in preparation for those drafts. Although the editors of the critical edition include both versions of this section in the revised volume (previously the first draft had been included in the *Gesammelte Schriften*), they offer no explanation for the quite considerable differences between the two. Within the secondary literature, there is a short discussion of the two editions in Stephen Plant's thesis, where he comments:

> The re-appraisal of ethics Bonhoeffer undertakes in his prison letters is evident in the contrast between the use of the Bible on the one hand in 'History and Good 1' and on the other in 'History and Good 2' and 'The Love of God and the Decay of the World'.[489]

Much of the material familiar to the reader of the second edition of 'History and Good' is already present, at least *in nuce*, in the first draft. The revised version retains the strong incarnational focus and a number of themes such as deputyship, correspondence with reality and guilt, which appeared in less developed form in the earlier version now receive more detailed treatment. However, a major feature of the early draft which does not re-emerge, either in the second edition of 'History and Good', or indeed in other chapters written later, is the sustained treatment of the 'Sermon on the Mount'. In this first draft, the relationship between the Sermon on the Mount, political involvement and responsible action forms a major motif. The Sermon on the Mount 'places humanity before the necessity of historical responsible action.'[490] It 'calls him to the love which proves itself in responsible action towards his neighbour.'[491] Because these are the

---

[487] Schrieber M. *Friedrich Justus Perels: Ein Weg vom Rechtskampf der Bekennenden Kirche in den politischen Widerstand* (München: Chr. Kaiser 1989), 170.

[488] Both version seem to have been written in the first months of 1942.

[489] Plant Stephen J. *Uses of the Bible in the 'Ethics' of Dietrich Bonhoeffer* Unpublished PhD Dissertation Cambridge 1993, 189-90. Plant does not explain his remark or make any suggestion as to why this section should have been so extensively rewritten within the period of a few months.

[490] DBW 6, 241.

[491] Ibid., 242.

words of the incarnate Christ, they are no abstract ethic, even an 'ethic of Jesus' but 'the words of one who lived in concrete responsibility for humanity.'[492]

However, where there are seventeen explicit references to this teaching in the first draft, only two survive in the second edition. Although Zettel 19, which sets out a draft outline of the second edition suggests that a discussion of the relationship between politics and the Sermon on the Mount was planned as part of a concluding section to the chapter, this section was never written and the Zettel suggests that even if it had been, what had operated as a central motif in the earlier draft would have been reduced to a more peripheral discussion.[493] Certainly there are several places within the second edition as we have it, where the text closely follows that of the first edition but references to the 'Sermon on the Mount' seem to have been deliberately omitted.[494] Given that, as we have seen, Bonhoeffer's discovery of the Sermon on the Mount was central to his espousal of pacifism, the omission or sidelining of this text at a time when Bonhoeffer has begun to countenance the possibility of tyrannicide is striking. Furthermore, one of the major additions to the second draft of 'History and Good', is the discussion of the political concept of *necessità* first coined by Machiavelli, in which Bonhoeffer argues that some circumstances are so exceptional that the normal rule of law is superseded. Such situations 'appeal directly to the free responsibility of the one who acts, a responsibility which is bound by no law'[495] and responsible and appropriate action steps outside the sphere of the legal and the rational into the realm of the *ultima ratio*.[496] The one who would act in freedom and responsibility can no longer look to a law to justify his action. Indeed, in such circumstances, the acknowledgement of the law's validity lies in breaking it. The implication is an acceptance, albeit, we would suggest a reluctant one, that in certain circumstances, the recourse to violence is the only appropriate (*sachgemäß*) response. However the one who acts in such

---

[492] Ibid., 234.

[493] The draft provides for a final section on 'Love and Responsibility' which was to have included a section on 'Politics and the Sermon on the Mount'. The heading appears at p.299 in DBW 6.

[494] e.g. DBW 6, 235 (first edition) 'The words of Jesus, for example the Sermon on the Mount, are the interpretation of his existence, the interpretation of that reality in which history comes to its fulfilment in the incarnation of God.' cf. DBW 6, 263 (second edition) 'The word of Jesus Christ is the interpretation of his existence and therefore the interpretation of that reality in which history comes to its fulfilment.' cf. also DBW 6, 237 and 252.

[495] DBW 6, 273; ET 238.

[496] Ibid., 274; ET 239.

free responsibility must acknowledge their guilt and can look only to God for justification.

At least some concrete support for our reconstruction can be found among the Zettel, the notes made in preparation for the various *Ethics* chapters, which were found at Bonhoeffer's death. Two are particularly relevant to our argument.[497] Zettel Nr. 28[498] offers the first concrete evidence to suggest that Bonhoeffer wrestled with the relationship between *necessità* and the Sermon on the Mount. Bonhoeffer writes:

> I myself can freely and willingly sacrifice my property, life etc. But because the property etc. of my family, people etc. does not belong to me, I cannot sacrifice it, not because it has in itself a greater right, but because I am <u>called</u> to the defence of <u>the property of another</u>, in order that the <u>freedom</u> of control over life, property etc. might be <u>preserved</u> for the individual.[499]

He lists qualities such as self sacrifice, endurance, love of enemies and innocence with their apparent opposites: self-assertion, rebellion, destruction of the enemy and guilt and argues that there is a 'false purity' a 'worldly form of love' which overlooks responsibility for one's neighbour. He asserts: 'Love is not a method, a frame of mind, but a being, namely a belonging to others, a being for others, a being in Christ etc. The command of love means nothing other than to actualise this being.'[500] The note concludes with an explicit reference to the Sermon on the Mount and *necessità*.[501] As we have already seen above, Zettel Nr. 19,[502] sets out what seems to be an outline for the revised version of 'History and Good'. There in the context of a discussion of *necessità*, Bonhoeffer asks 'what is the ultimate? an eternal law or free responsibility before God' and concludes

---

[497] Although this discussion does not appear as such in the finished work, the unpolished nature of these notes gives invaluable insight into the thought processes which resulted in the final version, and, gives at least some insight into the development between the two versions.

[498] According to the editor, Ilse Tödt, this Zettel dates from the period Winter 1941-Spring 1942 when it is assumed that the first draft of 'History and Good' was written. If so, it suggests that the conflict between the Sermon on the Mount and *necessità* was present in Bonhoeffer's thinking at this early stage, although at this point he seems to have thought some sort of reconciliation between the two might be possible.

[499] DBW 6 (Ergänzungsband) *Zettelnotizen für eine 'Ethik'* ed. Tödt I. (1993), 90 (in note form, underlining original).

[500] Ibid. cf. the discussion of 'being-for-one-another' in the previous chapter.

[501] The note reads:
'necessità - necessity - need
Sermon on the Mount - love - self-sacrifice - responsibility.

[502] DBW 6 (Ergänzungsband) op. cit.., 105f. According to Tödt, this Zettel dates from the first half of 1942.

'The dilemma must not be resolved! it remains open!'[503] There is no cheap resolution of the gulf between the resolute peace ethic of the Sermon on the Mount and involvement in a violent coup d'état. To attempt this would be to engage in precisely the sort of ethics which Bonhoeffer had set out to subvert and undermine, by attempting to justify an action which only God can judge and forgive. Instead, Bonhoeffer is clear that there can be no dissimulation. The one who engages in violent action against Hitler must recognise that he breaks the law, that in his action the teaching of the Sermon on the Mount is violated, that he becomes guilty.[504] We will discuss this question of the acceptance of guilt, which is perhaps the most radical of Bonhoeffer's contributions to ethical discussion in detail below. First, however, we must focus more broadly on the major motif of the second draft of 'History and Good', the question of responsible action.

## Freedom and Responsibility

Freedom, as we have seen throughout our discussion, is defined by Bonhoeffer christologically. Christ is the word of God's freedom, the one in whom God freely binds himself to humanity. But the one who embodies freedom is also the one who lives in response and responsibility before God and hence the parameters of the responsible life are given definition by the person and work of Christ. Christ is the one who supremely lived and died vicariously as the one for others. He is the sinless one who became guilty, the one in whom God's freedom for the world was exemplified in his free binding of himself to the world in incarnation, and finally on the cross. He is the one who entrusted the justification of his life and death wholly into the hands of God. Christ stands at the centre as the one who not only patterns and inspires, but also enables responsible action, the one who, as we have already seen, is both gift and example. It is such a life of responding to Christ as a whole person which Bonhoeffer calls responsibility. 'Responsibility means therefore that the whole of life is put at stake, it becomes a matter of life and death.'[505] It is here that Bonhoeffer hints at the vicarious, almost intercessory nature of responsibility, which

---

[503] Ibid., 106 (underlining original). cf. DBW 6, 275; ET 240.
[504] Bethge records a meeting in 1940 or 1941 when Hans von Dohnanyi questioned Bonhoeffer about the biblical text 'The one who takes up the sword shall perish by the sword' (Matt 26:52) and recalls that Bonhoeffer' replied: 'Yes, that is true, we will all be guilty. But people who are prepared to accept that are the ones needed at this time.' (DB 530).
[505] DBW 6, 254; ET 222.

was touched upon in the early academic treatises,[506] and will be spelt out more clearly later, when he writes: 'I stand at the same time for Christ before others and for others before Christ. My responsibility which I assume for Christ in the hearing of humanity is at the same time my responsibility for humanity in the hearing of Christ.'[507] In our earlier discussion of freedom, we noted the close connection between freedom for God and freedom for the other. Responsibility too is a personal rather than abstract concept, arising in the context of relationship. I stand in responsibility before God or before my neighbour and, as we shall discuss below in further detail, although God and neighbour never lose their discrete identities, neither can they be separated. The concept of responsibility is not a new departure for Bonhoeffer, but although it played an important role in his earlier writings, it is in *Ethics* that it becomes a major motif. Within the fragment 'History and Good', it can be seen as a fresh improvisation upon the recurrent theme of the creative relationship between constraint and freedom. Bonhoeffer writes:

> The structure of the responsible life is conditioned by two factors; that life is bound to humanity and to God and that each person's own life is free. It is this commitment of life to humanity and to God which sets it in the freedom of a person's own life. Without this bond and without this freedom, there is no responsibility.[508]

It is only in being bound to God and to one's neighbour that humanity can live in freedom. In being bound to others, the Christian acts vicariously for the other and reckons with the realities of the particular social and historical situation, which must always inform the responsible act. In freedom the Christian takes the risk of concrete action and incurs guilt. It is these key characteristics of responsible action, on which we must now focus, beginning with the one which has caused most controversy, vicarious action or deputyship.

*Vicarious Action*

Although the term *Stellvertretung*, which we will render 'vicarious action'[509] is only one aspect of the responsible life discussed here in

---

[506] DBW 1, 121ff esp. 123, 125.
[507] DBW 6, 255; ET 223.
[508] DBW 6, 256; ET 224, cf. Bachtell op. cit. 266.
[509] The standard English translation of *Ethics* renders *Stellvertretung* as 'Deputyship'. The German word embraces the concepts of substitution and representation which are often strictly distinguished - and used by opposing theological 'camps' in English. The

'History and Good', it is a concept of such fundamental importance to our understanding of divine and human freedom, that we must discuss it in some detail and engage with some of the major criticisms of Bonhoeffer's approach. The first significant discussion of vicarious action arises in *Sanctorum Communio*, where, in the context of a discussion of the realisation of the church through Christ, Bonhoeffer argues that the vicarious action of Christ is the life principle (*Lebensprinzip*) of the new humanity. Although he notes the controversy surrounding penal theories of atonement, Bonhoeffer follows Luther in maintaining that Christ's vicarious action is to be understood in terms of guilt and penalty:

> As the innocent one, Christ takes the guilt and punishment of the other upon himself, and in that he dies as a criminal, he is cursed, for he carries the sins of the world and is punished for them; but on the criminal's cross, vicarious love triumphs, obedience to God triumphs over guilt, and so guilt is really punished and overcome.[510]

Bonhoeffer suggests that it is erroneous to view Christ's vicarious action in ethical terms, as something which might or might not be possible or morally acceptable in the light of some human standard of morality. Instead, it must be seen as the reality of the gracious gift of God, which has taken place in Christ.[511] However, although Christ's action is unique, in that only he can act vicariously in a way which operates salvifically for another, Bonhoeffer argues that 'there is an ethical concept of vicarious action by which is meant the willing taking upon oneself of an evil in the place of another.'[512] Such human action is limited to its particular facts and circumstances and cannot operate salvifically. Indeed, the capacity of the Christian community to act vicariously for one another is entirely dependent upon and derivative of God's love, as demonstrated in the vicarious action of Christ. Bonhoeffer writes: 'One sustains the other in active love, intercession and the forgiveness of sins in the wholly vicarious

---

translation of Sölle's work renders *Stellvertretung* as 'representation', whereas Jüngel's essay translates the same word as 'substitution.' I have used the term 'vicarious action' both to avoid the 'political' luggage attached to 'substitution' and 'representation' and to make it clear that this same word is used throughout Bonhoeffer's writings to describe both Christ's action on behalf of humanity and the Christian's action for the other. However I am conscious that this choice is not without its shortcomings, in that it tends to privilege act over being.

[510] DBW 1, 99.
[511] Ibid.
[512] Ibid., footnote 17.

action, which is only possible in the community of Christ, which is wholly founded on the principle of vicarious action, that is on the love of God.'[513]

In the *Christology* lectures, Bonhoeffer had argued that the very ontological structure of the person of Christ was 'pro me'. Christ did not merely act 'pro me' in his atoning work on the cross, but *is* 'pro me'; the person and work are inextricably united. As God freely bound himself to humanity in the incarnation, death and resurrection of Christ, so Christ continues freely to bind himself to humanity in word, sacrament and church community.[514] Menke, in his definitive discussion of the concept of *Stellvertretung*,[515] suggests that because for Bonhoeffer, act and being are identical in Christ, 'Christ *is* vicarious action, he *is* the antithesis of isolation'.[516] He continues: 'Christ acts 'for us' in such a way that he is identical with his act. Therefore his gift is not something outside himself.'[517] In view of Bonhoeffer's insistence on speaking of Christ in personal terms, even to the extent of preferring to refer to 'the incarnate one' rather than 'the incarnation',[518] it is unlikely that he would find Menke's use of impersonal language acceptable. However Menke's underlying point that acting vicariously for others is something essential to the very being of Christ, is clearly in line with Bonhoeffer's conviction that there can be no valid discussion of some abstract Christ, apart from his activity in the economy of salvation. In redemption, humanity is liberated from the self absorption of the *cor curvum in se*, to the freedom of life in Christ, a freedom exhibited in a life lived for God and for others. Those redeemed by the vicarious life, death and resurrection of Christ are called and enabled to live vicariously, in conformation to Christ.[519] However, it is this concept of vicarious action or deputyship in Bonhoeffer's ethics which has been subjected to the most vehement criticism. As some of this criticism issues from such highly respected scholars as Dorothee Sölle, Eberhard Jüngel and Heinrich Vogel, it is clear that this is an issue which cannot lightly be dismissed, but must be addressed with care.

---

[513] DBW 1, 128.
[514] C, passim.
[515] Menke K-M. *Stellvertretung: Schlüsselbegriff christlichen Lebens und theologische Grundkategorie* (Freiburg Johannes Verlag 1991) pp 207-219.
[516] 'Als Identität von Akt und Sein *ist* er Stellvertretung, *ist* er das Gegenteil der Vereinzelung.' Ibid., 210.
[517] Ibid., 211.
[518] C, 104.
[519] Plant Stephen J. *Uses of the Bible in the 'Ethics' of Dietrich Bonhoeffer* Unpublished PhD Dissertation Cambridge 1993, 189-90.

*Dorothee Sölle* Sölle, in her important work on this subject, discusses Bonhoeffer's understanding of vicarious action in a chapter headed 'The Dialectic of Dependence and Responsibility'.[520] She contrasts Bonhoeffer with Barth, suggesting that the latter 'absolutises man's dependence at the expense of his irreplaceability and responsibility',[521] whilst the former falls into the opposite danger, as she sees it, of conceiving *Stellvertretung* in terms of 'responsibility without dependence'.[522] This is not the place to respond to Sölle's assessment of Barth. With regard to Bonhoeffer, however, we must take issue with her appraisal. Sölle's contention is that, with the exception of *Sanctorum Communio*, where *Stellvertretung* 'is taken in the narrow theological sense', relating to guilt and punishment, and is always discussed in terms of Christ's relationship to us, all reference to *Stellvertretung* in later works 'moves strictly within the sphere of ethics.'[523] However, the concept of Christ as *Stellvertreter*, in what Sölle terms 'the narrow theological sense', is not confined to *Sanctorum Communio*. In his lecture series *The Essence of the Church*, delivered in Berlin in Summer 1932, Bonhoeffer devotes a section to *Stellvertretung Christi*,[524] in which he emphasises the uniqueness of Christ's act: 'Jesus does what no other could do'.[525] In the *Christology* lectures Bonhoeffer speaks of Christ standing before God in the place of humanity[526] and in *The Cost of Discipleship*, although the precise word *Stellvertretung* is not used to describe Christ's redemptive activity, the concept is clearly implied when Bonhoeffer writes of Christ standing in our place before God, in terms very similar to those used in the *Christology* lectures.[527] Similarly, in the teaching material used at Finkenwalde, where the concept appears repeatedly in sermon classes and instructions for Confirmation, Bonhoeffer repeatedly emphasises the uniqueness of Christ's vicarious work.[528]

Perhaps more significantly, whilst it is true that in *Sanctorum Communio* the unique role of Christ as *Stellvertreter*, is clearly emphasised, and indeed is considered at greater length than in the later writings, even in that early dissertation, Christians too are called to live vicariously for one another, in the power of the love of Christ, in sacrificial, active work for

---

[520] Sölle D. *Stellvertretung - Ein Kapital Theologie nach dem 'Tode Gottes'* translated by David Lewis under the title *Christ the Representative* (London SCM 1967) 92-7.
[521] Ibid., 92.
[522] Ibid.
[523] Ibid., 93.
[524] DBW 11, 267.
[525] Ibid. 269, 273.
[526] DBW 12, 296 'er steht an ihrer Stelle, stellvertretend für sie vor Gott'; cf. C 48.
[527] DBW 4, 231.
[528] DBW 14, 339, 346, 804.

one's neighbour, in intercession and in the forgiveness of sins.[529] Indeed, given Bonhoeffer's christological understanding of the church as 'Christ existing as the community of the church',[530] it could hardly be otherwise. Hence, from Bonhoeffer's earliest writings, the unique vicarious activity of Christ in the redemption of humanity has had ethical implications for the way in which his followers live. These implications are not merely at the level of example, but are enabled and empowered by the presence of Christ among his people. The relationship between the unique salvific work of Christ and the vocation of the Christian is expressed with admirable clarity in *After Ten Years*, a paper written by Bonhoeffer around Christmas 1942 for his friends within the conspiracy:

> We are certainly not Christ; we are not called on to redeem the world by our own deeds and sufferings ... We are not Christ, but if we want to be Christians, we must have some share in Christ's large-heartedness by acting with responsibility and in freedom when the hour of danger comes, and by showing a real sympathy that springs not from fear, but from the liberating and redeeming love of Christ for all who suffer.[531]

Christ's atoning work cannot be repeated or emulated, but his 'liberating and redeeming love' motivates and enables the Christian to act in freedom and responsibility for others. The two, though distinct, cannot be separated. If, as we have argued, Bonhoeffer's christology is ethical and his ethics christological, then the distinction which Sölle seeks to draw between the 'narrow theological sense' and 'the sphere of ethics' becomes meaningless.

Sölle's further and related point is that 'in Bonhoeffer's account, representation fuses with responsibility, and the other aspect of representation - dependence on a representative, a specifically 'religious' problem - is ignored.'[532] However, as we will argue again below, for Bonhoeffer, responsible action is never something abstract, detached from relationship to Christ. Christ is the reality to whom responsible action must correspond, and it is into the likeness of Christ, incarnate, crucified and risen that the Christian is to be conformed, not through his own efforts, but by the working of Christ within him.[533] The stress on the Lutheran concept of *justitia passiva* discussed above, and on the relationship of creature to creator, is surely sufficient to demonstrate the essentially gracious

---

[529] The word *stellvertretend* is used in DBW 1, 121 in this context.
[530] *Christus als Gemeinde existierend* DBW 1, 76, 87, 126ff etc.
[531] LPP 14.
[532] Sölle op. cit., 94.
[533] DBW 6, 80.

foundation of all Bonhoeffer's ethics. By setting responsibility and dependence in antithesis, Sölle somehow misses the christological undergirding of all Bonhoeffer's ethics, in accordance with which, it is grace which enables true responsibility, just as the acceptance of creatureliness before God enables true freedom in his image, restored in Christ.

*Eberhard Jüngel and Heinrich Vogel* Jüngel's critique of Bonhoeffer's concept of vicarious action as a characteristic of responsible human life, arises in his discussion of the work of Heinrich Vogel.[534] Jüngel characterises Vogel as someone whose life's work has been to explore the mystery of *Stellvertretung*, to the extent that he can rightly be called a theologian of *Stellvertretung*. For Vogel, the crucial affirmation is 'He came in our place', something which can be said only of God's redemptive work in Christ. Jüngel's primary concern seems to be that where Christ's sacrifice is seen as exemplary, the danger of ethics eclipsing theology arises. However, whilst we would argue that the existence of an exemplary strand of interpretation of the cross in the New Testament and in Christian tradition should not be too lightly dismissed, this is not what Bonhoeffer is propounding, as is clear from his forceful rejection of a reductionist understanding of Christ as example.[535] We have already noted the reiteration throughout Bonhoeffer's writings of the unique and unrepeatable nature of Christ's vicarious action and the distinction he draws between Christ's vicarious action and the concept within the realm of ethics. Instead his concern lies in the healing of the false dichotomy between theology and ethics, faith and life, a reconciliation which has been effected in Christ. Jüngel suggests that Bonhoeffer saw *Stellvertretung* as 'some anthropologically identifiable substitutionary structure'[536] which is taken as a starting point for an understanding of Christ, a claim he supports by selective quotations from the section on vicarious action. However, as we have argued, the true case is precisely the opposite. Bonhoeffer's theology and ethics are always grounded christologically; it is Christ the incarnate Son of God who defines true humanity, never vice versa. Again, Jüngel's assertion that 'The concept [of *Stellvertretung*] is only meaningful as a *dogmatic recollection* of an *event* which may be provisionally paraphrased

---

[534] Das Geheimnis der Stellvertretung: Ein dogmatisches Gespräch mit Heinrich Vogel, translated as 'The Mystery of Substitution' in *Eberhard Jüngel: Theological Essays II* trans. Webster J B (1995 T&T Clark) 145-62.
[535] GS III, 177; C, 38 'If Jesus was the idealistic founder of a religion, I can be elevated by his work and stimulated to follow his example. But my sin is not forgiven ... the work of Jesus drives me to despair because I cannot follow his example.'
[536] Op. cit., 154.

with the statement *"In the person of Jesus Christ God took our human place"*,[537] has no obvious theological basis which would require the privileging of this one concept. For Bonhoeffer, being-for-others goes to the very heart of who God is. Hence for humanity to live in redeemed freedom, to live in Christ, as participants in his life, death and resurrection in the restored image of God, takes nothing away from the unique and unrepeatable work of Christ and indeed is only made possible through that work. As Bonhoeffer states in *After Ten Years*, as human beings, we cannot live the life Christ lived or die the death he died, nor are we called to do so. But by the grace of God we are called to participate in his risen life. Again this serves to emphasise the point we have made repeatedly, that Bonhoeffer avoids viewing divine and human freedom or action in terms of competition. It is the concept of vicarious action or deputyship which gives content to the intrinsic connection between freedom and responsibility, ensuring that the ethical implications of redeemed freedom are not obscured by a purely forensic understanding of justification which has no impact on life.

*Correspondence with Reality*

It is this concern to craft an ethic which reckons with the realities of life which informs Bonhoeffer's discussion of 'correspondence with reality'. As early as 1931, in a lecture 'The History of Systematic Theology in the Twentieth Century', Bonhoeffer had argued that theology had failed adequately to answer Feuerbach's two questions to religion.[538] In Chapter 2, we noted Bonhoeffer's concern to address Feuerbach's first question about truth. However, Feuerbach's second question concerning 'correspondence with real life',[539] was of equal concern to him. Bonhoeffer begins the section 'History and Good' with the assertion that there can be no theoretical concept of 'the good' abstracted from the particularity of human existence in history and in society. Hence the responsible life must be characterised by action in 'correspondence with reality' (*Wirklichkeitgemäßheit*). Once again, the person of Christ is central to Bonhoeffer's argument. In the section 'Christ, Reality and Good', he had defined reality christologically. The 'realisation of the real'[540] is action in conformity with Christ. So action which is in accordance with reality recognises that humanity and the world are both judged by God and

---

[537] Ibid. 155.
[538] DBW 11, 140 at 148-9.
[539] *Übereinstimmung mit dem wirklichen Leben.*
[540] DBW 6, 34.

reconciled to God in Christ, 'the real one, that is the incarnate God'.[541] However, argues Bonhoeffer, the decision as to whether an action is really in conformation to Christ is a judgement which must be left to God. The agent acts in the knowledge that in Christ, God became human and in so doing said 'Yes' to humanity. In the light of that knowledge, he makes no attempt to justify himself or to claim the rightness of his action, but places it into the hands of God.[542] 'The responsible, historical act is essentially characterised by ultimate ignorance of one's own good and evil and hence dependence on grace.'[543] However, this concept must be sharply distinguished from the 'servile consideration in the face of the facts', rightly derided by Nietzsche.[544] James Burtness, who characterises Bonhoeffer's ethics as consequentialist or teleological does not seem to have given this disclaimer sufficient credence. He equates the will of God with 'the future' and asserts: 'The emphasis upon the future places Bonhoeffer with those ethicists who concentrate on the consequences of actions rather than on the motives out of which the actions are done. It is not the rightness of an action but the result of an action which commends it.'[545] However, for Bonhoeffer, true responsible action neither colludes with the factual situation, taking success as a plumbline, nor does it set itself on a collision course against the facts. The distinction between the two emerges clearly in Bethge's comments on Bonhoeffer's response to the early successes of the German military offensive. The person of responsibility must recognise the historical 'Yes' to Hitler's victory over France, without confusing this with a theological or ethical 'Yes'. He must acknowledge that theology cannot undo what has happened, but must reckon with it, rather than live in unreality.[546]

*Guilt and Conscience*

In the light of this analysis, the close connection between freedom and guilt at which we have already hinted, becomes apparent. Given the traditional preoccupation with freedom from guilt in much ethical theory, Bonhoeffer's insistence that acceptance of guilt is constitutive of

---

[541] Ibid., 261; Bonhoeffer continues 'Action in accordance with Christ is in accordance with reality, because it lets the world be the world, because it reckons with the world as world and yet never loses sight of the fact that in Jesus Christ, the world is loved, judged and reconciled by God.' Ibid., 263.
[542] Ibid., 268; ET 234.
[543] Ibid.
[544] Ibid., 260.
[545] Burtness J. *Shaping the Future: The Ethics of Dietrich Bonhoeffer* (Fortress 1985), 16.
[546] DB 587.

responsible action is one of the most radical and perceptive insights in his attempt to re-formulate Christian ethics. The one who acts responsibly is not promised freedom from guilt but is given the freedom to be guilty. However, closer examination of the *Ethics* texts makes it clear that Bonhoeffer distinguishes between the two quite distinct types of guilt. The first type of guilt is the subject under discussion in the fragment 'Guilt, Justification and Renewal', which was probably written during the second half of 1941.[547] At the heart of this section lies a 'Confession of Guilt' on behalf of the church in which Bonhoeffer argues that the root cause of this guilt is to be traced not primarily to a catalogue of individual sins, but to a much more fundamental falling away from a destiny of conformation to Christ and hence from true humanity.[548] We might define this as the guilt of inaction and failure to take responsibility, which arises from freedom for self, rather than freedom for God and for others. When Bonhoeffer moves on to address the specific outworking of this alienation from Christ, it is telling that, at the heart of his indictment lies not wrong action, but inaction, not active evil, but the failure to speak out which colludes with evil and leaves it unchecked. The church's silence, her failure to proclaim the truth or to raise her voice against evil, and in particular the treatment of the Jews, runs as a recurrent motif throughout.[549] Where, as we have seen, on Bonhoeffer's definition, free and responsible action steps out in faith and takes risks, the hallmark of the church within Germany, including the Confessing Church, has been a concern for her own self-preservation and safety, epitomised by her inactivity in the face of evil. Bonhoeffer writes: 'The Church confesses that she has craved security, tranquillity, peace, possessions, honour, to which she had no right and so has not restrained peoples desires but encouraged them.'[550] Writing later from prison on the occasion of his godson's baptism, the indictment is even more sharply focused: 'Our church which has been fighting in these years only for its self preservation, as though that were an end in itself, is incapable of taking the word of reconciliation and redemption to humanity and the world.'[551] The church has sought freedom for itself, rather than seeking to be free for God and for others. However, despite the focus in the confession on the collective guilt of the church, as we have seen throughout our discussion,

---

[547] Editors' Introduction to DBW 6, 17, 19.
[548] DBW 6, 125; ET 110.
[549] 'She was silent when she should have cried out because the blood of the innocent was crying aloud to heaven.' (DBW 6, 129; ET 113), '[S]he has not raised her voice on behalf of the victims... She is guilty of the deaths of the weakest and most defenceless brothers of Jesus Christ' (Ibid., 130; ET 114).
[550] Ibid., 131, ET 115.
[551] LPP 300.

individual responsibility is never subsumed or obliterated within the corporate. The individual, unequivocally including Bonhoeffer himself, is equally implicated in the guilt of the church.[552] But it is only in the light of the grace and forgiveness of Christ that an individual is set free to take responsibility for his own guilt and is freed from the tendency to apportion blame, to point to others as more guilty than him or herself.

The second exploration of guilt comes in 'History and Good', in the section on the structure of the responsible life. If, as we have suggested, the first type of guilt is characterised by the failure to act which is rooted in the preservation of one's own freedom, the second, in contrast, is the guilt which is the inevitable corollary of responsible action, life lived in freedom for God and for others. Once again the discussion is framed christologically. Jesus Christ, the one in whom all responsible action originates, is the one in whom freedom from sin and the bearing of guilt are inextricably connected. It is 'in this sinless-guilty Jesus Christ that each vicarious, responsible act has its origin.'[553] Bonhoeffer traces an intrinsic relationship between the free venture of faith and the risk of loss of reputation and the incurring of guilt, and concludes that to act responsibly means inevitably to incur guilt. This reality, as Bonhoeffer recognises, flies directly in the face of the universal human concern to avoid guilt and to maintain a clear conscience and turns traditional Christian ethics on its head. Later, writing from Tegel, Bonhoeffer would reflect that the prevailing sin of the German middle classes was 'fear of free responsibility.'[554] True responsible action does not offer either the luxury of a clear conscience or the guarantee that the intrinsic virtue of an action will be recognised by all right-thinking people, but only the freedom to be guilty, trusting in the grace and forgiveness of God.

The paper *After Ten Years*, offers further reflection upon the same theme. Bonhoeffer argues that for most of German history, it could safely be assumed that to act in freedom and to serve one's nation amounted to the same thing. However, amidst an evil regime, where the sense of national vocation had become distorted, what was required was 'free and

---

[552] It is surely the case that Bonhoeffer's decision to return from America was fuelled by the sense that to sit out the war in safety would be to evade responsibility and so to incur guilt.

[553] DBW 6, 276; ET 241. cf. the discussion of the ambiguity of Christ as sinner and sinless one in C, 107-8.

[554] LPP 345; Bonhoeffer seems to have the same idea in view in a letter to Maria where he writes 'I think that the weakness of our class stems mainly from its misgivings' ... Simple folk (sic) ... make more mistakes, but they also do more good because the road to action doesn't traverse so many misgivings.' *Love Letters from Cell 92* ed. von Bismarck R-A. and Kabitz U. Trans. Brownjohn J. (Harper Collins 1994), 195.

responsible action, even in opposition to one's calling and mission.'[555] In such a situation, true Christian freedom was possible only at the expense of freedom as a German and loyalty to the Fatherland. 'Only today', he writes, 'are Germans beginning to discover what free responsibility means. It depends on a God who demands the free faith venture of responsible action and who promises forgiveness and consolation to the one who becomes guilty in the process.'[556] To act responsibly is not to find a way to emerge from the situation unspotted by guilt, but to look to the needs of the future generation. 'It is only from this question, with its responsibility towards history, that fruitful solutions can come, even if for the time being they are very humiliating.'[557]

It is in this context of acceptance of guilt that the question of conscience emerges.[558] Although the parameters of this discussion preclude a detailed exploration, there are a number of points which need to be emphasised at this juncture, particularly in terms of the relationship between conscience and guilt.[559] Where for Luther, conscience was viewed as a positive asset which awakens a knowledge of guilt and so leads the sinner to the justifying grace of Christ, for Bonhoeffer, conscience is generally seen negatively in terms of self-justification and avoidance of guilt.[560] Conscience, asserts Bonhoeffer, did not exist in the primeval state, but epitomises fallen humanity's ill-fated attempt to acquire absolute freedom, to become *sicut deus*, to be his own arbiter of good and evil.[561] It testifies to humanity's internal division, and to a continual quest for some universal law of good against which to measure its actions and so achieve unity within itself. Hence, asserts Bonhoeffer:

> The call of conscience has its origin and its goal in the *autonomy* of the individual I. In obeying the call, it is a matter of the individual himself, each time realising anew this autonomy, which has its origin beyond his own will and knowledge 'in Adam'.[562]

---

[555] LPP 6.
[556] Ibid.
[557] Ibid.
[558] cf. also the discussion of conscience in DBWE 2, 139ff, 148, 155.
[559] James Burtness in *Shaping the Future: The Ethics of Dietrich Bonhoeffer* op. cit., lists the major references to conscience within Bonhoeffer's work at pp 93-5.
[560] Bonhoeffer is critical of Karl Holl's appraisal of Luther's theology as a 'theology of conscience'. cf. 'The Question of Humanity in Contemporary Philosophy and Theology' DBW 10, 357 at 370.
[561] cf. DBW 1, 69.
[562] DBW 6, 278 (my italics).

Conscience is the reflection of the self-constituting I which seeks to justify itself before God, before other human beings and before itself. In marked contrast, for the Christian, the unity of his human existence no longer consists in his own autonomy, but is found beyond his own existence in Christ, in the surrender of his autonomy in exchange for true freedom in Christ. For the Christian, the natural conscience, which looks only for self-justification 'is overcome by the conscience which is set free in Jesus Christ and which calls me to unity with myself in Jesus Christ. Jesus Christ has become my conscience'.[563] But, as we have already seen, Jesus Christ is himself the one who, though without sin, incurred guilt. So, it is Jesus Christ who 'frees the conscience for the service of God and our neighbour, the one who frees the conscience even and precisely where the person enters into the fellowship of human guilt.'[564] The conscience freed from the law is free to incur guilt for the sake of the other. 'The freed conscience is not anxious, like one bound by the law, but is wide open to the neighbour and their concrete need.'[565] Its motivation is no longer self-justification, but obedience to the call of God.

Nevertheless, for Bonhoeffer, there remains a tension between the redeemed conscience and responsibility. Even the conscience set free in Christ is a call to unity within the self, and responsible action should never be at the expense of the destruction of that internal unity. Such action would be self-defeating because it would render true responsibility impossible. It follows that some individuals may be able to carry a greater burden of guilt than others and hence the truly responsible act in any given situation will differ according to the capacity of the agent.[566] Furthermore, even the freed conscience must reckon with the law, which Bonhoeffer sees in terms of the Decalogue, the Sermon on the Mount and the ethical teaching of the apostles. However, as he had argued in the section on 'The Ultimate and the Penultimate', Bonhoeffer continues to insist that Jesus Christ, not the law is the ultimate. For this reason, when the law and responsible action come into conflict, the free decision must be made for Christ.[567] So, asserts Bonhoeffer, 'Responsibility is bound by conscience, but conscience is free through responsibility.'[568] Bonhoeffer reiterates that the one who incurs guilt in this way does not do so:

---

[563] Ibid. 279.
[564] DBW 6, 279; ET 244.
[565] Ibid.
[566] Ibid., 281-2; ET 246-7.
[567] Ibid., 283; ET 247.
[568] Ibid.

[I]n the impious insolence of his own power, but in the knowledge that he is compelled towards this freedom and that in it, he is dependent upon mercy. Before other people, it is necessity which justifies the one who acts in free responsibility, before himself, his free conscience speaks for him, but before God, he hopes only for mercy. [569]

*Freedom and Simplicity*

It might well be objected at this point that Bonhoeffer is altogether too sanguine in his assumption that the will of God is any given situation is sufficiently clear to enable the free and responsible act. Surely the individual will be paralysed by the bewildering array of possible ethical choices. However, Bonhoeffer argues that precisely the opposite is the case, because true freedom, in marked contrast to the oppression of unending moral dilemma which results from the absolutising of freedom, is the freedom of simplicity. Hence for Bonhoeffer, unlike the standard approach to ethics, freedom is not essentially about being genuinely unconstrained when confronted by ethical dilemma, the freedom to choose between good and evil, but a freedom *from* ethical dilemma. In the fragment 'God's Love and the Decay of the World', written shortly after 'History and Good', Bonhoeffer points to the figure of Jesus portrayed in the Gospels, as the true image of God, who lives out of 'a complete freedom which is not bound by the law of logical alternatives'[570]. Although in the eyes of the Pharisees Jesus is a lawbreaker and a nihilist, his freedom is not antinomian but arises out of the simplicity of obedience to the will of God. The relevant section merits quoting at length:

> No one can discern in Jesus the uncertainty and timidity of one who acts arbitrarily, but his freedom gives to him and to his followers in all their actions a peculiar quality of sureness, unquestionableness and radiance...The freedom of Jesus is not the arbitrary choice of one amongst innumerable possibilities; it consists on the contrary precisely in the complete *simplicity* of his action, which is never confronted by a plurality of possibilities, conflicts or alternatives, but always only by one thing. This one thing Jesus calls the will of God...This will of God is his life. He lives and acts not by the knowledge of good and evil but by the will of God. There is only one will of God. In it the origin is recovered; in it there is established the freedom and the *simplicity* of all action.[571]

---

[569] Ibid., 283.
[570] Ibid., 314; ET 29.
[571] Ibid., 315 ET 30 (italics mine).

For Bonhoeffer, the idealising of unrestrained freedom had brought humanity face to face with the impossibility of making the right choice. However, where the absolutising of freedom and choice confronts humanity with an oppressive array of options, Jesus acts out of his centre in God and hence the call to life in Jesus is the 'liberating call to simplicity and to conversion',[572] the call to participation in Christ's life in union with God. Simplicity is not of course to be equated with the simplistic or the ill-considered, nor with the psuedo-piety which is actually self-deception. Bonhoeffer fully accepts that 'The will of God may lie very deeply concealed beneath a great number of available possibilities.'[573] However, the key to the weighing up of alternatives, the earnest struggle and prayerful consideration which he calls the 'proving' of the will of God arises primarily out of relationship with Christ, the one to whom the Christian seeks continually to be conformed. In the reality of that relationship, where the agent's primary concern is not self-justification or the avoidance of guilt, but obedience to Christ, there is 'freedom to make a real decision.'[574]

*Freedom, Obedience and Responsibility*

However, this reference to 'obedience to Christ' raises a further issue. We have already noted the way in which Bonhoeffer's discussions of creatureliness, obedience and responsibility can be seen as offering complementary reflections on the relationship between freedom and constraint. However, although these three concepts fulfil a similar function within the discussion, there is a clear difference in emphasis. In the discussion of creatureliness and obedience, the primary focus was human freedom as freedom for God, although the ethical implications in terms of freedom for others were always in view. In our discussion of responsibility, the emphasis has fallen more clearly on freedom for others.

The question which immediately arises concerns the relationship between responsibility and obedience. Has responsibility replaced or eclipsed obedience in Bonhoeffer's thinking and if so, is this ethic of free responsibility an ethic for the ruling elite, those whose place in society affords them the opportunity to influence events, whilst for most, the daily reality is obedience and subservience? Certainly in so far as a discussion of responsibility is rooted in the context of opposition to Hitler, a brief survey of the various groups involved in the resistance movement show that a

---

[572] Ibid., 321; ET 35.
[573] Ibid., 323; ET 38.
[574] Ibid., 327; ET 40.

majority, although by no means all came from the German ruling classes. The group centred on the *Abwehr*, of which Bonhoeffer was a member, was largely drawn from among the upper echelons of society. The Kreisau circle was headed up by Helmuth von Moltke and Peter Yorck von Wartenburg both sons of the Prussian aristocracy. Another group gained the sobriquet 'the Counts' Group', on account of the number of titled individuals involved.[575] Bonhoeffer anticipates the question and agrees that for all but the privileged few, daily life is hedged around by restrictions which allow little scope for true freedom of action. However, whilst recognising the tendency of social order to rob people of 'the creative ethical power, freedom',[576] he argues that to see responsibility as the privilege or the responsibility of the elite is to misunderstand the nature of the concept. Responsibility is not the preserve of the few, but, as Bonhoeffer had argued in his earliest academic dissertation and in particular his discussion of personhood, responsibility arises in every personal encounter. Hence responsible action is not limited to major ethical decisions, the preserve of the few, but arises wherever people are in relationship with another. Every personal relationship, even hierarchical relationships and relationships of dependence, offers the potential for a mutuality of free responsibility for the other. Obedience and responsibility are complementary:

> Obedience without freedom is slavery; freedom without obedience is arbitrary self-will. Obedience restrains freedom and freedom ennobles obedience. Obedience binds the creature to the Creator and freedom enables the creature to stand before the Creator as one who is made in his image.' [577]

Once again, at the root of this analysis lies Bonhoeffer's christological focus. Obedience, like vicarious action or correspondence with reality, is given content and can truly be understood only in the light of Jesus Christ, who redefines the concepts of freedom and obedience. Christ 'stands before God as one who is both obedient and free. As the obedient one, he does his Father's will in blind compliance with the law which is commanded him, and as the free one, he says yes to his will out of his own most personal knowledge, with open eyes and a joyous heart.'[578] Freedom and obedience

---

[575] As research by Allen and others has demonstrated, Hitler gained strong support amongst the German middle classes. Allen W. S. *The Nazi Seizure of Power: The Experience of a Single German Town 1922-1945* Revised Edition (New York: Franklin Watts 1984). Groups led by workers and students emerged but were destroyed with relative ease.
[576] DBW 6, 286; ET 251
[577] Ibid., 288.
[578] Ibid.

or constraint are understood relationally on the model of the relationship between Father and Son. It is in responsibility, argues Bonhoeffer that both freedom and obedience are realised. To act responsibly means to live in the tension between freedom and obedience. The two are held together in a unity which both transcends and affirms their distinctiveness. To separate them leads either to a Kantian ethic of duty or to an ethic of irresponsible genius. The one who acts in responsibility is responsible only to Christ and can look nowhere else for justification of his action.

> The responsible person who stands between obligation and freedom, who must dare to act in freedom as one under obligation, finds his justification neither in his obligation nor in his freedom, but solely in him who has put him in this (humanly impossible) situation and who requires this deed of him. [579]

Where in *Cost*, the tension between freedom and obedience is expressed paradoxically: obedience is freedom, freedom is obedience, in *Ethics*, obedience and freedom operate, as it were as twin poles, which designate the parameters of responsible action.

## A Responsible Ethic - Concluding Observations

In this chapter we have focused on the relationship between freedom and responsibility, seeing the latter both as a variation on the theme of freedom within limits and as the foundation for the articulation of Bonhoeffer's radical challenge to traditional ethics. This is a robustly Christian ethic, an ethic of Christ-shaped living, which resists any attempt to reduce it to a set of principles to be sieved off and applied more generally. We have noted repeatedly the christological foundation to the different ingredients of the schema. Jesus Christ is the responsible person par excellence, the one who embodies vicarious action, the reality to which all ethical action must conform, the innocent one who accepted guilt for others. But it is also an ethic that takes seriously the realities of human existence and fallibility. The backdrop to our discussion has been Bonhoeffer's involvement in the conspiracy against Hitler. We traced the move away from a traditional Lutheran 'two spheres' approach towards a commitment to political involvement and finally an attempted coup d'état. We suggested that the decisive issue was the persecution of the Jews, which highlighted the inadequacy of an ethic of passive resistance when the innocent suffering of others is at issue. In our discussion of responsible action, we engaged with

---

[579] Ibid., 289.

the criticisms levelled at Bonhoeffer's understanding of vicarious action or deputyship and argued that this concept is fundamental to Bonhoeffer's insistence on the inseparability of life and faith, ethics and doctrine. However, we suggested that Bonhoeffer's most original and radical contribution to the ethical debate lies in his discussion of guilt, which subverts traditional ethics' implicit goal of maintaining freedom from guilt.

Undoubtedly Bonhoeffer's understanding of free and responsible action arose and was sharpened as he wrestled with issues forced upon him and his fellow conspirators in a situation of 'extraordinary necessity'. However, whilst the dilemma of those forced to choose between treason or collusion with an evil regime is an exceptional one, as we suggested in our introduction, it may be that the extremity of the situation actually serves to highlight the some of the inadequacies of a more traditional approach of much ethical theory. Where, as Bonhoeffer suggests, traditional ethics concerns itself with doing good and being good, the agent is frequently paralysed into inaction in the face of the range of possible choices or opts for passivity to avoid making the wrong decision and incurring guilt. Bonhoeffer constructs an ethic which 'frees for action',[580] in which the parameters are marked not by the deceptive safety of norms or principles but by the person of Christ, the one who both models and enables the responsible life of freedom for others.

---

[580] cf. our discussion of Bethge's comment above.

# Chapter Six
# Freedom in a World Come of Age

**Introduction**

Eberhard Bethge has written memorably of the gradual silencing of Bonhoeffer by the Nazi regime.[581] However, from the perspective of our theme, Bonhoeffer's life can also be seen as an individual embodiment of the gradual but relentless erosion of human freedom which characterised National Socialism. To reformulate Bethge's well known account: In 1936, Bonhoeffer's freedom as an academic was curtailed when he was barred from his lecturer's post at Berlin; in 1940 his freedom as a preacher was abruptly terminated when he was banned from the pulpit; in 1941 his freedom as a writer was severely limited, when he was forbidden by the regime to publish his written work; in 1943, freedom of movement and even the freedom for theological conversation was denied as he was arrested and imprisoned. Finally, in 1945, even the freedom of life itself was surrendered on the gallows at Flossenbürg. Ironically, however, it was perhaps in those final months in prison, denied most of the basic human freedoms, that Bonhoeffer's life was most clearly marked by the 'hilaritas' of the one who is free in Christ.[582] Although he continued to pray for his own physical freedom,[583] the overriding impression of the Tegel correspondence is of one who had discovered a new freedom for theological reflection. By November 1943, Bonhoeffer had arranged a system for smuggling letters out of prison which meant that he could write freely, without concern for censorship, to his friend Eberhard Bethge.

---

[581] WCOA, 22.
[582] cf. the accounts of fellow prisoners Harald Poelchau and Fabian von Schlabrendorff in IKDB.
[583] LPP 132 'I'm now praying quite simply for freedom ... I sometimes get very angry at not being free yet.'

## The Tegel Theology in Context

In the scholarly discussion of *Letters and Papers*, most interest has inevitably been focused on the explicitly theological letters, beginning with the one dated 30th April 1944 which contains some of Bonhoeffer's most frequently cited words: 'What is bothering me incessantly is the question of what Christianity really is and who Jesus Christ is for us today',[584] and ending with the last extant letter which is dated 23rd August 1944. Hence the material available to us covers a period of less than four months and is incomplete, given that the later correspondence which did not survive, would almost certainly have continued the theological discussion.[585] Within the so-called 'theological letters', attention has centred on a number of apparently enigmatic phrases,[586] now well known and often cited, in particular 'religionless Christianity', the 'non-religious interpretation of Biblical concepts' and 'world come of age'.

I have already argued that the temptation to privilege the theology of the Tegel correspondence or to use it as a plumbline against which to measure the earlier writings should be avoided, and I do not propose to enter upon a detailed discussion as to evidence of the themes of *Letters and Papers* in the earlier writings. That task has already been undertaken by Ernst Feil, who gave particular attention to discussions of 'the world' and 'worldliness' within Bonhoeffer's writings,[587] and more recently by Ralf Wüstenberg, who focused on the criticism of religion within the Bonhoeffer corpus.[588] However, I will make frequent reference, throughout the chapter, to the relationship between these *Letters* and parts of *Ethics*, where I will suggest some striking parallels which have received inadequate scholarly attention.

In view of the parameters of this study, I will confine my attention to those sections and ideas which impinge most directly upon our theme,

---

[584] LPP 379.

[585] Bethge was forced to destroy a number of letters and notes from September and October 1944, at the time of his own arrest on 28th October 1944. cf. Bethge E. 'Wie die Tegeler Briefe überlebten' in *In Zitz gab es keine Juden* (Chr. Kaiser Verlag 1989) 152. Later letters to his fiancée Maria von Wedemeyer and poems dating from September, November and December 1944 have survived.

[586] In a letter to Bethge in 1967, Barth speaks somewhat dismissively of 'catchy phrases'. Karl Barth, *Letters 1961-1968*, tr. Bromiley G. W. ed. Fangmeier J. and Stoevesandt H. cited by Marsh C. *Reclaiming Dietrich Bonhoeffer* (Oxford OUP 1994), 26.

[587] Feil E. *The Theology of Dietrich Bonhoeffer* Op. cit.

[588] Wüstenberg R. K. *Glauben als Leben Dietrich Bonhoeffer und die nichtreligiöse Interpretation biblischer Begriffe* (Peter Lang 1996).

although, as will become apparent, my case is that a number of these well known, but apparently esoteric ideas and phrases, are cast in a fresh light when encountered against the backdrop of *Ethics,* and Bonhoeffer's reflections upon freedom. In particular, I will suggest that, read in the light of our discussion of divine and human freedom, Bonhoeffer's theological reflections in the *Letters* can be seen in terms of a deliberation upon three possible responses to the crucial question, posed in the letter of 30th April 1944: 'Who is Jesus Christ for us today', that is, in a 'world come of age'?

The first response has its roots in a false interpretation of 'worldliness' and, in Bonhoeffer's terms involves leaving the world 'to its own devices', endorsing its pursuit of an inauthentic freedom *from* God. The second, is the negative response of religion to the 'world come of age', a response which colludes with a competitive view of divine and human freedom and so sets itself in opposition to human autonomy, in a misguided attempt to keep the world in infancy and so preserve space for God. The third, firmly rooted within a *theologia crucis*, sees authentic freedom in terms the whole of life lived for God and for others, in the fullness of God-given potential and destiny and in recognition of Christ's claim on the whole of life, a world freed to be worldly, humanity freed to be fully human. In order to test this thesis, I will examine some of the main themes which arise in the so-called theological letters, 'worldliness', 'world come of age', 'non-religious interpretation of biblical concepts' and the *'theologia crucis'*. I will then examine the 'Outline for a Book', sketched during the latter months of Bonhoeffer's imprisonment, which as I will argue below, deserves particular attention, before concluding with a discussion of the poem 'Stations on the Road to Freedom'.

However, as a preliminary to our main discussion, I must first refer in some detail to the *Ethics* fragment 'The Concrete Command and the Divine Mandates'. This was the section of *Ethics* on which Bonhoeffer had been working at the time of his arrest in April 1943 and hence constitutes Bonhoeffer's last concentrated theological thinking before the theological sections of the letters from prison.[589] I hope to show that despite the year which separates the two, a careful examination of the *Ethics* fragment both demonstrates a number of dramatic parallels with the theological letters and offers a constructive way into these tantalising later writings.

---

[589] DB 625.

*The Ethics Fragment 'The Concrete Command and the Divine Mandates'*

The focus of this section of *Ethics* is the church's mandate to proclaim Christ, and, as elsewhere in *Ethics*, Bonhoeffer reiterates his conviction that the whole Christ, the eternal Son, the incarnate God, the crucified reconciler and the risen and ascended Lord must be proclaimed.[590] I will be referring back to this section at various points throughout this chapter, but at this stage will focus specifically on the sub-section headed 'The crucified reconciler'. Here, Bonhoeffer's discussion of the cross is particularly revealing when considered in the light of the prison writings, where, as we will see, the cross and indeed a *theologia crucis*, is at the centre of Bonhoeffer's thoughts on the relationship between Christ and the 'world come of age'. Bonhoeffer claims: 'The cross of reconciliation is the *setting free for life before God* in the midst of the godless world; it is the *setting free for life in genuine worldliness*.'[591] The argument here clearly builds on the discussion in 'Christ, Reality and Good' where, as we saw in Chapter 5, Bonhoeffer mounted a vigorous assault on the Lutheran doctrine of 'two spheres', the tendency to speak of God and the world in isolation from one another which failed to recognise Christ's radical work of reconciliation. For Bonhoeffer, the cross is the place where judgement and reconciliation are polemically united in a way which frees both humanity and the world fully to realise their potential, precisely as humanity and as world. Bonhoeffer continues, by way of explanation: 'The proclamation of the cross of reconciliation is a *setting free* because it leaves behind the vain attempts to deify the world and because it has overcome the divisions, tensions and conflicts between "Christian" and "worldly" and calls for simple action and life in faith in the reconciliation of God and the world which has been accomplished.'[592]

The two sides of this last assertion are equally critical to Bonhoeffer's argument. The cross frees the world from the propensity to self-deification, the desire to be *sicut deus*, which had constituted the fall out of original created freedom into the bondage of solipsistic self-assertion and self-absorption. But it also destroys the dualisms and polarisations between God and his world, which are ultimately denials of the breadth of Christ's lordship over the whole of life. Where Luther's concept of the Christian as

---

[590] Interestingly, Bonhoeffer adds a fourth category 'The Eternal Son' to the three-fold expression of the ministry of Christ, which appears regularly in *Ethics* and featured in the closing chapter of *Cost*.
[591] DBW 6, 404; ET 297 (my italics).
[592] Ibid., my italics.

*simul iustus et peccator* had often been applied individualistically, Bonhoeffer asserts its cosmic significance. Only in the cross can the apparently contradictory realities of the godlessness of the world and its reconciliation to God in Christ, be held together. In a section which both points back to the *imago dei* theology of *Creation and Fall* and forward to the Tegel theology, he asserts:

> Left to its own devices, the worldly neither wants nor is able to be merely worldly, but desperately and frantically searches for the deification of the worldly with the result that precisely this emphatically declared and exclusively worldly life lapses into an inauthentic semi-worldliness; *it lacks the freedom* and the courage for an authentic and thorough-going worldliness, which means letting the world be what in reality it is before God, namely a world reconciled with God in its godlessness.[593]

Bonhoeffer argues that without the reconciling work of Christ, the world is incapable of fulfilling its God given purpose and becoming fully itself as world. Instead it becomes caught up in the futile and ultimately destructive quest for self-deification and in the process forfeits its authentic worldliness. The parallels with Bonhoeffer's understanding of the fall of human beings are clear. The section concludes with the startling claim that '*authentic worldliness exists precisely and only on the basis of the proclamation of the cross of Jesus Christ.*'[594] As I will argue, the relationship between the cross of Christ and the worldliness of the world is foundational to an understanding of the Tegel theology.

Although it would be an over-statement to claim that this fragment of *Ethics* offers some sort of exclusive hermeneutical key to *Letters and Papers*, it seems clear, even from a superficial reading of the section, that a number of the key themes which will emerge again in the theological sections of *Letters and Papers* are, at least *in nuce*, already very much at the forefront of Bonhoeffer's thinking. Furthermore, whilst, as we will see below, the influence of Bonhoeffer's prison reading, particularly of Dilthey must be given its full weight, there are remarkable congruencies between this section and the Tegel theology, not merely in terms of subject matter, but at the level of language and phraseology. The question of the godlessness of the world, the quest for an authentic worldliness, the concern for Christ's lordship over the whole of life, not just the 'religious' parts, and the place of the cross, all feature prominently in the theology of

---

[593] Ibid., my italics.
[594] Ibid., italics original.

the Tegel correspondence. But equally the presence of ideas familiar to the reader of *Letters and Papers*, such as 'life before God' and the leaving of the world 'to its own devices' as well as the language of 'worldliness' and 'godlessness' is striking. The connections between this section of *Ethics* and the Tegel letters have received only sparse scholarly attention. Although Feil, in *The Theology of Dietrich Bonhoeffer*,[595] alludes briefly to the relevant paragraph as part of his historical survey of Bonhoeffer's understanding of the world and notes the link between a theology of the cross and the worldliness of the world, he makes no explicit reference to the connections between this section of *Ethics* and the Tegel theology, or to the marked congruity in language and subject matter. However, it is our case that any serious reflection upon the theology of the prison letters must reckon with this discussion.

## The Theological Letters

### Worldliness

I begin by focusing on the concept of 'worldliness', both because it will lead us on to other related ideas such as 'world come of age', and because interpretations of this term, without regard to its context, have been responsible to serious misreadings of the Tegel theology. In particular such renderings have encouraged a facile equation between the 'godlessness' or 'religionlessness' which Bonhoeffer perceived in Germany in the 1940s and the secularity of the 1960s, a correlation which at a distance of thirty years seems to say the least, questionable and a number of theologians who eagerly embraced Bonhoeffer on those terms in the 1960s seem prepared to concede that de Gruchy's assessment of the period is terms of the 'creative misuse of Bonhoeffer' is not so far off the mark.[596] These difficulties are compounded by the current translation of 'weltlich' as 'secular'.[597]

---

[595] Op. cit., 149.
[596] De Gruchy J. ed. *Dietrich Bonhoeffer, Witness to Jesus Christ* (Collins 1988) 36, cited with approval by Peter Selby in 'Who is Jesus Christ for us today?' in de Gruchy ed. *Bonhoeffer for a New Day: Theology in a Time of Transition* (Eerdmans 1997).
[597] Ironically the 1953 and 1967 editions rendered 'weltlich' and its cognates as 'worldly', but the current (1971) edition, presumably influenced by interpretations of Bonhoeffer in the 1960s which viewed him as an advocate of secularity, translates it as 'secular'. As a result, Bonhoeffer's comments are often assumed to carry the weight of arguments which attached to the concept of secularism in the 1960s. An exception comes at LPP 286, where 'weltlich' is translated as 'worldly' cf. DBW 8 416.

Although no translation is without its problems, I take the view that the use of 'secular' and its cognates is particularly infelicitous, because it enshrines precisely the polarisation between sacred and secular, religious life and 'the rest of life' to which Bonhoeffer, both in *Ethics* and in the Tegel correspondence, is so implacably opposed. For this reason, in my translations I will use the word 'worldly'.[598] For Bonhoeffer, 'Weltlichkeit' is not a term which endorses a dichotomy between the sacred and the secular, an approach which he has already dismissed in his discussion of 'thinking in two spheres' in *Ethics*,[599] but which embraces the whole of life. It is concerned with the world, and humanity as part of that world, becoming fully itself, precisely because Christ is Lord of the whole world. Indeed 'wholeness' is a crucial underlying theme in both *Ethics* and *Letters*. As we shall see, an important key to an understanding of Bonhoeffer's opposition of 'religion' to 'worldliness', or to the 'world come of age', arises precisely out of what he saw as religion's failure to recognise and affirm the wholeness of life, which had been such a crucial element in the christologically centred theology of *Ethics*. The fact that the same concern pervades the Tegel correspondence is masked, at least to some extent by the translator's equation of 'worldliness' with secularism.

For Bonhoeffer, the 'worldly world' is not an aberration to be regretted or opposed, but is precisely what the world is supposed to be. The problem, as Bonhoeffer perceives it, is that instead of calling the world into true worldliness, into the freedom to fulfil its true potential as world, religion, in its opposition to human development, has tended to affirm the world in its [false] assumption that human progress is inherently anti-Christian.[600] Religion in its various forms has signally failed to proclaim Christ's place at the centre of life,[601] the fact that 'Jesus claims for himself and the kingdom of God the whole of human life in all its manifestations', and so has failed to point the way to authentic freedom in Christ.[602] Where the pietists sought to hold the world in tutelage, calling Canute-like for a return to intellectual infancy, despite the evidence of water lapping around their ankles, Bonhoeffer's contemporary Paul Althaus struggled to preserve a place for the church, but was otherwise content to leave the world 'to its

---

[598] This choice is of course not unproblematic, given the pejorative use of the term within some religious circles. Where I offer my own translation, the footnote will refer first to the German edition DBW 8, before giving the parallel reference in LPP.
[599] DBW 6, 41ff; ET 196ff.
[600] LPP 326.
[601] LPP 312.
[602] LPP 342.

own devices',[603] and the ultimately destructive quest for self-deification. In contrast, but with equally fatal results, religion in its Liberal Protestant manifestation, '[conceded] to the world the right to determine Christ's place in the world.'[604]

All these approaches, argues Bonhoeffer, bring religion into conflict with its own scriptures, particularly the Old Testament which never compartmentalised life into sacred and secular. Hence in the letter of 5th May, Bonhoeffer muses 'I'm thinking about how we can reinterpret in a 'worldly' sense - in the sense of the Old Testament and of John 1.14 - the concepts of repentance, faith, justification, rebirth and sanctification.'[605] Within the context of the letter, it is clear that for Bonhoeffer a 'worldly' interpretation is one which takes the incarnation, the reality that God took upon himself human flesh, with due seriousness. In the final section of the *Ethics* manuscript on which we reflected at the beginning of this chapter, Bonhoeffer had argued that the incarnation means that:

> [I]n Jesus Christ, the human being is made free to be really human (*wirklich Mensch*) before God. The 'Christian' element is not now something beyond the human element, but it must be in the midst of the human element. The Christian element is not an end in itself, but it consists in the fact that human beings both may and should live as human beings before God.[606]

In the incarnation, God frees humanity to be fully human, to fulfil its God-given potential and, by extension, frees the world to be fully itself. In an earlier *Ethics* fragment, 'Church and World', Bonhoeffer had reflected on the apparently contradictory Gospel texts Mk 9:40 ('Whoever is not against us is for us.') and Mt. 12:30 ('Whoever is not with me is against me.'), and had argued 'The greater the exclusiveness, the greater the freedom ...The more exclusively we acknowledge and confess Christ as our Lord, the more fully the wide range of his dominion will be disclosed to us.'[607] In *Letters*, these same ideas re-emerge. It is when Christ's claim to the whole of life is recognised and engaged with, that the world is most fully free to be itself, or to take up the musical imagery of the letter of 20th May 1944, 'Where the *cantus firmus* is clear and plain, the counterpoint

---

[603] cf. LPP 286, 327.
[604] LPP 327.
[605] LPP 286; John 1.14 reads 'And the Word became flesh and lived among us, and we have seen his glory, the glory as of a father's only son, full of grace and truth.'
[606] DBW 6, 404; ET 296-7.
[607] Ibid., 347; ET 58.

can be developed to its limits.'[608] Although Bonhoeffer never uses the precise term the *menschliche Mensch*, as a parallel to the worldliness of the world, he does speak of *Menschlichkeit*, which seems to embrace a similar idea of full humanity. The truly worldly world is made up of human beings who live their humanity to the full. Irenaeus's words, 'the glory of God is a person fully alive',[609] whilst never quoted by Bonhoeffer, in many ways encapsulate the heart of the Tegel theology.

I have already indicated my unease with any easy identification of the secularity of Europe in the 1960s and the Germany of 1944. In fact, it seems likely that the secularity of the 1960s may, in Bonhoeffer's eyes, have had more in common with the 'cheap grace' of *The Cost of Discipleship*, than with the worldliness of which he speaks from Tegel. I am encouraged in this suggestion by Bonhoeffer's letter of 21st July 1944, written just after the failure of the 20th July plot against Hitler, in which he speaks of the 'this-worldliness' (*Diessseitigkeit*) of Christianity, defining it first negatively and then positively. The relevant sections are worth quoting in full:

> In recent years I've come to recognise and understand more and more the profound this-worldliness of Christianity. The Christian is not a *homo religiosus* but a human being pure and simple, as Jesus - in clear distinction from John the Baptist - was a human being. I don't mean the shallow and banal this-worldliness of the enlightened, the busy, the comfortable or the lascivious but the profound this-worldliness characterised by discipline and in which the knowledge of death and resurrection is always present. [610]

To equate the secularism of the 1960s with 'the shallow and banal this-worldliness of the enlightened, the busy, the comfortable or the lascivious' would be too harsh a judgement, but it remains the case that the generation enjoying the freedom and fruits of the post-war recovery, the advent of consumerism and the sexual revolution, was scarcely one 'characterised by discipline and in which the knowledge of death and resurrection is always present.' Those marching in the streets of Paris in the heady days of 1968, or even those protesting against the war in Vietnam bore little in common with those standing, in 1944, like the biblical Jeremiah with whom

---

[608] LPP 303 cf. also 305, 311.
[609] Irenaeus *Adversus Haereses* IV XX.7, cited in Cocksworth C. *Holy, Holy, Holy: Worshipping the Trinitarian God* (London: Darton, Longmann & Todd 1997), 145.
[610] DBW 8 541; LPP 369.

Bonhoeffer identified so closely,[611] amid the ashes of their country's imminent defeat. Bonhoeffer continues with the positive side of the equation:

> By this-worldliness I mean to live in the fullness of life's duties, questions, successes and failures, experiences and perplexities. In so doing we throw ourselves completely into the arms of God, no longer taking seriously our own sufferings, but the sufferings of God in the world, then we watch with Christ in Gethsemane, and I think that is faith, that is metanoia: and that is how one becomes a human being and a Christian (cf. Jer. 45!).[612]

As with the concept of 'Weltlichkeit', 'this-worldliness' means living life to the full, not in some self-centred libertarianism, but a life fully given to God, participating in his sufferings. Hence when Bonhoeffer speaks of God as 'transcendent'[613] in the midst of life',[614] we should not make too facile an assumption that he is dissolving transcendence into immanence. On the contrary, Bonhoeffer is rejecting the picture of God as the *deus ex machina*, waiting passively in the wings for his prompt when human resources run out, and asserting God's claim to centre stage, in the whole of life.

## World Come of Age

Another closely related concept is that of the 'world come of age'. Although we cannot be certain as to the precise source for Bonhoeffer's use of the term (both Kant[615] and Dilthey[616] have been suggested, and for our purposes the origin of the phrase is of less importance than its usage by Bonhoeffer), it seems to have been in fairly common usage as an expression of humanity's status in the wake of the Enlightenment.[617] Kant's

---

[611] During this period, Bonhoeffer refers repeatedly to Jer 45.5 which reads 'And you, do you seek great things for yourself? Do not seek them; for I am going to bring disaster upon all flesh, says the LORD; but I will give you your life as a prize of war in every place to which you may go'.

[612] LPP 370.

[613] *jenseitig* translated as 'beyond' in LPP.

[614] DBW 8 408; LPP 282; the German 'mitten' conveys the sense of 'in the thick of'.

[615] Moltmann J. in 'Die Wirklichkeit der Welt und Gottes konkretes Gebot nach Dietrich Bonhoeffer' in *Mündige Welt* ed. Bethge E, Grunow R. in 4 volumes (Chr. Kaiser Verlag 1955-1963), 56.

[616] Feil op. cit. 178ff.

[617] 'Unmündigkeit' is commonly used in the German translation of the scriptures to convey a lack of Christian maturity, a remaining in infancy. cf. 1 Cor 3:1, 14:20; Eph. 4:14.

definition of 'enlightenment' (Aufklärung) as 'the departure of humanity from his self-inflicted immaturity...[from] the inability to use one's own reason without the guidance of someone else', is at heart a description of human autonomy.[618] Although Kant did not view God as a threat to human *Mündigkeit*, and indeed saw the existence of the deity as essential to his ethical understanding, the hegemony of reason, which became the enduring legacy of the Enlightenment, was often expressed in terms of a struggle for freedom from clericalism, and from a world view which was perceived to denigrate humanity and keep it in dependence. Both Nietzsche and Feuerbach viewed faith in God and human autonomy as in competition, with the corollary that human freedom was only achievable at the expense of faith in God, who was reduced to a dispensable obstacle to human maturity.

Feil writes that '[Bonhoeffer] tried to accept the autonomy and adulthood of humanity without reserve. But the decisive question for him was whether autonomy was necessarily the tribunal before which faith had to account for itself or, conversely whether autonomy was infringed upon by the mere fact that people follow Jesus Christ.'[619] However, if we take seriously the understanding of divine and human freedom which emerges from Bonhoeffer's earlier writings, the issue can be seen instead in terms of a choice between authentic freedom, which arises in relationship with Christ, as freedom for God and for others, and inauthentic freedom, the illegitimate and ultimately destructive attempt to be free for self, from God and others. In *Ethics*, Bonhoeffer had suggested that the standard ethical dichotomy between autonomy and heteronomy is to be resolved in the higher unity of christonomy,[620] and although this is not stated in such explicit terms in the prison letters, the christocentric nature of the Tegel theology, and in particular the repeated concern for the centrality of the lordship of Christ, would suggest that Bonhoeffer's convictions in this respect remain unchanged. Freedom in Christ is the solution to the dichotomy between religious infantalisation and the idolatrous absolutising of human autonomy.

What is really at issue here is the most fundamental of all questions, the nature of God himself. Where 'God' is a construct of Enlightenment thinking, the all powerful, all knowing Cartesian thinking subject writ large, rather than the biblical 'God and Father of our Lord Jesus Christ', who chooses, in his freedom, to be free for the world and not for himself, a

---

[618] Kant I. *Werke* VIII 35 'Was ist Aufklärung?' 1874 cited by Bethge in DB 770.
[619] Feil op. cit. 182.
[620] DBW 6, 406 footnote 3; ET 299 footnote.

false view of divine freedom emerges which sees it as constituted in God's aseity, his freedom from others. Clearly such a God, who stands over against me rather than with me and for me would threaten my autonomy. Such a God will absorb me into himself like the human thinking subject absorbs its object. If I do not resist, if I do not compete for my own freedom, he will keep me in bondage. In such a scenario, God is reduced to the cosmic Jailer who can only maintain his sovereignty by keeping his world in subjection, a somewhat pitiable deity, threatened by advances in human knowledge, who through his agent the church must thrust his presumptuous subjects back into infancy and dependence.

However, as we have already noted, for Bonhoeffer, God, far from enslaving humanity is precisely the one, and indeed the only one who gives authentic freedom. Through his revelation in Christ, God defines himself as the giver of freedom, the one who creates humanity in his image, in freedom, and restores its fallen freedom through redemption in Christ, the true image of the Father. It is humanity apart from God, trapped in the *cor curvum in se*, which cannot place itself into true freedom, any the more than it can place itself into truth. All human attempts to create or grasp at freedom are but poor counterfeits of the genuine currency. True freedom can only be received as gift, not seized or demanded at the expense of another, and only the God who is person, the God who reveals himself in Jesus Christ gives true freedom and releases human beings to be most fully human. However as Bonhoeffer appraises the response of the church to the growth of modernity, his diagnosis is that in the years after the Enlightenment, theology all too readily embraced the premises of Enlightenment thinking, even when struggling against it. Instead of questioning the assumption promulgated by Nietzsche and Feuerbach, that faith in God and human freedom were mutually exclusive possibilities, the church accepted this assessment without question and responded by trying to force humanity back into infancy and dependence. In fighting a rearguard action to preserve ground for itself and for God, it in fact endorsed the exclusion of God from daily life. At the same time, its uncritical opposition to human progress, as epitomised in the polemical reaction to Darwinism,[621] served only to strengthen and endorse the increasingly widely held view that active belief in God was incompatible with humanity's aspirations to reach its full intellectual and emotional potential.

However, Bonhoeffer rejects with equal vehemence the attempt of Christian apologetics to retain a place for God within the inner life, as the

---

[621] cf. LPP 341.

answer to questions of guilt and the fear of death, so that people would be kept in dependence on God, at least when it came to the so-called 'ultimate questions'. These vain attempts to find some last remaining gaps where humanity has not yet got all the answers, are dismissed as 'in the first place pointless, secondly as ignoble and thirdly as unChristian'.[622] Instead, Bonhoeffer maintains firmly that the church must accept the world come of age. However, this acceptance does not imply uncritical endorsement. Freedom from the tutelage of childhood does not necessarily mean maturity or the right use of freedom. It is telling that in his discussion of 'sins of strength', (which he sees as more urgently in need of confrontation with the Gospel than 'sins of weakness'), Bonhoeffer identifies 'fear of free responsibility' as the prevailing sin of the German middle classes.[623] Human 'Mündigkeit', like the adolescent's transition from childhood to adulthood implies a freedom from the constraints of childhood, but not necessarily the capacity to use that freedom in responsible action. Bethge, in his biography, makes a helpful and indeed vital distinction when he argues that in Bonhoeffer's thinking, an historical 'yes' must never be equated with or allowed to subsume a theological or ethical yes.[624] Bethge's immediate concern is with misinterpretations of Bonhoeffer's reaction to Hitler's victory over France, where his acceptance of the reality of the situation led some to fear that he had changed his view of Hitler, but the point is equally valid in the context of human *Mündigkeit*. What is at issue is not a value judgement on humanity's coming of age, but a concern that theology recognise that it cannot undo that reality, but must reckon with it.[625] As Bonhoeffer writes to Bethge at Christmas 1943 'Of course, not everything that happens is simply "God's will"; yet in the last resort nothing happens "without God's will" (Matt 10.29), i.e. through every event, however untoward, there is access to God.'[626] As we have seen, Bonhoeffer's concern is how the realities of human autonomy and a world free to make its own mistakes, can be faced with the claim of Christ, and it is within this context that his critique of religion and proposals for a 'non-religious Christianity' are to be understood.

---

[622] LPP 327.
[623] LPP 345.
[624] DB 587.
[625] cf. Bonhoeffer's stress on the need for responsible and free action to be in 'correspondence with reality' (Chapter 5 above).
[626] LPP 167. The text reads 'Are not two sparrows sold for a penny? Yet not one of them will fall to the ground apart from your Father.'

## The Critique of Religion and the Non-religious Interpretation of Biblical Concepts

Bonhoeffer suggests that the right response to the 'world come of age' is to be found neither in a denial of the reality of human freedom, nor in an uncritical endorsement of it. Instead, he argues, the answer is to break the connection between Christianity and religion once and for all because 'Only in that way will Liberal theology really be overcome... and at the same time its question be genuinely taken up and answered.'[627] When Christianity is released from the baggage which comes with 'religion',[628] the autonomy of the world can be both recognised and yet really addressed by Christ and by the Gospel. Bonhoeffer reiterates and clarifies the same point in his letter of 30th June 1944, where he writes 'Jesus claims for himself and for the kingdom of God, the whole of human life in all its manifestations.'[629] Forced to break off in mid paragraph, Bonhoeffer repeats that the issue at stake is 'the laying claim to the world which has come of age by Jesus Christ.'[630]

Bonhoeffer's criticism of religion has been the subject of much speculation and interpreters are hampered by the fact that, as Ralf Wüstenberg has demonstrated, he never provides a precise definition of 'religion'.[631] Nevertheless, a close reading of *Letters and Papers* reveals a number of characteristics which Bonhoeffer repeatedly ascribes to religion and against which, the vehemence of his criticism is directed. Most frequently cited are metaphysics, individualism, partiality, privilege, inwardness and the desire to create dependency.[632] For our purposes, it is striking that all of these attributes tend, potentially at least, towards dualism, towards the polarisation of life into sacred and secular. If I am correct in viewing Bonhoeffer's understanding of authentic freedom in terms of wholeness of life and fulfilment of God-created potential, (the worldly world and the fully human person), his opposition to religion, at least in the terms in which he characterises it, becomes not only comprehensible but inevitable. The strength of Bonhoeffer's convictions in this respect are perhaps most evident when he draws a striking and

---

[627] Ibid., 329.
[628] We will discuss the basis of Bonhoeffer's negative view of religion below.
[629] Ibid., 342.
[630] Ibid.
[631] Wüstenberg R. K. *Glauben als Leben* Op. cit.
[632] LPP 280, 286, 327 etc.

provocative parallel between religion and the New Testament debate over circumcision[633] and writes:

> The Pauline question whether περιτομη [circumcision] is a condition of justification seems to me in present-day terms to be whether religion is a condition of salvation. Freedom from περιτομη is also freedom from religion.[634]

What is being asserted is that in the Germany of the Third Reich, religion provides an obstacle to the freedom of the true Gospel equivalent to that of circumcision in the first century Gentile context. From the perspective of our discussion of freedom, it is striking that the heart of Paul's message in Galatians is to proclaim the true freedom of the Gospel as the way between and beyond the legalism[635] and partiality of religious requirements such as circumcision, and the antinomianism which appeared to be its alternative.[636] So for Bonhoeffer, Christ and the Gospel must be freed from the cultural trappings of religion in its Protestant form, so that human beings can be set free, not for the unbridled autonomy of self-

---

[633] The major discussion comes in the second half of the letter of 30th April 1944 (LPP 281), but the issue is referred to again in parentheses in the letter of 8th June 1944, in the context of a discussion of religion and the 'positivism of revelation.'

[634] LPP 281. Bonhoeffer had previously reflected upon parallels between the situation in Galatia and the contemporary German context in his paper on *The Church and the Jewish Question* (GS II 44-53 esp. pp 51-52). There he argues that the German Christians, in setting up a law for church membership which excludes those of Jewish descent, are in fact behaving analogously to Paul's judaizing (Jewish Christian) opponents in their requirement that Gentiles become Jews. In both cases a law of membership, whether requiring Jewish or non-Jewish identity, was being set up against the Gospel, which knows no qualification for membership except the call of Christ. The question of circumcision is not expressly discussed in that paper.

[635] Although the work of E. P. Sanders, J. Dunn and others has done much to alert post-Holocaust theologians to the twin dangers of equating first century Judaism with legalism and of reading Galatians through the spectacles of Luther's search for freedom from guilt, for Bonhoeffer this would have been the traditional and at that time almost unquestioned interpretation. Nevertheless, even if, with Dunn and Sanders, we view circumcision as a 'badge of the covenant', a mark of ethnic identity and nationalistic pride rather than a 'work' to earn salvation, (a detailed appraisal of the Sanders/Dunn line falls outside the remit of this thesis), it clearly comes within the scope of a condition or requirement of salvation and hence the analogy with 'religion' still holds good.

[636] In Gal 5:1 Paul contrasts the freedom Christ brings with the 'yoke' of religious requirements: 'For freedom Christ has set us free. Stand firm, therefore, and do not submit again to a yoke of slavery.' In Gal 5:13 he contrasts the authentic freedom of the Christian with the selfishness of a freedom from one another rather than for one another: 'For you were called to freedom, brothers and sisters; only do not use your freedom as an opportunity for self-indulgence, but through love become slaves to one another.' (NRSV).

deification, which ultimately proves illusory, but for authentic freedom from self, for God and for others.

The issue of language, especially language about God and the Gospel is of crucial importance here. Some of the more superficial interpretations have assumed that Bonhoeffer's quest for a 'non-religious interpretation of biblical concepts' was motivated by a concern to make Christianity relevant and easily accessible to a secular age. However, as more perceptive commentators have noted, in fact Bonhoeffer's aim is in many ways quite the opposite. Rowan Williams provocatively but accurately asserts: '[Bonhoeffer] is not out to make religious language easier; he's out to make it more difficult. I don't think we begin to understand the agenda of the letters unless we understand that ... he is going to make it more difficult to talk about God.'[637] For our purposes, the 'Thoughts' which Bonhoeffer wrote for the baptism of his godchild are particularly illuminating. There he suggests that the problem with religious language is that it has ceased to be authentic language about God, and so has ceased to set people free. Somehow, he urges, the church must find a new language, which like the language of Jesus is 'liberating and redeeming'.[638] Such a language will not be the comfortable rhetoric of the secular agenda, God in the tones of the newspaper editorial or the soap opera. Instead 'it will shock people and yet overcome them by his power; it will be the language of a new righteousness and truth, proclaiming God's peace with humanity and the coming of his kingdom.'[639]

A significant contribution to our understanding of the concept of the 'Non-religious interpretation of biblical concepts' is to be found in Ralf Wüstenberg's admirable recent reassessment entitled *Glauben als Leben*.[640] Wüstenberg's thesis is that when the letters are read both in the light of the earlier writings and with due attention to the major external influences upon Bonhoeffer, in particular Karl Barth and Wilhelm Dilthey, it becomes clear that the non-religious interpretation can best be viewed as a *lebenschristologische* interpretation, a christological re-pristination of the *Lebensphilosophie* of Dilthey.[641] He argues that rather that setting faith and religion in opposition, as in Barth's dialectical theology, Bonhoeffer

---

[637] Williams R. *Bonhoeffer, the Sixties and After* op. cit. 1; cf. also Williams R. *Arius: Heresy and Tradition* (Darton, Longman and Todd 1987), 236-7.
[638] LPP 300.
[639] Ibid.
[640] Wüstenberg R. K. op. cit.
[641] Ibid., 205ff and passim. Wüstenberg also points to the influence of William James and the Spanish philosopher J. Ortega y Gasset.

opposes religion and life.⁶⁴² Whilst Wüstenberg's thesis is compelling, I would suggest that in his apparent equation of faith and life, Wüstenberg fails to do justice to the strong presence of faith as a discrete theme within in *Letters and Papers*. For Bonhoeffer faith and life must never be separated, but nor can faith be reduced to or subsumed in life. As Bonhoeffer writes on 21st July 1944 'I'm still discovering right up to this moment that it is only by living completely in this world that one learns to have faith.'⁶⁴³ It is the *cantus firmus* of faith in Christ which releases and enables the polyphony of life. Nevertheless, the importance of 'life' as a unifying theme within the Tegel correspondence can scarcely be stressed too strongly.⁶⁴⁴

*Positivism of Revelation*

I would suggest that Bonhoeffer's understanding of 'religion' and 'life' as irreconcilable opposing forces, might also throw some light on his much cited and apparently enigmatic criticism of both Karl Barth and the Confessing Church, in terms of 'positivism of revelation'. Wüstenberg has made a detailed study of the three passages in which the phrase occurs in connection with Barth and has shown, convincingly, that the context is always one of the criticism of religion.⁶⁴⁵ On this basis, he argues, cogently in my view, that the focus of Bonhoeffer's concern is Barth's move from the unambiguous opposition of religion and grace in the commentary on *Romans*, to the rehabilitation of a true religion 'justified by faith' in *Church Dogmatics*.⁶⁴⁶ If we accept Wüstenberg's thesis at this point, it is fascinating, from the standpoint of our theme, to note that Barth's discussion of 'religion' in *Romans*, which Bonhoeffer praises as 'his greatest service, in spite of all the Neo-Kantian eggshells',⁶⁴⁷ comes in a chapter entitled 'Freedom', in which he expounds Romans 7. There, religion is equated with 'life under the law', a life of slavery. As 'the last and noblest human possibility' of humanity,⁶⁴⁸ religion compromises the

---

⁶⁴² Ibid., 250.
⁶⁴³ LPP 369.
⁶⁴⁴ Bonhoeffer uses similar language of fullness of life in his correspondence with Maria. In the letter of 23rd April 1944 he writes 'Praying confidently and following readily: there's a full life for you.' *Love Letters from Cell 92* op. cit., 187.
⁶⁴⁵ Op. cit., 116ff. The relevant pages in LPP are 280, 286 and 328.
⁶⁴⁶ CD I/2 § 17, 325ff.
⁶⁴⁷ LPP 328.
⁶⁴⁸ Barth K *The Epistle to the Romans* trans. Hoskyns E. C. (from the Sixth German Edition 1928) (Oxford University Press Paperback Edition 1968), 240.

freedom of God because 'the one, pre-eminent, victorious, free God [is] degraded to the god of this world, who is "No-God"',[649] 'a thing in this world.'[650] In religion, human beings are 'limited, enclosed and fettered by [religion's] ambiguity'[651] and yet, as rebellious slaves, they overlook their utter separation from God and 'become to themselves what God should be to them.'[652] In contrast, 'Grace is the freedom of God by which men are seized',[653] the possibility beyond all human possibility. 'Beyond the humanism which reaches its culminating point in religion, we encounter the freedom which is ours by grace.'[654]

Echoes of Barth's critique of religion as a human possibility can be traced at various points in Bonhoeffer's earlier writings, for example in his characterisation of the serpent's question as 'the religious question' in *Creation and Fall*.[655] However, only a year later, in the *Christology* lectures, the 'Who?' question is described as '*the* religious question', without any pejorative connotations.[656] I have already argued, that whilst Bonhoeffer never provides a precise definition of religion, the heart of his critique, especially in *Letters and Papers*, centres on the failure of religion to affirm the whole of life as Christ's. Religion enslaves because it fails to address life in all its fullness. Like circumcision in the Galatian church, it has become an unwarranted pre-condition of salvation.[657] If we examine the four places where Bonhoeffer uses the term 'positivism of revelation',[658] (including the occasion when the phrase is used in connection with the Confessing Church which is not included in Wüstenberg's appraisal),[659] it becomes clear that the criticisms of religion in terms of metaphysics, individualism, inwardness, privilege, partiality and the desire to keep others in dependence, which we have already noted, are all present. For Barth, the picture of a true religion, justified by faith and hence a gift of God's free grace, which he sketches in *Church Dogmatics* 1/2 §17, is not incompatible with his earlier condemnation of religion as a human possibility. However, for Bonhoeffer, the rehabilitation of religion, even a so-called 'true

---

[649] Ibid., 231.
[650] Ibid., 244.
[651] Ibid., 233.
[652] Ibid. cf. Bonhoeffer's reflections on the human endeavour to be *sicut deus* in Chapter 3.
[653] Ibid., 240.
[654] Ibid., 230-231.
[655] 'Die fromme Frage' DBW 3, 96ff.
[656] C, 31.
[657] LPP 281.
[658] LPP 280, 286, 328 and 329.
[659] LPP 329.

religion' is an unthinkable return to the sort of dualism, in which the worldly world is either 'left to its own devices'[660] or forced back into infancy. What is at stake for Bonhoeffer is a return to the world of two spheres, which privileges sacred over secular, supernatural over natural, in which the church is a church free from the world rather than free for it, continuing to concern itself with its privileged position, rather than recognising the Gospel imperative to be there for others and so to free the world for true worldliness.

Charles Marsh, in his discussion of 'positivism of revelation', traces Bonhoeffer's unease with Barth's approach to a concern that the latter's understanding of grace as 'all-embracing, *totalitarian*'[661] fails to leave room for the created freedom of the world to be other than God. In that Barth had once accused the young Bonhoeffer of 'killing everything' with grace,[662] this would be an interesting reversal of positions. However, whilst I agree with Marsh that questions of divine and human freedom are at the root of the issue, I would suggest that the position is more complicated than he suggests. As I argued at the outset of this chapter, in the Tegel theology, Bonhoeffer's concern is not with human freedom *per se*, but with the authentic human freedom in which human beings are fully themselves, rather than the inauthentic freedom from God and others which is characteristic of humanity estranged from God. Hence, I would suggest that for Bonhoeffer the problem is not that Barth's theology of grace denigrates human freedom, but that 'religion' either leaves the world trapped in an illusory and inauthentic freedom or attempts to keep it in infantile dependence. Marsh does not seem to have noted the parallels between the fragment of *Ethics* with which we began our discussion, and the letters, and hence finds negative comments about the world being 'left to its own devices' misleading and at odds with what he understands to be Bonhoeffer's concern to affirm the 'relative autonomy of humanity'.[663] However, as we saw in our discussion of 'The Concrete Command and the Divine Mandates', the world 'left to its own devices' is precisely not free to be truly worldly, but falls into the desperate and ultimately destructive pursuit of self-deification. For Bonhoeffer, only the cross frees the world

---

[660] LPP 286.
[661] Marsh C. *Reclaiming Dietrich Bonhoeffer: The Promise of his Theology* op. cit., 24 citing Karl Barth's *Letter to a Pastor in the German Democratic Republic* pp. 54-58.
[662] Letter from Bonhoeffer to Erwin Sutz 24/7/31, reflecting on his first meeting with Barth. DBW 11, 18 at 20.
[663] Marsh op. cit. 21.

for true worldliness and it is to a discussion of Bonhoeffer's theology of the cross that we now turn.

## The Tegel Theology as a 'Theologia Crucis'

The call of the Christian to suffer with Christ is a strong theme in Bonhoeffer's Lutheran heritage and resonates through the earlier writings.[664] However, the place of the cross in the Tegel theology has received far less scholarly attention than the more enticing motifs of 'worldliness' and 'religionless Christianity'. An recent exception to this tendency is Leslie Alford, who, in her doctoral dissertation, makes a detailed study of the *theologia crucis* in Bonhoeffer's writings, arguing that *Letters and Papers* is 'the pinnacle of Bonhoeffer's theology of the cross.'[665] Although her interpretation of Bonhoeffer's work as 'a steady progression away from omnipotent, glorious imagery for God to terms characterised by weakness, suffering and hiddenness'[666] relies too heavily, in my view, on the sort of linear model of development criticised in the opening chapter, her exploration of the theology of the *Letters* in terms of a *theologia crucis*, offers a timely reminder of the centrality of the cross in the Tegel theology. I have already expounded the relational foundations to Bonhoeffer's understanding of divine and human freedom. However, where some of the more facile relational theologies can sideline the cross as an unfortunate interruption within Trinitarian harmony, Bonhoeffer, in focusing primarily on God's relationship to the world in the economy of salvation, always keeps the cross at the centre. It is only through the cross that the world can be related to God. It is God's freedom for humanity, even to the point of the cross, which sets human beings free to be fully human.

As we noted in our analysis of the *Ethics* fragment 'The Concrete Command and the Divine Mandates', at the beginning of this chapter, Bonhoeffer saw a clear and indeed essential connection between the cross and the authentic worldliness of the world. It is the cross that sets people free for genuine worldliness. In the Tegel theology, Bonhoeffer argues that it is precisely in the weakness of the cross that God 'is with us and helps us.'[667] It is God's weakness, supremely demonstrated in his willingness to

---

[664] cf. especially CD 80, 192-3, 273.
[665] Alford L. M. *Toward a dialectical understanding of power: Dietrich Bonhoeffer and the theology of the cross* New College Edinburgh 1994 (unpublished doctoral thesis), 125.
[666] Ibid., 30.
[667] DBW 8 534; LPP 360.

*Freedom in a World Come of Age* 167

be 'pushed out of the world on to the cross' that epitomises the difference between Christianity and religions of whatever sort.[668] Where religious humanity looks for the powerful *deus ex machina*, Bonhoeffer asserts: 'the Bible directs us to God's powerlessness and suffering; only the suffering God can help.'[669] It is this very powerlessness of God in the cross which he suggests as a 'starting-point for our "worldly interpretation"',[670] because it is an understanding of the cross which destroys false understandings of God, pointing instead to the true God who reverses the expectations of the religious, by calling his followers to watch with him in Gethsemane and to share in his sufferings.[671] Bonhoeffer continues:

> [The Christian] must really live in the godless world and should not attempt to cover over or explain its godlessness in some religious way or other; he must live in a worldly way and so participate in the sufferings of God; he *may* live in a worldly way, that is, he is freed from all false religious ties and scruples. To be a Christian does not mean to be religious in a particular way ... but to be a human being, not a type of human being, but the human being Christ creates in us. It is not the religious act which makes the Christian, but the participation in the sufferings of God in worldly life. [672]

The cross frees *from* false religion and *for* authentic worldliness. In Christ the Christian is free to become the fully human person he is created to be, sharing in the sufferings of Christ. For Bonhoeffer, of course, this participation in the sufferings of Christ is never abstract theology, but, as we saw in Chapter 5, is worked out in free and responsible action for others. This connection between theology and its outworking in ethical living is once again made explicit when Bonhoeffer attempts to order his reflections in the so-called 'Outline for a book', to which we must now direct our attention.[673]

---

[668] LPP 360-1.
[669] DBW 8 534; LPP 361; In a letter to his sister Sabine, (21/5/1942) Bonhoeffer had written 'for me the idea that God himself is suffering has always been one of the most convincing teachings of Christianity'. GS VI 557 (written in English).
[670] Ibid., The English translation renders 'weltlich' here and in the following section as 'secular'.
[671] cf. the poem *Christians and Pagans* which illustrates the same reversal of expectations. 'Christians stand by God in his hour of grieving.' LPP 348-9.
[672] DBW8 535; LPP 361.
[673] LPP 380ff (DBW8, 553 *Entwürf für ein Arbeit*), enclosed with letter of 3/8/97, hereafter 'Outline'.

## The Outline for a Book

Although much discussion of the Tegel theology has tended to focus on the letters, this sketch for a projected book merits particular attention. In contrast to the letters, where Bonhoeffer is using Bethge, to some extent at least, as a sounding board for his theological ideas,[674] in *Outline*, he sketches three draft chapters for a book, aimed at contributing to the church's call to 'move out again into the open air of intellectual discussion [and to] risk saying controversial things if we are to get down to the serious problems of life.'[675] Hence, although *Outline* would never have been published, it constitutes a serious attempt by Bonhoeffer to arrange and refine his thoughts, in preparation for a concentrated piece of theological writing.[676]

The first chapter, to be headed, 'A Stocktaking of Christianity' was to deal with the issues of humanity's coming of age, God as an insurance policy or stop-gap, and the various attempts by the Protestant church to preserve Christianity as a religion, which had failed to reach beyond the confines of the middle classes. Bonhoeffer argues that the church tends to defend itself, rather than taking risks for others. These questions, as Bonhoeffer notes, have already featured in the theological letters and do not require further discussion here.[677] However, the terse comment 'no risk for others' at the end of the subsection on the response of the church to the world come of age, leads into a discussion of the concept 'existence for others',[678] which features in the drafts for the second and third chapters, headed respectively 'What does the Christian faith really mean' and 'Conclusions'. The roots of this motif in Bonhoeffer's earlier exploration of the idea of 'freedom for others', *Stellvertretung* and the 'responsible life' are clear, and have already been discussed in an earlier chapter. In the final *Ethics* fragment to which I have referred throughout this chapter, Bonhoeffer had written:

---

[674] cf. LPP 287 'I've written more to clear my own mind than to edify you ... .but I can't help sharing my thoughts with you, simply because that is the best way to make them clear to myself.' cf. also LPP 346.

[675] LPP 378.

[676] The work on the book itself which Bonhoeffer continued until his execution, is lost, presumably burnt at Flossenbürg.

[677] It seems that Bonhoeffer was satisfied that his discussion on these matters in correspondence set out the main points he intended to make.

[678] *Dasein für andere.*

In the incarnation, God proclaims himself as the one who does not wish to be for himself, but 'for us'. In view of the incarnation, to live as a human being before God can only mean to exist not for oneself but for God and for other human beings.[679]

A similar christological focus is evident in the draft outline for Chapter Two, where Bonhoeffer addresses the question 'Who is God?' by arguing: 'The being-there-for-others of Jesus is the experience of transcendence.'[680] A genuine experience of God is not primarily about belief in certain attributes, but encounter with Jesus Christ. In a brief but telling section which encapsulates the distinction and relationship between divine and human freedom, Bonhoeffer continues: 'Omnipotence, omniscience, omnipresence arise only out of freedom from self, out of 'being-there-for-others' to the point of death. Faith is the participation in this being of Jesus. (Incarnation, cross and resurrection).'[681] In other words, it is Jesus Christ, the one in whom the image of God as freedom for others was perfectly realised, the one free from self, who is there for others to the ultimate extent of the cross, who is the measure and interpreter of the divine attributes.

But that same Christ is also the epitome of full humanity. Human beings, those created to be free for others but trapped in self-absorption through the fall, are freed by faith and through participation in the existence of Christ, the one for others, to be those who exist for others, those for whom life is whole, because life is seen christologically. 'Participation' was, of course, a critically important concept in *Ethics*. Although in the earlier correspondence with Bethge, Bonhoeffer has focused particularly on the Christian life as participation in the sufferings of Christ,[682] in *Outline*, he reiterates the theme insistently echoed in *Ethics*, that the Christian is called to participate in the threefold form of Christ, the incarnate, crucified and risen one.[683] Bonhoeffer now speaks in terms of participation in the 'being' (*Sein*) of Jesus, rather than 'form' (*Gestaltung*), as in *Ethics* and in the *Christology* lectures. Wüstenberg suggests that this reflects a movement from a predominant interest in the person of Christ in the *Christology* lectures towards a greater stress on the being of Christ in the *Outline*, a

---

[679] DBW 6, 404; ET 296-7.
[680] DBW 8 208; LPP 381.
[681] Ibid. (Unaccountably, the reference to freedom '*Aus der Freiheit von sich selbst*' is not reflected in the English translation).
[682] Especially letters of 27/6/44 LPP 337 and 16/7/97 LPP 360-361 and the poem 'Christians and Pagans' LPP 348f.
[683] LPP 381.

shift which he attributes to the influence of Dilthey.[684] However, such a distinction would seem difficult to maintain, given that in *Christology*, Bonhoeffer refers regularly to the 'pro-me-being' of Christ,[685] whilst the stress on encounter with Christ as the answer to the question 'Who is God?' in the *Outline*, is surely a reiteration of the importance of Christ as person rather than idea.

As we have already noted, in his early essay on *The Nature of the Church*, Bonhoeffer had spoken of Christ as both gift and example.[686] Here in *Outline*, Christ is both a model and enabler of freedom from self, for others. Unless the background of the earlier writings, and in particular of *Ethics* is appreciated, there is a clear danger of understanding Bonhoeffer's concept of 'being-there-for-others' in terms of a reductionist Christianity evacuated of content, in which religion is replaced by ethics.[687] That, of course, was one response to the Enlightenment, as epitomised in the work of Richard Rothe, who had reduced the Christian faith to the ethical autonomy of humanity. Bonhoeffer had read his five volume *Theological Ethics*, in preparation for writing his *Ethics*.[688] However, whilst Bonhoeffer in this passage, rightly points out the use of 'example' language in the Pauline epistles, it is clear that the call of the church and of Christians is not to a sterile moral endeavour, but arises out of and is sustained by participation in Christ.

Hence, although we can trace clear differences in the way in which the ideas are articulated in *Outline*, there are equally clear roots in the earlier writings. As we saw in our discussion of *Act and Being*, divine freedom is not the freedom of a transcendent aseity, but is christologically expressed in terms of freedom for the world. In *Creation and Fall*, human creation in the image of God is understood as a creation in freedom for God and for others. Redemption, as we noted in our discussion of *Cost* and of *Ethics* is seen in terms of the emancipation of the Christian from the *cor curvum in se* to a freedom for God and for others which is expressed in community. It is a restoration of the lost image, a participation in the image of Christ the true image of God. Hence, I would argue that Bonhoeffer's understanding of 'being-there-for-others', in *Outline*, whilst enriched by his reading of

---

[684] Wüstenberg op. cit. 242.
[685] C, 49; DBW 12, 295.
[686] In Chapter 3 above. DBW 11, 298 cf. also DBW 1 170.
[687] Although the ethical aspects are not excluded. In a letter to Maria dated 13th August 1944, Bonhoeffer writes 'You've no idea how liberated I myself would feel if I were once more able to work for others instead of solely for myself.' *Love Letters from Cell 92* op. cit., 220.
[688] Bethge in DB 619.

Dilthey and others, is entirely consistent with the understanding of creation, fall and redemption expressed in the earlier writings.

**Freedom in the Prison Poetry**

In the introduction to this chapter, I commented on the fact that the curtailment of Bonhoeffer's physical freedom seems to have released him into a new emotional and psychological freedom. In particular, the experience of imprisonment seems to have unlocked reserves of creativity in Bonhoeffer, so that one of the most intriguing aspects of the Tegel theology is the variety of genres in which it is expressed. Apart from letters, the outline for a book and miscellaneous notes, which we have already discussed, Bonhoeffer also attempted to write a novel and a play and produced a number of poems. The poetry has not received a great deal of critical attention, although Johann Christoph Hampe's *Von Guten Mächten*,[689] S. F. Wiltshire's short article 'Dietrich Bonhoeffer's Prison Poetry',[690] and Albert Altenähr's discussion of the poem 'Stations on the Road to Freedom',[691] are notable exceptions. From the perspective of our theme, I will confine our discussion to the two poems which reflect explicitly upon the theme of freedom, *The Friend* and *Stations on the Road to Freedom*.[692]

*Freedom and Friendship*

The poem *The Friend*, which was probably written on 27th August 1944, is one of the last surviving documents from Tegel.[693] I will discuss it prior to *Stations*, because the ideas embodied in the poem have their roots a much earlier letter, addressed to Eberhard and Renate Bethge, in which Bonhoeffer discussed the nature of friendship and its relationship to the divine mandates.[694] When the poem is read in the context of that letter, it

---

[689] *Dietrich Bonhoeffer Von Guten Mächten* (Chr. Kaiser/Gütersloher Verlaghaus 1976).
[690] In *Religion in Life* 38, 4 Winter 1969, 522- 534.
[691] Altenähr A. 'Dietrich Bonhoeffers Gedicht "Stationen auf dem Weg zur Freiheit" als Theologie und Zeugnis' in *In Libertatum Vocati Estis* eds. Boelaars H. and Tremblay R. (Roma: Academia Alfonsiana 1977) 283-309.
[692] (hereafter *Stations*).
[693] There are later letters to Maria and the poems 'Jonah', 'The Death of Moses' and 'Power of Good'.
[694] Letter of 23rd January 1944, LPP 190ff. It is possible that the concentrated deliberation on the theme of freedom in *Stations*, brought the link between freedom and friendship

seems clear that Bonhoeffer is reflecting specifically on his friendship with Bethge, and the way in which the relationship has freed and sustained him to live in free responsibility.

The concept of the divine mandates, to which we have already made brief reference,[695] is first developed in *Ethics*. Bonhoeffer is clear that the mandates are God given and give freedom to live before God, and as such are to be carefully distinguished from the 'orders of creation', a concept which had been so abused by the German Christians. In Tegel, Bonhoeffer speaks for the first time of what he terms 'the broad area of freedom, which surrounds all three areas of the divine mandates.' He continues: 'The one who is ignorant of this area of freedom may be a good father, citizen and worker, indeed even a Christian, but I doubt whether he is a complete person (and therefore a Christian in the widest sense of the term).' As we have already noted, for Bonhoeffer, there is a clear connection between freedom and the wholehearted embracing of life in all its fullness. He continues 'Our Protestant (not Lutheran) Prussian world has been so strongly defined by the four mandates that the sphere of freedom has receded into the background. I wonder whether it is possible... to regain the idea of the church as providing an understanding of the area of freedom (art, education, friendship, play) so that the 'aesthetic existence' (Kierkegaard), would not be banished from the sphere of the church but rather would be established anew in it?'[696] Then in words which recur in the poem some seven months later, Bonhoeffer makes explicit the link between freedom and friendship, when he writes: 'within the sphere of freedom, friendship is by far the rarest and most priceless treasure.'[697]

It seems that over the intervening months, Bonhoeffer continued to reflect on the relationship between freedom and friendship, and that these thoughts culminated in the poem *The Friend* in which freedom is a strong and unifying theme.[698] In the first stanza he writes that friendship is a gift

---

back to the forefront of Bonhoeffer's consciousness, although the two poems differ significantly in both style and content.

[695] cf. Chapter 3 above. In the *Ethics* fragment 'Christ, Reality and Good', these are listed as work, marriage, government and the church, but in a later section, 'The Concrete Commandment and the Divine Mandates', Bonhoeffer refers to 'church, marriage and the family, culture and government'.

[696] WE 105; LPP 193.

[697] LPP 193; The words 'rare' (seltenste) and 'priceless' (kostbarste) are repeated in the poem 'The Friend' discussed below.

[698] I have worked from the German text (WE 213ff) because the English translation (LPP 388ff) is a paraphrase which is concerned to render the words as poetry rather than to render a literal translation and hence at times obscures the strength of the theme of freedom.

which arises not from 'blood, race and oath',[699] but from 'the free delight and free longing of the spirit'. This link between freedom and gift continues in the second verse, where Bonhoeffer compares the one who is free to the cornflower which 'no one has planted, no one waters, which grows without protection in freedom'.[700] Friendship is 'the rarest and most precious blossom arising from the freedom of the carefree, daring, trusting spirit in a propitious hour.' The fourth stanza is resonant with Bonhoeffer's joy in Bethge's friendship and letters, when he speaks of friendship as refreshing water and as a refuge for the one who in freedom has 'faced the world with clear eyes and free action', whilst the fifth verse focuses on the trust between friends who 'disclose themselves fully to the one they trust and are united in freedom and faithfulness with the other.' The mature man[701] looks to his friend 'not for orders or for peremptory extraneous laws and precepts, but for the good and earnest counsel which sets him free.' The poem ends with the claim that each friend recognises in the other 'the true helper to freedom and full humanity' (*Menschlichkeit*). Once again we are reminded of the relational nature of freedom as Bonhoeffer perceived it and the intrinsic connection between authentic freedom and life lived to the full. In friendship each is free for the other and in that freedom sets the other free to be fully themselves.

## Stations on the Road to Freedom

*Stations* is one of the more tightly structured and polished of the Tegel poems. The existence of an earlier draft and of notes for the four stanzas suggests that Bonhoeffer worked on it over a period of time. The whole poem is set out in the Appendix below.[702] The English edition of the *Letters* places *Stations* directly after the letter to Bethge dated 21st July 1944, (the first letter written after news reached Bonhoeffer of the failure of the 20th July assassination attempt on Hitler's life,[703] which includes a note

---

[699] A clear reference to the Nazi preoccupation with such ties.
[700] In the letter of 23/1/44 (LPP 193) Bonhoeffer had spoken of friendship's relationship to the mandates as comparable to the cornflower's relationship to the cornfield and this same comparison is taken up in the poem.
[701] This is one of the rare occasions where Bonhoeffer uses 'Mann' rather than 'Mensch', presumably because the friendship which inspires the poem is that between him and Bethge.
[702] The translation is my own.
[703] Bethge tells us that Bonhoeffer heard the news broadcast from foreign radio stations in the sick bay at Tegel on 21st July. DB 730.

referring to a poem written 'in a few hours this evening').[704] However, it seems unlikely Bonhoeffer would have produced such a 'finished' poem within so short a time. More tellingly perhaps, references to the themes of suffering and death in the letter of 28th July, but the absence of any allusion to the poem, suggest that Bonhoeffer wrestled with the ideas over a period of time before crafting them into poetic format.[705] Bethge's letter of 26th August 1944 refers to receipt of a poem with the 'birthday letter', (probably that of 14th August 1944) and the reference to four 'strophes', the last of which Bethge finds 'most striking and least comprehensible',[706] (almost certainly the stanza on death which I will discuss in detail below), would seem to fit *Stations*.[707] Whatever the date, Bonhoeffer is almost certainly writing in the recognition that he will be implicated in the plot, and that death must be the inevitable outcome of his freely chosen action in becoming involved in the conspiracy. It is against this background that the poem is to be understood. If the later dating is correct, and the *Stations* poem is the culmination of the reflections on the theme of freedom in correspondence, the letter of 28th July can be seen as Bonhoeffer's own prospective commentary on the poem, or at least three of the four 'stations', action, suffering and death. He writes:

> To turn to an entirely different point: not only action but also suffering is a way to freedom. In suffering, the liberation consists in our being able to put the matter out of our own hands into God's hands. In this sense, death is the crowning of human freedom. Whether the human deed is a matter of faith or not depends on whether or not we understand our suffering as a continuation of our action and as a perfection of freedom. I consider that very important and very comforting. [708]

These thoughts suggest that the 'stations' in the poem are not necessarily consecutive or mutually exclusive but inextricably connected. In the 'Miscellaneous Thoughts', enclosed with the letter, Bonhoeffer takes up the theme of purity which features strongly in the first stanza of the poem.[709] The same 'Thoughts' echo the final stanza of the poem as they speak of death as 'the greatest festival on the road to freedom.' Albert

---

[704] LPP 372.
[705] Altenähr's paper includes a detailed discussion of the possible dating of the poem and suggests 14th August 1944 as the most likely option. op. cit. 307f.
[706] LPP 395.
[707] Volume 8 of the DBW, published in October 1998, followed Altenähr's suggestion that the poem be dated 14th August.
[708] LPP 375.
[709] LPP 376; cf. also reference to the same theme at LPP 212.

Altenähr, whose detailed commentary on the poem will be referred to throughout this section, makes the interesting comment that the formal hexametric structure of the poem (which he terms the '"objectivierende" Gedichtform') 'frees Bonhoeffer's existential testimony from the purely individualistic sphere of validity of his person, without taking away any of its existential persuasive power. The verses bear testimony to distance and to engagement at the same time.'[710] In other words, the discipline of the structure frees the poem from introspective individualism, a dialectic which we encountered in our discussion of freedom and discipline in worship.[711]

The four stanzas are headed 'Discipline', 'Action', 'Suffering' and 'Death'. In a note sketched out in preparation for the poem, found with his papers, Bonhoeffer summarises the content of the four stanzas in terms of the learning process; 'learn to have control of oneself', 'learn to act: taking hold of reality, not hovering between possibilities', 'learn to suffer: to lay in other hands' and 'learn to die: highest festival on the way to freedom'.[712] In the final version, the stanzas build cumulatively to a climax, from exhortation in verses one and two, through exclamation in the third and transitional verse on suffering, culminating in invocation and prayer in the closing stanza. It is striking how many of the themes which we have already noted in our discussion of freedom emerge once again.

The first stanza reflects upon the paradoxical but intrinsic connection between freedom and discipline or self-restraint which we have already noted: 'No one comes to know the mystery of freedom except through discipline.' Altenähr comments 'Discipline grounded in the word of God is not the high-handedness (*Eigenmächtigkeit*) of titanic or pharisaical humanity, but the simple answer to the call of freedom. In discipline we affirm freedom as *costly* grace.'[713] At Finkenwalde Bonhoeffer had seen the dialectic of freedom and discipline as the key to the formation of his students. In prison, he valued the pattern of the church's year with its seasons and feast days and found that the discipline of a structured daily routine freed him from excessive introspection.[714] In the second stanza headed 'Action', Bonhoeffer's comment, 'Freedom exists not in hovering between possibilities but in courageously grasping reality, not in the flight

---

[710] Altenähr A. op. cit., 289.
[711] cf. Chapter 4.
[712] *Nachlass Dietrich Bonhoeffer* Microfiche 1678, 67A, (c) (Bonhoeffer's original note) and (d) (Eberhard Bethge's transcript of (c) ( University Library Cambridge).
[713] Ibid., 294 (italics original).
[714] e.g. LPP 168 where Bonhoeffer describes resisting the temptation to stay in bed after 6 am. and recommends the value of exercises and a cold wash in the morning. cf. also Altenähr op. cit., 295.

of ideas, but only in action', can be seen as his own reflection on the decision to take part in the conspiracy. Again we hear the call to responsible action and the risk of faith, even to the extent of incurring guilt, which was the subject of our last chapter. The third verse speaks of suffering, which has been such a strong theme throughout the *Letters*. However, as we have seen, the focus has never been on Bonhoeffer's personal sufferings, but on the call of the Christian to participate in the sufferings of Christ.[715] In the light of Bonhoeffer's reflections on the forsakenness and powerlessness of God on the cross in the letter of 16th July,[716] the christological undertones of this stanza seem unmistakable. Christ, the one with bound hands, who in confidence commits his cause to God, is both example and enabler.

We have already noted Bethge's view of the closing stanza of the poem entitled 'Death' as 'least comprehensible'. It is not difficult to trace the cause of Bethge's unease. Coming against the backdrop of the failure of the coup, the verse with its almost eager embracing of death seems to strike a discordant note in the light of all that Bonhoeffer has written about 'this worldiness'. Are earthly life and the human body, which Bonhoeffer had affirmed so powerfully, now to be viewed as a prison from which death provides the welcome release? Certainly some have thought so. M.E.M. Van den Berk in his thesis *Bonhoeffer, boeiend en geboeid: de theologie van Dietrich Bonhoeffer in het licht van zijn persoonlijkheid* has propounded the thesis that Bonhoeffer had an unhealthy fascination with death, even a death wish.[717] In an article based on the thesis, entitled 'Bonhoeffer and Death', he writes: 'Bonhoeffer suffered from a melancholy so deeply rooted that the idea that he might die terrified him far less than that he must remain alive.'[718] Van den Berk's thesis, which is based upon a discussion of Bonhoeffer's life as a whole, sees the return from America in 1939 as the acting out of a death wish. However, such an interpretation is difficult to maintain both in the light of the life-affirming content of the prison correspondence and against the background of

---

[715] Altenähr comments 'the suffering which counts in Bonhoeffer's eyes is a christological suffering, that is the participation in the suffering of God in the godless world.' (op. cit., 302).

[716] LPP 360-361.

[717] (Boom Mepel, 1974) cited in Peck W. J. (ed.) *New studies in Bonhoeffer's Ethics* (New York Edwin Mellen Press 1987), 177. His thesis discusses Bonhoeffer's life as a whole, seeing the return from America in 1939 as the acting out of a death wish.

[718] 'Bonhoeffer en de dood' in *Tijdschrift voor Theologie* (Nijmegen 1995), 158-51, cited in Peck W. J.(ed.) *New studies in Bonhoeffer's Ethics* (New York Edwin Mellen Press 1987), 179.

Bonhoeffer's earlier discussion of the relationship between death and freedom in the section on suicide in his *Ethics*. There, Bonhoeffer had argued that one of the things which distinguishes the human creation from the animal kingdom is humanity's freedom to accept or reject God's gift of life:

> Only because a human being is free towards death, can he choose to lay down his bodily life for the sake of a higher good. Without the freedom to sacrifice his life in death, there would be no freedom in relation to God, there would be no human life.[719]

However, he draws a clear distinction between suicide, which in his view is not an option for the Christian,[720] and the freedom to give one's life for others. It seems to me that the distinction between uncritical affirmation and acceptance of reality, which I sought to draw out in the discussion of 'the world come of age', is again applicable here. In other words, we must distinguish between the sort of death wish which is escapism and the calm acceptance of a reality which has become inevitable. The former, we would argue, would be strangely out of tune with the Bonhoeffer, embracing life in its fullness, who emerges from the prison letters, (including those written after this poem). However, the latter reflects the traditional theme of Christian hope. Bonhoeffer makes a similar point in his letter of 18th December 1943. 'I believe that we ought so to love and trust God in our *lives,* and in all the good things that he sends us, that when the time comes (but not before) we may go to him with love, trust and joy.'[721] As long as God gives life, we must live it to the full, but for Bonhoeffer writing in August 1944, that time was past. Far from reflecting a death wish, the poem concludes on a note of almost childlike trust and joy: 'Freedom, we have long searched for you in discipline, in action and in suffering. Dying, we recognise you in the face of God himself.'[722]

In *After Ten Years*, Bonhoeffer had presciently reflected: 'It is we ourselves, and not outward circumstances, who make death what it can be,

---

[719] Ibid. 192 As the editors point out in a footnote 'freedom toward death' is a concept which appears in Heidegger's *Sein und Zeit*. Bonhoeffer discusses the related idea of 'being towards death' in *Act and Being*.

[720] Bonhoeffer's approach is non-judgmental and concludes 'But who would say that God's grace and mercy cannot embrace and sustain even a person's failure to resist this hardest of all temptations.' DBW 6, 199; ET 172.

[721] LPP 168 (italics original).

[722] LPP 371.

a death freely and voluntarily accepted.'[723] This conviction, rather than any escapist death wish, is the perspective from which *Stations* should be read. Bethge, would seem to have come to a similar conviction with hindsight. In a radio interview he commented: 'Death for him was not just a cruel, senseless destruction of a human being without any free will, but he was able to make that horrible Flossenbürg death into an act of his free will. It was a free entering into death, and in this way made out of a death which is a witness for more than death, a witness for life.'[724] This, I would maintain is the perspective from which the concluding stanza of *Stations* is to be understood. The climax is an eschatological and relational vision of freedom, an encapsulation of the Christian hope. Humanity created and redeemed for freedom in the image of God, at last beholds the image face to face.

As we have already noted, the poem recapitulates much of the theology of freedom which we have discussed in this and the previous chapters. Freedom is both grace and obedience, God's gift and human responsibility. However, given the context discussed above, the poem must surely also be seen as Bonhoeffer's own reflection on his life from the perspective of imminent death.[725] As such, it is telling that he should choose to encapsulate his life in terms of a movement towards freedom, or, to invoke musical imagery, in terms of improvisation on the theme of freedom.

## Conclusion

In this final chapter, we have offered a re-reading of *Letters and Papers from Prison* in the light of our discussion of freedom and particularly within the context of the theology in which Bonhoeffer was engaged at the time of his arrest. We have argued that the strong continuities between the *Ethics* fragment 'The Concrete Command and the Divine Mandates' and the ideas which emerge from the short but fertile period between April and August 1944, make the case for some sort of radical shift in Bonhoeffer's thinking difficult to maintain. This is not to suggest that the theology of the

---

[723] LPP 16.

[724] Comment made in BBC interview with Keith Clements broadcast Sept. 1986 as 'Striking the Serpent's Head.' in Clements K. *What Freedom: The Persistent Challenge of Dietrich Bonhoeffer* (Bristol Baptist College 1990 ), 52.

[725] cf. Peter Zimmerling's 'Dietrich Bonhoeffer - Leben und Werk' in Mayer R. and Zimmerling P. eds. *Dietrich Bonhoeffer Heute: Die Aktualität seines Lebens und Werkes* (Brunnen Verlag Giessen 1992) 13ff, which uses the stanzas of the poem to structure a discussion of Bonhoeffer's life.

*Letters* is merely some stale re-working of earlier ideas. As I argued in the opening chapter, attempts to address the development of Bonhoeffer's theology in linear terms fail to do justice to the rich and multi-layered texture of his writing. Perhaps, in the light of the musical imagery in the Tegel correspondence, the language of intensification or improvisation on a theme might be more helpful. So here in the prison theology, what would have been a relatively small section within Bonhoeffer's ethical writings, summarised in the sentence 'The cross of reconciliation is the setting free for life before God in the midst of the godless world; it is the setting free for life in genuine worldliness',[726] emerges again to become the theme upon which Bonhoeffer improvises so fruitfully.

From this starting point, we proposed a reading of the Tegel theology in terms of an exposition of authentic life-affirming freedom in Christ, which transcends and subverts the dualism between an uncritical affirmation of human autonomy and the attempts of religion to keep humanity in dependence. We discussed the familiar concepts of 'worldliness', 'world come of age' and 'non-religious interpretation of biblical concepts' from this perspective and suggested how such a reading might throw fresh light on Bonhoeffer's much disputed critique of Barth in terms of 'positivism of revelation.' We argued that Bonhoeffer's theology of the cross, a recurrent but much under-rated theme within the *Letters*, lay at the heart of his understanding of authentic freedom. It is the cross which sets the world free for true worldliness.

In our discussion of *Outline for a Book*, we traced the development of Bonhoeffer's concept of freedom for God and for others, in the concept of being-there-for-others. It is by participation in the life, death and resurrection of Christ, the one who perfectly epitomised freedom from self for others, that Christians find authentic freedom, from self, for others and for God. Finally, we noted how the poem *Stations* offers a meditation on a number of the theological and ethical questions with which our study has engaged. Throughout this study, I have sought to show how a consideration of the relationship between divine and human freedom in Bonhoeffer's writings offers a fresh and illuminating perspective on his life and work, and takes with due seriousness Bonhoeffer's own concern that theology should never be abstracted from the concrete realities of life. I would suggest that *Stations* reflects that inextricable connection between faith and life, belief and action which is so much Bonhoeffer's hallmark and as such provides a fitting conclusion to this study.

---

[726] DBW 6, 404; ET 297.

# Bibliography

**Primary Sources in German**

*Dietrich Bonhoeffer Werke in 16 Bande (Chr. Kaiser Verlag, München 1986-present)*

DBW 1 *Sanctorum Communio* ed. von Soosten, J. (1986).
DBW 2 *Act und Sein* ed. Reuter, H-R. (1988).
DBW 3 *Schöpfung und Fall* ed. Rüter, M. and Tödt, I. (1989).
DBW 4 *Nachfolge* ed. Kuske, M. and Tödt, I. (1994).
DBW 5 *Gemeinsames Leben;Das Gebetbuch der Bibel* ed. Müller, G.L and Schönherr, A. (1987).
DBW 6 *Ethik* ed. Tödt, I., Tödt, H.E. and Green, C.J. (1992).
DBW 6 (Ergänzungsband) *Zettelnotizen für eine 'Ethik'* ed. Tödt, I. (1993).
DBW 7 *Fragmente aus Tegel* ed. Bethge, R. and Tödt, I. (1994).
DBW 9 *Jugend und Studium 1918-1927* ed. Pfeifer, H. (1986).
DBW 10 *Barcelona, Berlin, Amerika 1928-31* ed. Staats, R. and von Hase, H.E. (1991).
DBW 11 *Ökumene, Universität, Pfarramt 1931-1932* ed. Amerlung, E. and Strohm, C. (1994).
DBW 13 *London 1933-1935* ed. Goedeking, H., Heimbucher, M. and Schleicher, H-W. (1994).
DBW 14 *Illegal Theologen-ausbildung Finkenwalde 1935-1937* ed. Dudzus, O. and Henkys, J. (1996).
DBW 15 *Illegale Theologen-ausbildung Sammelvikariate 1937-1940* ed. Schulz, D. (1998).
DBW 16 *Konspiration und Haft 1940-1945* ed. Glenthøj, J., Kabitz, U. and Krötke, W. (1996).

**Other Primary Works in German**

*Gesammelte Schriften Bds I-VI* (München: Chr. Kaiser Verlag 1965-1974).
*Widerstand und Ergebung* (Chr. Kaiser/Gütersloher Verlaghaus, Gütersloh 1951; 15, durchgesehene Auflage, 1994).

*Schweitzer Korrespondenz 1941/2: im Gespräch mit Karl Barth/Dietrich Bonhoeffer* (München: Kaiser 1982).

## Primary Works in English

### English Translations of the DBW

DBW 1 *Sanctorum Communio* ed. Green, C.J. trans. Krauss, R. and Lukens, N. (Minneapolis: Fortress 1998).
DBW 2 *Act and Being* ed. Floyd, W.W. trans. Rumscheidt H.M. (Minneapolis: Fortress 1996).
DBW 3 *Creation and Fall* ed. de Gruchy, J.W. trans. Bax S. D. (Minneapolis: Fortress 1997).
DBW 4 *Discipleship* ed. Godsey, J. and Kelly, G.B. trans. Green, B. and Krauss, R. (Minneapolis: Fortress 2000).
DBW 5 *Life Together* ed. Kelly, G. B., trans. Bloesch, D. (Minneapolis: Fortress 1996).

### Other English Translations

*Sanctorum Communio* trans. Gregor Smith, R. (London: Collins 1963).
*Act and Being* trans. Noble, B. (London: Collins 1961).
*Creation and Fall* trans. Fletcher, J. C. (London: SCM 1959).
*Christology* trans. Robertson, E.H. (London: Collins 1978).
*Spiritual Care* trans. Rochelle, J. (Minneapolis: Fortress 1985).
*Ethics* trans. Horton Smith, N. (London: SCM 1955).
*Letters and Papers from Prison* trans. Fuller, R., Clarke, F. and Bowden, J. (London: SCM 1971).
*Love Letters from Cell 92* ed. von Bismarck, R-A. and Kabitz, U. trans. Brownjohn, J. (London: Harper Collins 1994).
*No Rusty Swords* ed. Robertson, E.H. (London: Collins 1965).
*The Way to Freedom* ed. Robertson, E.H. (London: Collins 1966).
*True Patriotism* ed. Robertson, E.H. (London: Collins 1973).

## Bibliographies and Reference Material

Meyer, D. and Bethge, E. *Nachlass Dietrich Bonhoeffer* (Microfiche 1678, University Library Cambridge).
Floyd, W.W. Jr. and Green, C.J. *Bonhoeffer Bibliography: Primary and Secondary Literature in English* (Illinois: American Theological Library Association 1992).

## Secondary Literature

Alford, L.M. (1994), *Toward a Dialectical Understanding of Power: Dietrich Bonhoeffer and the Theology of the Cross,* Unpublished PhD. Dissertation, New College Edinburgh.
Allen, W.S. (1984), *The Nazi Seizure of Power: The Experience of a Single German Town 1922-1945*, Franklin Watts, New York.
Altenähr, A. (1977), 'Dietrich Bonhoeffers Gedicht "Stationen auf dem Weg zur Freiheit" als Theologie und Zeugnis', in Boelaars, H. and Tremblay, R. (eds), *In Libertatum Vocati Estis*, Academia Alfonsiana, Roma, pp.283-309.
Anderson, R.S. (1975), *Historical Transcendence and the Reality of God: A Christological Critique*, Eerdmans, Grand Rapids.
Bachtell, D.S. (1973), *Freedom in the Theology of Dietrich Bonhoeffer*, Unpublished PhD. Dissertation, Drew University (Microfilm British Library)
Baillie, D.M. (1956), *God was in Christ*, Faber, London.
Balfour, M., and Frisby, J. (1972), *Helmuth von Moltke*, Macmillan, London.
Barker, G. (1992), 'Cross of Reality: The Role of Luther's "theologia crucis" in the development of Dietrich Bonhoeffer's Theology', paper presented at the International Bonhoeffer Society Conference, New York.
Barth, K. *The Epistle to the Romans* trans. Hoskyns, E.C. (from the Sixth German Edition 1928) (Oxford University Press Paperback Edition 1968).
_____ *Church Dogmatics I/1* trans. Bromiley, G.W. and Torrance, T.F. (Edinburgh: T & T Clark 1975).
_____ *Church Dogmatics I/2* trans. Bromiley, G.W. and Torrance, T.F. (Edinburgh: T & T Clark 1956).

_____ *Church Dogmatics II/1* trans. Bromiley, G.W. and Torrance, T.F. (Edinburgh: T & T Clark 1957).
_____ *Church Dogmatics III/1* trans. Bromiley, G.W. and Torrance, T.F. (Edinburgh: T & T Clark 1958).
_____ *Church Dogmatics IV/1* trans. Bromiley, G.W. and Torrance, T.F. (Edinburgh: T & T Clark 1956)
Bayer, O. (1992), *Leibliches Wort: Reformation und Neuzeit im Konflikt*, Mohr, Tübingen.
Bethge, E. (1970), *Dietrich Bonhoeffer: Theologian, Christian, Contemporary*, Collins, London.
Bethge, E. (1975), *Bonhoeffer: Exile and Martyr*, Seabury Press, New York.
Bethge, E. (1979), 'Freiheit und Gehorsam bei Bonhoeffer', in *Am gegebenen Ort: Aufsätze und Reden*, Chr. Kaiser Verlag, München.
Bethge, E. (1982) (ed.), *Dietrich Bonhoeffers Schweitzer Korrespondenz 1941-2* (München: Chr. Kaiser Verlag 1982).
Bethge, E. (1984), *Bekennen und Widerstehen*, Chr. Kaiser Verlag, München.
Bethge, E. (1989), 'Wie die Tegeler Briefe überlebten', in *In Zitz gab es keine Juden*, Chr. Kaiser Verlag, München.
Bethge, E. (1991), 'Dietrich Bonhoeffer unter den Verstummten?' in *Erst Gebot und Zeitgeschichte: Aufsätze und Reden 1980-1990*, Chr. Kaiser München: Verlag, München.
Bethge, E. and Bethge, R. (1984). *Letzte Briefe im Widerstand: Aus dem Kreis der Familie Bonhoeffer*, Chr. Kaiser Verlag, München.
Bocker, M.S. (1996), *The Community of God, Jesus Christ and Responsibility*, Unpublished PhD. Dissertation, University of Chicago, Chicago.
Burtness, J. (1980), 'As though God were not given: Barth, Bonhoeffer and the Finitum Capax Infiniti', *Dialog* (Minnesota) vol 19, pp. 249-255.
Burtness, J. (1985), *Shaping the Future: The Ethics of Dietrich Bonhoeffer*, Fortress Press, Philadelphia.
Carter G., Van Eyden R., Van Hoogstraten H.D., Wiersma J. (eds) (1991), *Bonhoeffer's Ethics, Old Europe and New Frontiers*, Kok Pharos, Kampen.
Chandler A. (1995), 'Have we an Ethic of Resistance?', in *Theology* vol XCVIII (March-April 1995), pp. 82-92.
Clements, K. (1990), *What Freedom: The Persistent Challenge of Dietrich Bonhoeffer*, Bristol Baptist College, Bristol.

Cocksworth, C. (1997), *Holy, Holy, Holy: Worshipping the Trinitarian God*, Darton, Longmann & Todd, London.

Conway, J.S. (1968), *The Nazi Persecution of the Churches*, Weidenfeld and Nicolson, London.

Day, T.I. (1981), 'Conviviality and Common Sense: The Meaning of Christian Community for Dietrich Bonhoeffer', in Klassen, A.J. (ed.), *A Bonhoeffer Legacy: Essays in Understanding*, Eerdmans, Grand Rapids, pp. 213-236.

De Gruchy, J. (1984), *Bonhoeffer and South Africa: theology in dialogue*, Eerdmans, Grand Rapids.

De Gruchy, J. (1988), (ed.), *Dietrich Bonhoeffer, Witness to Jesus Christ*, Collins, London.

De Gruchy, J. (1996), 'Dietrich Bonhoeffer and the Transition to Democracy in the German Democratic Republic and South Africa', in *Modern Theology* vol. 12:3, pp. 345-366.

De Gruchy, J. (1997) (ed.), *Bonhoeffer for a New Day: Theology in a Time of Transition*, Eerdmans, Grand Rapids.

Dicker, G.S. (1971), *The Concept Simul Justus et Peccator in Relation to the Thought of Luther, Wesley and Bonhoeffer, and its Significance for a Doctrine of the Christian Life,* Unpublished ThD. Thesis, Union Theological Seminary, New York.

Dillenberger, J. (1962) (ed.), *Martin Luther: A Selection from his Writings*, Doubleday, New York.

Dostoyevsky, F. (1993), *The Brothers Karamazov*, trans. McDuff D., Penguin, London.

Dülffer, J. (1996), *Nazi Germany 1933-1945: Faith and Annihilation*, Arnold, London.

Dumas, A. (1971), *Dietrich Bonhoeffer Theologian of Reality*, trans. McAfee Brown, R., SCM, London.

Ericksen, R.P. (1985), *Theologians Under Hitler: Gerhard Kittel, Paul Althaus and Emmanuel Hirsch*, Yale University Press, Yale.

Feil, E. (1985), *The Theology of Dietrich Bonhoeffer*, trans. Rumscheidt, M., Fortress, Philadelphia.

Feil, E. (1997), *Bonhoeffer Studies in Germany: A Survey of Recent Literature*, trans. Sorum J., International Bonhoeffer Society, English Language Section.

Floyd, W.W. Jr. (1979), *The Function of the Person of Christ in Bonhoeffer's Theology of Creation*, Unpublished Paper, Bonhoeffer Society Collection, Union Theological Seminary, New York.

Floyd, W.W. Jr. (1988), *Theology and the Dialectics of Otherness*, University Press of America, Washington D. C.

Floyd, W.W. Jr. (1995), 'Re-visioning Bonhoeffer for the Coming Generation: Challenges in Translating the Dietrich Bonhoeffer Works', *Dialog* vol. 34, pp. 32-38

Floyd, W.W. Jr. and Marsh, C. (eds) (1994), *Theology and the Practice of Responsibility: Essays on Dietrich Bonhoeffer*, Trinity Press International, Valley Forge.

Ford, D.F. (1996) (ed.), *The Modern Theologians*, Blackwell, Oxford.

Fowl, S.E. and Jones, L.G. (1991), *Reading in Communion:Scripture and Ethics in Christian Life*, SPCK , London.

Fritz, W. (1983), 'Symphonie Bonhoeffer: Dietrich Bonhoeffer and Music', in *Journal of Church Music* vol. 25:7, pp. 3-7.

Glenthøj, J. (1993), 'Zwei neue Zeugnisse von der Ermordung Dietrich Bonhoeffers', in Mayer, R. and Zimmerling, P. (eds), *Dietrich Bonhoeffer: Mensch hinter Mauern*, Brunnen Verlag, Giessen.

Godsey, J.D. (1960), *The Theology of Dietrich Bonhoeffer*, SCM, London.

Godsey, J.D. (1965), *Preface to Bonhoeffer: The Man and Two of his Shorter Writings*, Fortress, Philadelphia.

Godsey, J.D. (1967), 'Reading Bonhoeffer in English Translation: Some Difficulties', in *Union Seminary Quarterly Review*, vol. XXIII.1, pp. 79-90.

Godsey, J.D. and Kelly G.B. (eds) (1981), *Ethical Responsibility: Bonhoeffer's Legacy to the Churches*, Edwin Mellen Press, New York.

Gordon, E. (1997), *And I Will Walk At Liberty: An eye-witness account of the Church Struggle in Germany 1933-1937*, Morrow & Co, Bungay.

Green, C.J. (1999), *Bonhoeffer: A Theology of Sociality*, (Revised Edition) Eerdmans, Grand Rapids, Michigan, first published in 1972 as *Bonhoeffer: The Sociality of Christ and Humanity*, Scholars Press American Academy of Religion, Missoula.

Gregor Smith, R. (1967) (ed.), *World Come of Age: A Symposium on Dietrich Bonhoeffer*, Collins, London.

Greenspan, P.S. (1993), *Practical Guilt: Moral Dilemmas, Emotions and Social Norms*, Oxford University Press, Oxford.

Hampe, J.C. (1976), *Dietrich Bonhoeffer Von Guten Mächten*, Chr. Kaiser/Gütersloher Verlaghaus, München.

Hardy, D. (1990), 'Response to David H. Hopper's Paper', in *International Bonhoeffer Society Newsletter*, pp. 7-10.

Harrelson, W. (1963), 'Bonhoeffer and the Bible', in Marty, M.E. (ed.), *The Place of Bonhoeffer*, SCM, London.

Hinchcliff, P. (1982), *Holiness and Politics*, Darton, Longman & Todd, London.

Hopper, D. (1989), *Bonhoeffer's 'Love of the World', 'The Dangers of that Book' and the Kierkegaard Question*, paper presented to the American Academy of Religion, Bonhoeffer Society Collection, Union Theological Seminary, New York.

Hunsinger, G. (1996), Review of 'Reclaiming Dietrich Bonhoeffer: The Promise of his Theology', by Charles Marsh in *Modern Theology* vol. 12.1, pp. 121-123.

Huntemann, G. (1993), *Dietrich Bonhoeffer, An Evangelical Reassessment* trans. Huizinga, T., Baker, Grand Rapids.

Jones, G.L. (1994), 'The Cost of Forgiveness - Bonhoeffer on Grace, Christian Community and the Politics of Worldly Discipleship', in Floyd, W.W. Jr. and Marsh, C. (eds.), *Theology and the Practice of Responsibility: Essays on Dietrich Bonhoeffer*, Trinity Press International, Valley Forge.

Jüngel, E. (1995), 'The Mystery of Substitution', in *Eberhard Jüngel: Theological Essays II* trans. Webster J. B., T&T Clark, Edinburgh, pp. 145-62.

Kelly, G.B. (1974), 'The Influence of Kierkegaard on Bonhoeffer's Concept of Discipleship', *Irish Theological Quarterly*, pp.148-154.

Kelly, G.B. (1974), 'Revelation in Christ: A Study of Bonhoeffer's Theology of Revelation', in *Ephemerides Theologicae Lovanienses* vol. 50, pp. 39-74.

Kelly, G.B. (1984), *Liberating Faith: Bonhoeffer's Message for Today*, Augsburg Press, Minneapolis.

Kelly, G.B. and Nelson, F.B. (1990) (eds), *A Testament to Freedom: The Essential Writings of Dietrich Bonhoeffer*, Harper, San Francisco.

Kemp, W.H. (1976), 'The "Polyphony of Life": References to Music in Bonhoeffer's *Letters and Papers from Prison*', in Schultz, E. (ed.), *Vita Laudanda: Essays in Memory of Ulrich S. Leopold*, Wilfred Laurier Univ. Press, Waterloo, pp. 137-154.

Kierkegaard, S. (1985), *Fear and Trembling*, Penguin, Harmondsworth.

Klassen, A.J. (1981), *A Bonhoeffer Legacy: Essays in Understanding*, Eerdmans, Grand Rapids.

Lash, N. (1988), *Easter in Ordinary*, SCM, London.

Lockley, H. (1993), *Dietrich Bonhoeffer: His Ethics and its Value for Christian Ethics Today*, Phoenix Press, Swansea.

Lowe, W. (1994), *Bonhoeffer and Deconstruction: Towards a Theology of the Crucified Logos*, in Floyd, W.W. and Marsh, C. (eds), *Theology and the Practice of Responsibility: Essays on Dietrich Bonhoeffer*, Trinity Press International, Valley Forge.

Macmurray, J. (1991), *Persons in Relation*, Humanities Press International, New Jersey.

McFadyen, A. (1990), *The Call to Personhood*, Cambridge University Press, Cambridge.

Marsh, C. (1992), 'Bonhoeffer on Heidegger and Togetherness', in *Modern Theology* vol. 8:3, pp. 263-283.

Marsh, C. (1992), 'Barth and Bonhoeffer on the Worldliness of Revelation', Paper presented to the International Bonhoeffer Society Conference, New York.

Marsh, C. (1992), 'Human Community and Divine Presence: Dietrich Bonhoeffer's Theological Critique of Hegel', in *Scottish Journal of Theology* vol. 45, 4, pp. 427-448.

Marsh, C. (1994), *Reclaiming Dietrich Bonhoeffer: The Promise of his Theology*, Oxford University Press, Oxford.

Marsh, C. (1996), 'Dietrich Bonhoeffer', in Ford, D. F. (ed.), *The Modern Theologians*, Blackwell, Oxford.

Marty, M.E. (ed.) (1963), *The Place of Bonhoeffer*, SCM, London.

Mayer, R. and Zimmerling, P. (1992) (eds), *Dietrich Bonhoeffer Heute: Die Aktualität seines Lebens und Werkes*, Brunnen Verlag, Giessen.

Mayer, R. and Zimmerling, P. (1993) (eds), *Dietrich Bonhoeffer: Mensch hinter Mauern*, Brunnen Verlag, Giessen.

Mayer, R. and Zimmerling, P. (1997) (eds), *Dietrich Bonhoeffer:Beten und Tun des Gerechten*, Brunnen Verlag, Giessen.

Menke, K-M. (1991), *Stellvertretung: Schlüsselbegriff christlichen Lebens und theologische Grundkategorie*, Johannes Verlag, Freiburg, pp. 207-219.

Meyer, W. (1993), *Unternehmen Sieben: Eine Rettungsaktion für vom Holocaust Bedrohte aus dem Amt Ausland/Abwehr im Oberkommando der Wehrmacht*, Verlag Anton Hain GmbH, Frankfurt am Main.

Moltmann, J. and Weissbach, J. (1967), *Two Studies in the Theology of Bonhoeffer*, trans. Fuller, R.H. and Fuller, I., Charles Scribner & Sons, New York.

Morse, C. (1995), 'The Need for Dogmatic Theology: Bonhoeffer's Challenge to the United States in the 1930s and the 1990s', in *The Ecumenical Review*, vol. 47.3, pp. 263-267.

Mottu, H. (1969), 'Feuerbach and Bonhoeffer's Criticism of Religion and the Last Period of Bonhoeffer's Thought', in *Union Seminary Quarterly Review* vol. XXV 1, pp. 1-18.

Müller, C-R. (1990), *Dietrich Bonhoeffers Kampf gegen die nationalsozialitische Verfolgung und Vernichtung der Juden*, Chr. Kaiser Verlag, München.

Müller, H. (1961), *Von der Kirche Zur Welt, ein Betreig zu der Beziehung des Wortes Gottes auf die Societas in Dietrich Bonhoeffers theologische Entwicklung*, Herbert Reich, Leipzig.

Nietzsche, F. (1968), *Twilight of the Idols* and *The Anti-Christ*, trans. Hollingdale, R.J., Penguin, Harmondsworth.

Nietzsche, F. (1973), *Beyond Good and Evil*, trans. Hollingdale, R.J., Penguin, Harmondsworth.

Nietzsche, F. (1978), *Thus Spoke Zarathustra*, trans. Kaufmann, W., Penguin, Harmondsworth.

Ott, H. (1971), *Reality and Faith: The Theological Legacy of Dietrich Bonhoeffer*, trans. Morrison, A.A., Lutterworth, London.

Pangritz, A. (1989), *Karl Barth in der Theologie Dietrich Bonhoeffers: eine notwendige Klarstellung*, Alektor Verlag, West Berlin.

Pangritz, A. (1992), *Continuity and Discontinuity in Bonhoeffer's Theological Development*, paper presented to the International Bonhoeffer Society Conference, New York.

Pangritz, A. (1994), *Polyphonie des Lebens: Zu Dietrich Bonhoeffers 'Theologie der Musik'*, Alektor Verlag, Berlin.

Peck, W. J. (ed.) (1987), *New studies in Bonhoeffer's Ethics*, Edwin Mellen Press, New York.

Peters, T.R. (1976), *Die Präesenz des Politischen in der Theologie Dietrich Bonhoeffers*, Chr. Kaiser Verlag, München.

Phillips, J.A. (1967), *The Form of Christ in the World*, Collins, London.

Pickstock, C. (1997), 'Necrophilia: The Middle of Modernity', in *Modern Theology*, vol. 12:4, pp. 405-433.

Plant, S.J. (1993), *Uses of the Bible in the 'Ethics' of Dietrich Bonhoeffer*, unpublished PhD. Dissertation, Cambridge.

Polanyi, M. (1962), *Personal Knowledge*, Routledge and Kegan, London.

Polanyi, M. (1969), *Knowing and Being*, Routledge and Kegan, London.

Rades, J. (1988), *Bonhoeffer and Hegel: From Sanctorum Communio to the Hegel Seminar with some Perspectives for the Later Works*, unpublished draft manuscript, University of St Andrews, St Andrews.

Rades, J. (undated), *Kierkegaard and Bonhoeffer*, unpublished draft manuscript, University of St Andrews, St Andrews.

Rades, J. (undated), *Nietzsche and Bonhoeffer*, unpublished draft manuscript, University of St Andrews, St Andrews.

Rades, J. (undated), *Luther and Bonhoeffer*, unpublished draft manuscript, University of St Andrews, St Andrews.
Rasmussen, L. (1988), *Human Power and Divine Presence in a new Era: A Comparison of Dietrich Bonhoeffer and Irving Greenberg*, unpublished paper presented to the International Bonhoeffer Society Conference, New York.
Rasmussen, L. (1990), and Bethge R., *Dietrich Bonhoeffer: His Significance for North Americans*, Fortress, Minneapolis.
Reist, B.A. (1969), *The Promise of Bonhoeffer*, J.B. Lippincott, Philadelphia.
Roberts, R. (1996), 'Theology and the Social Sciences', in Ford, D.F. (ed.), *The Modern Theologians*, Blackwell, Oxford.
Robinson, J.A.T. (1963), *Honest to God*, SCM, London.
Rupp, E.G. (1953), *The Righteousness of God*, Hodder and Stoughton, London.
Scholder, K. (1989), *A Requiem for Hitler and other Perspectives on the German Church Struggle*, SCM, London.
Schönherr, A. and Krötke, W. (1985), *Bonhoeffer-Studien: Beiträge zur Theologie und Wirkungsgeschichte Dietrich Bonhoeffers*, Evangelische Verlagsanstalt, Berlin.
Schrieber, M. (1989), *Friedrich Justus Perels: Ein Weg vom Rechtskampf der Bekennenden Kirche in den politischen Widerstand*, Chr. Kaiser Verlag, München.
Schwöbel, C. (1995), 'Imago Libertatis: Human and Divine Freedom', in Gunton, C.E. (ed.), *God and Freedom*, T & T Clark, Edinburgh.
Scott, J.S. (1993), 'From the Spirit's choice and free desire: Friendship as atheology in Dietrich Bonhoeffer's Letters and Papers from Prison', in *Studies in Religion/Sciences Religieuses* vol. 22/1, pp. 49-62.
Selby, P.S. (1995), *Regain Your Whole Image: 'Christ for us' in the Legacy of Dietrich Bonhoeffer*, unpublished lecture delivered in Durham.
Selby, P.S. (1997), *Grace and Mortgage*, Darton Longman and Todd, London.
Selby, P.S. (1997), 'Who is Jesus Christ for us today?', in De Gruchy, J. (ed.), *Bonhoeffer for a New Day: Theology in a Time of Transition*, Eerdmans, Grand Rapids.
Sherman, F. 'Act and Being', in Marty, M.E. (ed.), *The Place of Bonhoeffer*, SCM, London.
Sölle, D. (1967), *Christ the Representative: An Essay in Theology after the Death of God*, trans. Lewis, D., SCM, London.
Sölle, D. (1997), *Mystik und Widerstand*, Hoffmann und Campe, Hamburg.

Umidi, R.G. (1994), *Imaging God Together: The Image of God as 'Sociality' in the Thought and Life of Dietrich Bonhoeffer*, unpublished PhD. dissertation, Drew University.

Von Loewenich, W. (1976), *Luther's Theology of the Cross*, trans. Boumann, H.J.A., Christian Journals Ltd., Belfast.

Walker, H.N. (1968), 'The Incarnation and the Crucifixion in Bonhoeffer's Cost of Discipleship', in *Scottish Journal of Theology* vol. 21.4, pp. 407-415.

Williams, R.D. (1979), 'Barth on the Triune God', in Sykes, S. (ed.), *Karl Barth: Studies of his Theological Methods*, Clarendon, Oxford.

Williams, R.D. (1987), *Arius: Heresy and Tradition*, Darton, Longman and Todd, London.

Williams, R.D. (1991), *Bonhoeffer, the Sixties and After*, Paper presented to the Consultation on Bonhoeffer, Britain and British Theology.

Wiltshire, S.F. (1969), 'Dietrich Bonhoeffer's Prison Poetry', in *Religion in Life* vol. 38, 4, pp. 522-534.

Woelfel, J.W. (1970), *Bonhoeffer's Theology, Classical and Revolutionary*, Abingdon, Nashville.

Wolterstorff, N. (1998), 'Is it possible and desirable for theologians to recover from Kant?', in *Modern Theology* vol. 14, Nr.1 pp.1-18.

Wüstenberg, R.K. (1995), 'Dietrich Bonhoeffer on Theology and Philosophy', *Anvil* vol. 12.1, pp. 45-56.

Wüstenberg, R.K. (1996), *Glauben als Leben: Dietrich Bonhoeffer und die nichtreligiose Interpretation biblischer Begriffe*, Peter Lang, Frankfurt.

Zerner, R. (1976), 'Dietrich Bonhoeffer's American Experiences: People, Letters and Papers from Union Seminary', in *Union Seminary Quarterly Review*, vol. XXXI. 4, pp. 261-282.

Zimmermann, W-D. and Gregor Smith, R. (eds), *I Knew Dietrich Bonhoeffer*, Collins, London.

Zizioulas, J. (1975), 'Human Capacity and Incapacity', in *Scottish Journal of Theology* vol. 28, p. 420.

# Index

acceptance of guilt 117, 128–9
*Act and Being* 6
  community 85, 88–92
  creation 51, 55
  epistemology 14, 15–47
  justification 82
actuality 26–7
Adorno, Theodor 16
*After Ten Years* 134, 136, 139–40, 177–8
Alford, Leslie 166
Allen, W. 10
Altenähr, Albert 175
Althaus, Paul 73, 153–4
*analogia entis* 24
*analogia relationis* 61–2
*Arkandisziplin* 94
autonomy 157–9, 165, 170

Bachtell, D. S. 37, 50
baptism 100–1, 114
Barth, Karl
  critique of religion 162, 163–4
  divine freedom 17, 27–8, 29, 31, 88
  revelation 40–1
  Trinity 59
  vicarious action 133
*Basic Questions for a Christian Ethic* 79
Bethge, Eberhard 1–2, 7, 14
  censorship 147
  community 106
  confession 110
  *The Cost of Discipleship* 98
  *Ethics* 117–18
  Finkenwalde 93–4
  friendship 171–2
  obedience 103
  political involvement 122

  *Stations on the Road to Freedom* 173–4
  violence 124–5
  world come of age 159
body 63–5
boundary 37–8, 65–70, 83, 105–6, 116
Burtness, James 73, 137

Cartesianism 44, 84
centre, boundary 66, 67–9, 83
Christ
  boundary 67–9
  community 39–45, 87–92, 100–1, 103–4, 105–6
  Counter-logos 46, 67
  creation 54, 57–8
  divine freedom 29–30
  ethics 119
  Eucharist 113–14
  faith 40–1
  fall 73
  guilt 139–41
  justification 82
  obedience 144–5
  *Outline* 169–71
  personhood 35–6, 38
  potentiality 26
  preaching 42
  reality 4–5, 136–7
  redemption 78–82
  responsibility 145–6
  theology 42–4
  truth 45–6
  ultimate and penultimate 75–7
  vicarious action 129–36
  world come of age 149, 150–2
  worldliness 154–5
  *see also* crucifixion; incarnation; resurrection

*Christology* 3
  boundary 67
  Christ as reality 5
  community 91–2
  creation 50, 51
  epistemology 15
  fall 73
  God's word 56
  incarnation 78
  Kierkegaard 96
  personhood 37
  questioning of humanity 45–6
  vicarious action 132, 133
church 31, 39–45, 85–104, 134
*The Church and the Jewish Question* 121
Church Struggle 49
community 39–45, 84–115, 116
*Concerning the Christian Idea of God* 18, 36–7, 96
Confessing Church 92–3, 97, 122, 124, 138–9, 163
confession 110–13
conscience 137–42
*cor curvum in se* 60, 82, 158
  community 89
  confession 110, 111
  justification 102, 103
  knowledge 14, 25, 28–9
  vicarious action 132
*The Cost of Discipleship*
  community 85, 93–104, 114–15
  confession 112
  ecclesiology 3
  Eucharist 114
  grace 76
  obedience 145
  pacifism 117
  political involvement 121–2
  redemption 80–1
  vicarious action 133
  violence 124
creation 48–83
*Creation and Fall* 48–83
creatureliness
  boundary 116

community of faith 44
  fall 49, 70
  freedom within limits 65–9
  justification 82
  knowledge 24
  obedience 143
  personhood 33
  redemption 81
crucifixion
  redemption 78, 81
  ultimate and penultimate 75, 77
  vicarious action 129, 131–2, 135–6
  world come of age 150–2, 166–7

*Dasein* 24, 44
De Gruchy, J. 152
death 176–8
Decalogue 67–8, 141
deputyship *see* vicarious action
*Dietrich Bonhoeffer Werke* 7–8, 118–19
Dilthey, Wilhelm 162
discipleship 98, 102–3, 113
divine freedom
  christological 54
  church 39–40
  community 87–8
  creation 49, 52–65
  epistemology 25–31
  formal 27–9, 54
  and human freedom 17, 83, 169
  possibility 53
  substantial 29–31, 54, 57
  ultimate and penultimate 76
  unconditioned 52–4
divine mandates 73, 172
Dohnyani, Hans 122, 125
dualism 63–4
Dumas, A. 5

ecclesial knowing 31, 42–4, 46–7, 48, 51
ecclesiology 109
  christology 3
  community 85–104
ego 23

# Index

Enlightenment 21, 71, 157–8
epistemology 14–47, 48, 51–2, 70
eschatology 75, 76–7, 101, 105
*The Essence of the Church* 133
essential freedom 123–4
*Ethics*
  boundary 68
  confession 113
  creation and preservation 73–4
  Enlightenment 21
  fall 69, 70–1
  guilt 138–9
  human body 65
  incarnation 168–9
  justification 82, 111
  persecution of the Jews 125–6
  redemption 81
  relationship to *Letters and Papers* 2, 4–5
  responsibility 91, 116–20, 124–9, 130
  simplicity 142–3
  world come of age 149–52
  worldliness 153, 154
ethics
  boundary 67–8
  community 89
  Eucharist 114
  knowledge 21–2
  redemption 79–80
  responsibility 116–46
  revelation 28–9
Eucharist 113–14
evil 70–1, 138
existential knowing 40–1

faith
  community 105
  justification 82
  knowledge 40–1
  obedience 74, 76, 103
  possibility 26–7
fall 21, 27, 49, 69–77, 109–10
Feil, Ernst 3–4, 50, 67, 148, 152, 157
Feuerbach 136, 157
  Finkenwalde 85, 93, 101, 104, 106, 108–11
Floyd, Wayne Whitson 16, 20, 21
forgiveness 43, 110–13, 131–2, 134
*The Friend* 171–3

Genesis 50–2, 64–5
*Gesammelte Schriften* 7
*Gestalt* 5
God
  Christian concept of person 32
  church 40–1
  community 86–8, 92
  creation 52–6
  epistemology 15, 17–19
  fall 70–2
  image of 48–83, 103, 109–10
  nature 157–8
  objectification of 17–18, 22–3, 28
  personality 36–7
  redemption 78–82
  word 54–6
  *see also* divine freedom
Godwy, John 50
Gogarten, Friedrich 9, 17
grace
  'cheap' 95–6, 102–3
  community 104–5
  confession 111–12
  ethics 80
  fall 72–4
  redemption 81
  ultimate and penultimate 76–7
Green, Clifford 84, 85, 88, 90, 118, 120
Grisebach, Eberhard 28, 34
guilt 117, 128–9, 131, 137–42

*Habilitationschrift* 15, 17
Harrelson, Walter 50
Hegel, G.W.F. 5
  beginning 51–2
  community 89–90
  creation 53
  incarnation 97
  knowledge 23
  personhood 38

Heidegger, Martin 24
Hildebrandt, Franz 99
history 36–7, 136–7
*The History of Systematic Theology in the Twentieth Century* 18
Hitler, Adolf 1, 3
　assassination attempt 125–6, 155, 173–4
　resistance to 143–4
　rise of 9–10
Holy Spirit 58–60, 65, 89, 101
Hooft, Visser't 124
Hopper, David 94–5, 96–7, 119
human freedom
　*analogia relationis* 61–2
　boundary 37–8, 65–9
　Christian concept of person 33
　community 87–8
　and divine freedom 17, 53–4, 83, 169
　ethics 116
　Holy Spirit 58–60
　image of God 56–65
　knowledge 19, 46–7
　ultimate and penultimate 76
　within limits 65–9
*Humanity in Contemporary Philosophy and Theology* 26
Hunsinger, George 35, 61–2

I-Thou relationship 28–9, 32–4, 37–8, 87, 89, 90
Idealism 17–18, 19–23, 34, 37–8
incarnation
　baptism 100–1
　community 103–5
　redemption 78–9, 80–1
　ultimate and penultimate 75, 77
　vicarious action 129, 131–2, 135–6
　worldliness 154
individualism 11–12, 84
　*The Cost of Discipleship* 93–8
　epistemology 44
　fall 69
　revelation 39–40
International Bonhoeffer Society 7

Jüngel, Eberhard 132, 135–6
justification 74, 75–6, 81–2
　community 102, 103
　confession 111–12
　guilt 140–1
　vicarious action 136
*justitia passiva* 61, 134–5

Kant, Immanuel 17–18, 19–21, 22–3, 156–7
Kierkegaard, S. 34, 94–7
knowledge 14–47, 70
*Kristallnacht* 122, 125
Kütemeyer 95–6

last things 75
law 67–8, 127–9, 141–2
*Letters and Papers from Prison* 1–6, 9, 68–9, 94, 148–79
*Life Together* 85, 93, 104–14, 115
logos 37, 67
London 92
Lowe, Walter 21
Luther, Martin
　community 89, 91, 102, 114
　confession 112
　conscience 140
　creation 59
　*justitia passiva* 61
　sin 23

Marsh, Charles 16, 35, 61–2, 89–90, 165
Menke, K-M. 132
Moltke, Helmuth von 124–5, 144
Müller, Christine-Ruth 125

National Socialism 11
　censorship 147
　collusion with 138–40
　community 92, 100
　creation 49–50, 72
　freedom 9–10
　persecution of the Jews 120–2, 125–6
　resistance to 120–2, 125, 143–4

nationalism, freedom 9–10, 11
nature, fall 73–4
*The Nature of the Church* 85, 91, 170
Neo-Kantianism 22–3, 40
*nessessità* 127–9
Nietzsche, F. 79, 97, 157
non-religious Christianity 159, 160–3
Norway 124–5

obedience
  community 102–3, 104
  ethics 116
  faith 74, 76
  responsibility 143–5
ontology, knowledge 24–5
orders of creation 49, 72, 172
orders of preservation 49, 72–7
Ott, Heinrich 4–5
*Outline for a Book* 167, 168–71

pacifism 120, 124–9
participation 169–70
Paton, William 124
Paul 98, 161
penultimate 75–7
Perels, F. J. 125–6
personhood
  bodiliness 64
  Christian concept of 31–8
  community 86, 91, 101, 105–6, 109–10
  knowledge 23
  obedience 144
Phillips, John 2–3, 50
pietism 93–4, 97, 98, 100
Plant, Stephen 126
poetry 171–8
Polanyi, Michael 10
political involvement 120–2
positivism of revelation 163–6
possibility 26–7, 53, 71
potentiality 26–7
prayer, community 106–8
preaching, knowledge 40, 42
prison letters 1–6, 148–79
  *The Problems of a Theological Anthropology*, Kierkegaard 96
  *Protestantism Without Reformation* 122–4
Psalms 106–7

reality 4–5
  correspondence with 136–7
  possibility 26–7
  world come of age 159
reason 19–22, 24–31
*Recent Theology* 78–9
redemption 48–9, 78–82
  community 87, 105
  confession 111–12
  justification 82
  preservation 73–5
  ultimate and penultimate 75–6
relationship
  *analogia relationis* 61–2
  community 85
  ethics 116
  responsibility 130
religion, critique of 160–6
*The Religious Experience of grace and the Ethical Life* 79–80
responsibility 116–46
  community 91–2, 110
  God's word 56
  grace 76
resurrection
  creation 54
  human freedom 58
  redemption 81
  ultimate and penultimate 75, 77
Reuter, Hans-Richard 36
revelation
  epistemology 15, 17–21, 25–31, 46–7
  knowledge 24–5, 39–45
  personhood 36–7
  positivism of 163–6
  sociality 39–45, 85–6
Rieger, Julius 106
Robertson, Edwin 7, 50
Robinson, John 2

sacraments
  community 100–1, 104–5
  fall 73
  see also baptism; confession; Eucharist
Sanctorum Communio 6, 7
  actuality 26
  community 39, 84, 85–92, 105
  divine freedom 28
  epistemology 15, 20
  Eucharist 113
  fall 69
  Kierkegaard 96, 97
  personhood 32, 37–8
  vicarious action 131–2, 133
Seeberg, Reinhold 85
Selby, Peter 12
Sermon on the Mount 98–100, 125, 126–9, 141
simplicity, ethics 142–3
sin 23, 48–9
  community 90, 91
  confession 110–13
  creation 49
  orders of preservation 73
  possibility 27
  vicarious action 131–2, 134
sociality 84–115
  justification 82
  revelation and knowledge 39–45
Solle, Dorothee 132, 133–5
soul, bodiliness 63–4
sovereignty, creation 62–3
spirit, personhood 36
*Spiritual Care*, confession 111–12
*Stations on the Road to Freedom* 171, 173–8
*Stellvertretung* 5, 130–1
  see also vicarious action
structuralism 5
suicide 177

*theologia crucis* 149, 150, 166–7

theology
  epistemology 48
  knowledge 40, 42–4
  revelation 53–4
*The Theology of Crisis and its attitude towards Philosophy and Science* 16, 96
Thomism 24
Tödt, Ilse 118–19
transcendentalism 20–3, 28, 36–7
translations 6–8
Trinity 59–60
  *analogia relationis* 61–2
  community 91
  personhood 35
  see also Holy Spirit
truth
  Christ 45–6
  confession 110–13

ultimate 75–7
United States 122–3, 176–7

Van den Berk, M.E.M. 176–7
vicarious action 117, 129–36
violence 120, 121, 124–9
Vogel, Heinrich 132, 135–6

Williams, Rowan 60, 162
word
  community 104
  creation 54–6
  divine freedom 27–8, 29–30
  fall 71
world, human sovereignty 62–3
world come of age 71–2, 147–79
worldliness 149, 150–6, 160–1, 165–7
worship, community 106–8, 115
Wüstenberg, Ralf 148, 160, 162–3, 169–70

Zimmermann, Wolf-Dieter 110–11